The Metasta
of Enjoyme

WO ES WAR

A series from Verso edited by Slavoj Žižek

Wo es war, soll ich werden – Where it was, I shall come into being – is Freud's version of the Enlightenment goal of knowledge that is in itself an act of liberation. Is it still possible to pursue this goal today, in the conditions of late capitalism? If 'it' today is the twin rule of pragmatic-relativist New Sophists and New Age obscurantists, what 'shall come into being' in its place? The premiss of the series is that the explosive combination of Lacanian psychoanalysis and Marxist tradition detonates a dynamic freedom that enables us to question the very presuppositions of the circuit of Capital.

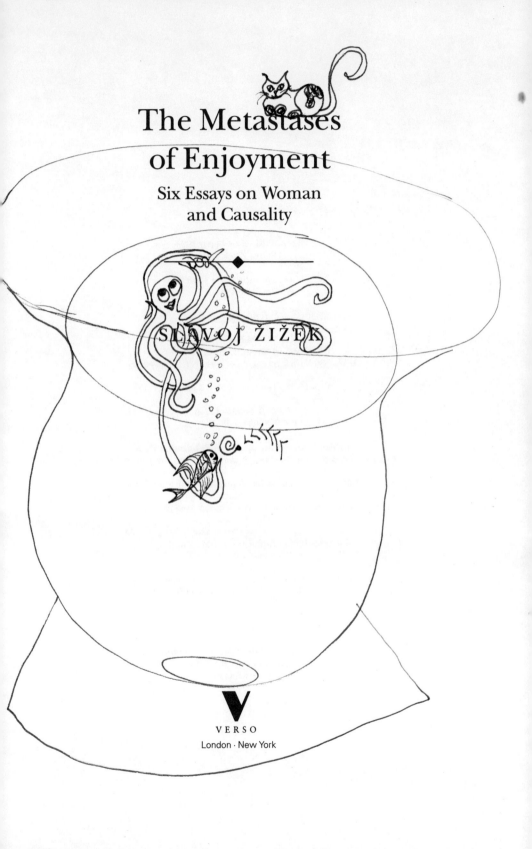

The Metastases
of Enjoyment

Six Essays on Woman
and Causality

◆

SLAVOJ ŽIŽEK

V
VERSO
London · New York

First published by Verso 1994
© Slavoj Žižek 1994

Second impression 1995
Reprinted 2001

Verso
UK: 6 Meard Street, London W1F 0EG
USA: 180 Varick Street, New York, NY 10014–4606

Verso is the imprint of New Left Books

ISBN 0–86091–444–5
ISBN 0–86091–688–X (pbk)

British Library Cataloguing in Publication Data
A catalogue record for this book is available from the British Library

Library of Congress Cataloging-in-Publication Data
Žižek, Slavoj.
The metastases of enjoyment: six essays on woman and casuality /
Slavoj Žižek.
p.   cm. — (Wo es war)
Includes bibliographical references and index.
ISBN 0–86091–444–5 : ISBN 0–86091–688–X
(pbk.)
1. Violence. 2. Women. 3. Pleasure. 4. Philosophy, Marxist.
5. Psychoanalysis and philosophy. I. Title. II. Series.
B105.V5Z58 1994   94–19936
306—dc20

Typeset by Solidus (Bristol) Limited
Printed and bound in Great Britain by Biddles Ltd
www.biddles.co.uk

Contents

INTRODUCTION: FROM SARAJEVO TO HITCHCOCK ...
AND BACK   1

PART I CAUSE   5

1   The Deadlock of 'Repressive Desublimation'   7

Critical Theory against Psychoanalytic 'Revisionism' 9 –
Contradiction as the Index of Theoretical Truth 13 –
'Repressive Desublimation' 16 – Habermas: Psychoanalysis as
Self-Reflection 22 – 'The Object's Preponderance' 26

2   Does the Subject Have a Cause?   29

Lacan: From Hermeneutics to the Cause 29 – Between Substance
and Subject 34 – The Syllogism of Christianity 38 – Why Isn't
Hegel a Humanist Atheist? 41 – The Enigma of 'Mechanical
Memory' 43 – Hegel's Logic of the Signifier 47

3   Superego by Default   54

A Law That Enjoys Itself 54 – The Split Subject of Interpellation
57 – Kundera, or, How to Enjoy Bureaucracy 62 – 'Do not give
up your desire!' 65 – Ego-Evil, Superego-Evil, Id-Evil 70 –
The Impotent Gaze and Its Guilt 73 – The War of Fantasies 75 –
Traversing the Fantasy 80

PART II WOMAN   87

4   Courtly Love, or, Woman as Thing   89

The Masochistic Theatre of Courtly Love 89 – The Courtly 'Imp
of the Perverse' 94 – Exemplifications 99 – From the Courtly
Game to *The Crying Game* 102 – *The Crying Game* Goes East 105

v

CONTENTS

5   David Lynch, or, the Feminine Depression   113

Lynch as a Pre-Raphaelite 113 – A Voice That Skins the Body 116 –
A Crack in the Causal Chain 117 – The Birth of Subjectivity out
of the Feminine Depression 119 – The Pure Surface of the
Sense-Event 122 – Deleuze as a Dialectical Materialist 125 –
The Problems of 'Real Genesis' 129

6   Otto Weininger, or, 'Woman doesn't exist'   137

'Woman is only and thoroughly sexual . . .' 137 – The Feminine
'Night of the World' 143 – Beyond the Phallus 148 – The
'Formulas of Sexuation' 153

APPENDIX   TAKING SIDES: A SELF-INTERVIEW   167

Subjective Destitution 167 – Why Popular Culture? 173 – Fantasy
and the *objet petit a* 177 – Psychoanalysis, Marxism, Philosophy 181
– The Decentred Subject 184 – Lacan and Hegel 188 – Lacan,
Derrida, Foucault 193 – 'Phallocentrism' 199 – Power 203 – From
Patriarchy to Cynicism 205 – Bosnia 210

INDEX   218

INTRODUCTION

From Sarajevo to Hitchcock
... and Back

Where can we grasp 'enjoyment as a political factor' at its purest? A famous photo from the time of Nazi anti-Semitic pogroms shows a frightened Jewish boy driven into a corner and surrounded by a group of Germans. This group is extremely interesting in so far as the facial expressions of its members render the entire scale of possible reactions: one of them 'enjoys it' in an immediate, idiotic way; another is clearly scared (perhaps he has a premonition that he might be next); the feigned indifference of the third conceals a freshly awakened curiosity; and so on, up to the unique expression of a young man who is obviously embarrassed, even disgusted, by the entire affair, unable to yield wholeheartedly to it, yet at the same time fascinated by it, enjoying it with an intensity that surpasses by far the idiocy of immediate pleasure. *He is the most dangerous*: his quavering indecision exactly corresponds to the unique expression of the Rat Man's face noticed by Freud when the Rat Man was relating the story of the rat torture: 'At all the more important moments while he was telling his story his face took on a very strange, composite expression. I could only interpret it as one of horror at pleasure of his own of which he himself was unaware.'[1]

This enjoyment is the primordial generative element, with its metastases spreading out in the two interconnected series, one political and one sexual, which account for the partition of this book into two parts. How, then, are we to conceive of this interconnection? In autumn 1992, after I had delivered a lecture on Hitchcock at an American campus, a member of the public asked me indignantly: How can you talk about such a trifling subject when your ex-country is dying in flames? My answer was: How is it that you in the USA *can* talk about Hitchcock? There is nothing traumatic in me behaving as befits a victim and testifying to the horrible events in my country – such behaviour cannot but arouse compassion and a false feeling of guilt that is the negative of a narcissistic satisfaction – that is, of my audience's awareness that they are all right while things are going badly for me. But I violate a silent

1

prohibition the moment I start to behave like them and talk about Hitchcock, not about the horrors of war in ex-Yugoslavia. . . .

This experience of mine tells us a lot about what is really unbearable to the Western gaze in the present Balkan conflict. Suffice it to recall a typical report from the besieged Sarajevo: reporters compete with each other on who will find a more repulsive scene – lacerated child bodies, raped women, starved prisoners: all this is good fodder for hungry Western eyes. However, the media are far more sparing of words apropos of how the residents of Sarajevo desperately endeavour to maintain the appearance of normal life. The tragedy of Sarajevo is epitomized in an elderly clerk who takes a walk to his office every day as usual, but has to quicken his pace at a certain crossroads because a Serbian sniper lurks on the nearby hill; in a disco that operates 'normally', although one can hear explosions in the background; in a young woman who forces her way through the ruins to the court in order to obtain a divorce so that she can start to live with her lover; in the issue of the Bosnian cinema monthly that appeared in Sarajevo in spring 1993 and published essays on Scorsese and Almodóvar. . . .

The unbearable is not the difference. The unbearable is the fact that in a sense *there is no difference*: there are no exotic bloodthirsty 'Balkanians' in Sarajevo, just normal citizens like us. The moment we take full note of this fact, the frontier that separates 'us' from 'them' is exposed in all its arbitrariness, and we are forced to renounce the safe distance of external observers: as in a Moebius band, the part and the whole coincide, so that it is no longer possible to draw a clear and unambiguous line of separation between us who live in a 'true' peace and the residents of Sarajevo who pretend as far as possible that they are living in peace – we are forced to admit that in a sense we also imitate peace, live in the fiction of peace. Sarajevo is not an island, an exception within the sea of normality; on the contrary, this alleged normality is itself an island of fictions within the common warfare. This is what we try to elude by stigmatizing the victim – that is, by locating the victim in the blemished domain between the two deaths: as if the victim were a *pariah*, a kind of living dead confined to the sacred fantasy-space.

This experience accounts for the theoretical and political context of this book. Part I analyses the structural role of violence in late capitalism, thereby providing the wider politico-ideological background to the recent horrors in Bosnia; Part II is centred on the vicissitudes of the figure of woman in modern art and ideology; the aim is to 'rescue' for progressive thought authors who are usually dismissed as hopeless reactionaries. The two parts of the book, far from belonging to two different domains, that of political analysis and that of cultural studies, relate to each other like the two surfaces of a Moebius band: by progressing far enough on one surface, we suddenly find ourselves on the opposite surface. In Part I, the inherent analysis of ideology leads to the link between violence and *jouissance féminine*; in Part II, the examination of the discursive status of women continuously shifts into the topic of power relations.

Notes

1. Sigmund Freud, 'Notes upon a Case of Obsessional Neurosis', in James Strachey, ed., *The Standard Edition of the Complete Psychological Works of Sigmund Freud*, vol. 10, London: Hogarth Press, 1955, pp. 166–7.

PART I

Cause

The Deadlock of
'Repressive Desublimation'

One of the seasonal rituals of our intellectual life is that every couple of years, psychoanalysis is pronounced *démodé*, surpassed, finally dead and buried. The strategy of these attacks is also well rehearsed – there are three main motifs:

- some new 'revelation' about Freud's 'scandalous' scientific or personal conduct – say, his alleged escape from the reality of paternal seduction (Jeffrey Masson's *The Assault on Truth*);
- raising doubts about the efficacy of psychoanalytic treatment: if such treatment works at all, it is as a result of the analyst's suggestion; this doubt is usually supported by news (which, again, pops up regularly every couple of years) of a great breakthrough in biology: finally, the neuronal, etc., basis of mental disorders has been discovered . . .
- disclaiming the scientific standing of psychoanalysis: psychoanalysis is at best an interesting and provocative literary-metaphorical description of the way our minds work; it is definitely not a science capable of formulating clear causal dependencies.

From the standpoint of historical materialism, far more interesting than the inherent critique of these attacks is their interpretation as indicators of the state of ideology at a given historical moment. It is easy to demonstrate how the recent revival of the theory of seduction (parental sexual abuse of the child as the cause of later psychic disturbances) is blind to Freud's fundamental insight into the phantasmic character of trauma – that is to say, how it denies the autonomy of the psychic domain and reasserts the traditional notion of a linear causal chain. It is more productive, however, to locate this revival in the context of the late-capitalist Narcissistic mode of subjectivity within which the 'other' as such – the real, desiring other – is experienced as a traumatic disturbance, as something that violently interrupts the closed equilibrium of my Ego. Whatever the other does – if s/he fondles me, if s/he smokes, if s/he utters a reproach, if s/he looks at me lustfully, even if s/he *doesn't* laugh at my joke heartily enough – it is (potentially, at least) a violent encroachment upon my space.[1]

At the inherently theoretical level, all these attacks centre on the problem of causality: one either assumes the 'scientific' standpoint and blames psychoanalysis for failing to formulate exact, verifiable causal laws, or one assumes the standpoint of *Geisteswissenschaften* and blames psychoanalysis for 'reifying' the intersubjective dialectic into the nexus of causal links, thus reducing the living individual to a puppet at the mercy of unconscious mechanisms. The only way to answer these charges effectively, therefore, is to provide a full account of how psychoanalysis stands with regard to the traditional couple of *Naturwissenschaften* and *Geisteswissenschaften* – that is, of causal determinism and hermeneutics. In order to keep our awareness of the true reach of the Freudian revolution alive, it is worth the trouble, from time to time, to return to the basics – that is, to the most 'naive', elementary questions. Is psychoanalysis the most radical version of psychic determinism, is Freud a 'biologist of the mind', does psychoanalysis denounce mind itself as the plaything of unconscious determinism and, consequently, its freedom as an illusion? Or, on the contrary, is psychoanalysis the 'in-depth hermeneutics' that opens up a new domain for the analysis of meaning by demonstrating how, even in the case of (what appear to be) purely physiological corporeal disturbances, we are still dealing with the dialectic of meaning, with the subject's distorted communication with himself and his Other? The first thing to be noted here is that this duality is reflected in the very Freudian theoretical edifice, in the guise of the duality of the meta-psychological *theory of drives* (oral, anal, phallic stage, etc.), which relies on the physicalist-biologist metaphorics of 'mechanisms', 'energy' and 'stages', and *interpretations* (of dreams, jokes, psychopathology of every-day life, symptoms . . .), which remain thoroughly within the domain of meaning.

Does this duality prove that Freud did not resolve the antagonism of causality and sense? Is it possible to bring both sides into a 'unified theory of the Freudian field', to evoke the suitable Einsteinian formula-tion of Jacques-Alain Miller? Clearly no solution is to be found in the pseudo-dialectical 'synthesis' of both sides, or in offering one side as the key to the other. We can no more conceive of the notion of causal determinism of the psyche as the paradigmatic case of objectivist 'reification', of the positivist misrecognition of the proper subjective dialectic of meaning, than we can reduce the domain of meaning to an illusory self-experience regulated by hidden causal mechanisms. What, however, if the true reach of the Freudian revolution is to be sought in the way it undermines the very opposition of hermeneutics and explanation, of sense and causality? Up to now, the explicit conception of psychoanalysis as a science that puts into question the opposition of hermeneutics and causal explanation has come from only two sources: the Frankfurt School and Jacques Lacan.

Critical Theory against Psychoanalytic 'Revisionism'

Well before Lacan, the Frankfurt School articulated its own project of a 'return to Freud' as a challenge to psychoanalytic 'revisionism'. In order to mark the contours of *this* 'return to Freud', Russell Jacoby's *Social Amnesia*[2] can serve as our initial reference: as indicated by its subtitle ('A Critique of Conformist Psychology from Adler to Laing'), the book surveys the analytical 'revisionism' in its entirety, from Adler and Jung up to anti-psychiatry, without omitting the neo-Freudians and post-Freudians (Fromm, Horney, Sullivan), as well as the different versions of 'existential' or 'humanist' psychoanalysis (Allport, Frankl, Maslow). Jacoby's main aim is to demonstrate how this entire orientation amounts to a progressive 'amnesia' concerning the social-critical kernel of the Freudian discovery. In one way or another, all those writers and analysts surveyed reproach Freud for his alleged 'biologism', 'pan-sexualism', 'naturalism' or 'determinism': Freud is supposed to have conceived of the subject as a 'monadic' entity, as an abstract individual at the mercy of objective determinants, as the battleground of reified 'agencies'. Freud supposedly embraced such a conception without considering the concrete context of the individual's intersubjective practice, without locating the individual's psychic structure within its sociohistorical totality.

The 'revisionists' oppose this 'narrow' conception in the name of man as a creative being who transcends himself in his existential project, whose objective instinctual determinants are merely 'inert' constituents that acquire their signification within the framework of man's active and totalizing relationship towards the world. At the properly psychoanalytic level, this approach, of course, amounts to reasserting the central role of the Ego as the agency of synthesis: the primary source of psychic trouble is not the repression of illicit desires but, rather, the hindering of man's creative potential. Thus, psychic troubles include thwarted 'existential fulfilment'; non-authentic interpersonal relations; the lack of love and confidence; the reified conditions of modern labour and the moral conflict provoked by the demands of an alienated environment, which force the individual to renounce his true Self and wear masks. Even when psychic troubles assume the form of sexual disturbances, sexuality remains a stage on which more fundamental conflicts (concerning the

Ego's creative fulfilment, the need for authentic communication, etc.) are enacted. (The nymphomaniac, for example, only expresses in an alienated and reified form, determined by society's insistence that women serve as objects of sexual satisfaction, her need for close interpersonal contact.) Within this perspective, the unconscious is not a storehouse of illicit drives but, rather, the result of moral conflicts and creative deadlocks that became unbearable for the subject.

Consequently, 'revisionism' advocates a 'socialization' and 'historicization' of the Freudian unconscious: Freud is reproached for projecting into the 'eternal human condition' features which are strictly dependent on specific historical circumstances (the sadomasochistic 'anal' character is embedded in capitalism, etc.). With Erich Fromm, this revisionist orientation takes an overt Marxist turn: he aims to detect in the superego the 'internalization' of the historically specified ideological agencies, and tries to integrate the Oedipus complex into the totality of the social process of production and reproduction. However, members of the Frankfurt School, particularly Theodor Adorno and Herbert Marcuse, fought this 'revisionist' tendency from the very beginning in the name of a strict historical-materialist approach: at stake in the so-called *Kulturismus-Debatte*, the first great splitting within the Frankfurt School, was precisely the repudiation of Fromm's neo-Freudian revisionism.

What, then, were the Frankfurt School's objections to this revisionist attempt to 'socialize' Freud by shifting the accent from the libidinal conflict between Ego and Id to the social-ethical conflicts within the Ego? While 'revisionism' replaces 'nature' ('archaic', 'pre-individual' drives) with 'culture' (the creative potential of the individual, his alienation in contemporary 'mass society'), for Adorno and Marcuse, the true problem resides *in this 'nature' itself*. In what appears as 'nature', as biological or, at least, philogenetic heritage, critical analysis must unearth the traces of historical mediation. Psychic 'nature' is the result of a historical process which, on account of the alienated character of history, assumes the 'reified', 'naturalized' form of its opposite, of a pre-historical given state of things:

> The 'sub-individual and pre-individual factors' that define the individual belong to the realm of the archaic and biological; but it is not a question of pure nature. Rather it is *second nature*: history that has hardened into nature. The distinction between nature and second nature, if unfamiliar to most social thought, is vital to critical theory. What is second nature to the individual is accumulated and sedimented history. It is history so long unliberated – history so long monotonously oppressive – that it congeals. Second nature is not simply nature or history, but frozen history that surfaces as nature.[3]

Such 'historicizing' of the Freudian theoretical edifice has nothing in common with focusing on sociocultural problems, on the Ego's moral and emotional conflicts: rather, it stands squarely against the revisionist gesture of 'domesticating' the unconscious – that is, of attenuating the fundamental and irresolvable tension between the Ego, which is structured according to the social norms, and the unconscious drives, which are opposed to the Ego – the very tension that confers on Freud's theory its critical potential. In an alienated society, the domain of 'culture' is founded upon the violent exclusion ('repression') of man's libidinal kernel which then assumes the form of a quasi-'nature': 'second nature' is the petrified evidence of the price paid for 'cultural progress', the barbarity inherent to 'culture' itself. Such a 'hieroglyphic' reading, which detects in the quasi-biological repository of drives the traces of congealed history, was practised above all by Marcuse:

> Unlike the revisionists Marcuse holds to Freud's quasi-biological concepts, but more faithfully than Freud himself – and against Freud, unfolds them. The revisionists introduce history, a social dynamic, into psychoanalysis from, as it were, the *outside* – by social values, norms, goals. Marcuse finds the history *inside* the concepts. He interprets Freud's 'biologism' as second nature, petrified history.[4]

It is impossible to miss the Hegelian background of this notion of the unconscious: the appearance of a positive objectivity, of a 'substantial' force that determines the subject from outside, is to be conceived of as resulting from the self-alienation of the subject who does not recognize himself in his own product – in short, the unconscious stands for the 'alienated psychic substance'. It is not sufficient, however, to say that the Frankfurt School discovers history where Freud saw only natural drives – in saying this one fails to take into account the *effective, actual* status of 'second nature'. The guise in which the unconscious appears as 'archaic', quasi-'biological' drives is in itself an indication of a 'reified' social reality; as such, this appearance is not a simple illusion to be abolished by 'historicizing' the unconscious but, rather, *the adequate manifestation of a historical reality which is itself 'false'* – that is to say, alienated, inverted. In contemporary society, individuals are not effectively subjects 'condemned to freedom', engaged in realizing their existential projects; they are atoms at the mercy of quasi-'natural' alienated forces, in no position to 'mediate' them or make any sense of them. For that reason the Freudian approach, which deprives the Ego of its autonomy and describes the dynamic of 'naturalized' drives to which the individual is submitted, is far closer to social reality than any glorification of human creativity.

11

Although one finds in Freud some passages which point towards the historical 'mediation' of the dynamic of the drives,[5] his theoretical position none the less implies the notion of the drives as objective determinations of psychic life. According to Adorno, this 'naturalistic' notion introduces into the Freudian edifice an irresolvable contradiction: on the one hand, the entire development of civilization is condemned, at least implicitly, for repressing drive-potentials in the service of social relations of domination and exploitation; on the other hand, repression as the renunciation of the satisfaction of drives is conceived as the necessary and insurmountable condition of the emergence of 'higher' human activities – that is to say, of culture. One intra-theoretical consequence of this contradiction is the impossibility of distinguishing in a theoretically relevant way between the *repression* of a drive and its *sublimation*: every attempt to draw a clear line of demarcation between these two concepts functions as an inapposite auxiliary construction. This theoretical failure points towards the social reality in which every sublimation (every psychic act that does not aim at the immediate satisfaction of a drive) is necessarily affected by the stigma of pathological, or at least pathogenic, repression. There is thus a radical and constitutive *indecision* which pertains to the fundamental intention of psychoanalytic theory and practice: it is split between the 'liberating' gesture of setting free repressed libidinal potential and the 'resigned conservatism' of accepting repression as the necessary price for the progress of civilization.

The same impasse repeats itself at the level of treatment: in its beginnings, psychoanalysis, inspired by the passion of radical Enlightenment, demanded the demolition of every agency of authoritarian control over the unconscious. However, with the topical differentiation between Id, Ego and Superego, analytic treatment increasingly aimed not to demolish the Superego but to establish the 'harmony' of the three agencies; analysts introduced the auxiliary distinction between the 'neurotic, compulsive' Superego and the 'sane', salutary Superego – pure theoretical nonsense, since the Superego is defined by its 'compulsive' nature. In the work of Freud himself, the Superego already emerges as an auxiliary construction whose function is to resolve the contradictory roles of the Ego. The Ego stands for the agency of consciousness and rational control that mediates between intra-psychic forces and external reality: it restrains the drives in the name of reality. However, this 'reality' – alienated social actuality – forces upon individuals renunciations which they cannot accept in a rational, conscious way.

Thus the Ego, as the representative of reality, paradoxically operates in support of unconscious, irrational prohibitions. In short, we necessarily get stuck in the contradiction according to which 'the Ego –

inasmuch as it stands for consciousness – must be the opposite of repression, yet simultaneously – inasmuch as it is itself unconscious – it must be the agency of repression'.[6] For this reason, all the postulates about the 'strong Ego' embraced by the revisionists remain deeply ambiguous: the two operations of the Ego (consciousness and repression) entwine inextricably, so that the 'cathartic' method of early psychoanalysis, prompted by the demand to tear down all barriers of repression, inevitably winds up tearing down the Ego itself – that is to say, disintegrating the 'defense mechanisms at work in resistances, without which it would be impossible to sustain the identity of the Ego as the opposition to the multiple urges of the drives';[7] on the other hand, any demand to 'strengthen the Ego' entails an even stronger repression.

Psychoanalysis escapes this deadlock by way of a compromise-formation, a 'practico-therapeutical absurdity according to which defense mechanisms must be in turn demolished and strengthened':[8] in the case of neuroses, where the Superego is too strong and the Ego is not strong enough to provide the minimal satisfaction of drives, the resistance of the Superego must be broken; whereas in the case of psychoses, where the Superego, the agency of social normality, is too weak, it must be reinforced. The goal of psychoanalysis and its contradictory character thereby reproduce the fundamental social antagonism, the tension between the individual's urges and the demands of society.

Contradiction as the Index of Theoretical Truth

At this point, we must be careful not to miss the epistemological and practical wagers at stake in Adorno: in no way does he aim at 'resolving' or 'abolishing' this contradiction by way of some conceptual 'clarification'; on the contrary, he aims at *conceiving of this contradiction as an immediate index of the 'contradiction' – that is, the antagonism – that pertains to social reality itself,* in which every development of 'superior' ('spiritual') capacities is paid for by the 'repression' of drives in the service of social domination; in which the underside of every 'sublimation' (redirection of libidinal energy towards 'higher', non-sexual, goals) is an indelibly 'barbaric', violent oppression. What first appears as Freud's 'theoretical insufficiency' or 'conceptual imprecision' possesses an inherent cognitive value, since it marks the very point at which his theory touches the truth. And it is precisely this unbearable 'contradiction' that the various revisionisms try to avoid, to soften its sting in the name of a 'culturalism' that advocates the possibility of a non-repressive 'sublimation', of a 'development of human creative potentials' not paid for by the mute suffering articulated in the formations of the unconscious. One thus constructs a consistent and homogeneous theoretical edifice, but what gets lost is simply the truth of the Freudian discovery. Critical theory, on the contrary,

> values Freud as a non-ideological thinker and theoretician of contradictions – contradictions which his successors sought to escape and mask. In this he was a 'classic' bourgeois thinker, while the revisionists were 'classic' ideologues. 'The greatness of Freud,' wrote Adorno, 'consists in that, like all great bourgeois thinkers, he left standing undissolved such contradictions and disdained the assertion of pretended harmony where the thing itself is contradictory. He revealed the antagonistic character of the social reality.'[9]

Here, those who align the Frankfurt School with 'Freudo–Marxism' encounter their first surprise: from the outset, Adorno denounces the failure and the inherent theoretical falsity of 'Freudo–Marxist' attempts to provide a common language for historical materialism and psychoanalysis – that is, a bridge between objective social relations and the concrete suffering of the individual. This failure cannot be 'thought away' by the immanent theoretical procedure of 'surmounting' the 'partial' character of both psychoanalysis and historical materialism through some kind of 'larger synthesis', since it registers the 'actual conflict between the Particular and the Universal',[10] between the individual's self-experience and the objective social totality. The 'autonomy' of the psychological subject is, of course, an ideological lure that results from the 'opaqueness of alienated objectivity':[11] the individual's impotence in the face of social objectivity is ideologically inverted into the glorification of the monadological subject. The notion of a 'psychological' subject, of an 'unconscious' reservoir of drives independent of social mediation, is thus unquestionably the ideological effect of social contradictions:

> The non-simultaneity of the unconscious and of the conscious merely reveals the stigmata of a contradictory social evolution. The unconscious accumulates what lags behind in the subject, what is not taken into account by progress and the Enlightenment.[12]

Notwithstanding the legitimate emphasis on social mediation of every psychic content, however, it is imperative to maintain the dialectical tension between the psychic and the social, in order to avoid the hasty 'socialization' of the unconscious: the socio-psychological complement to the naturalization of the unconscious

is merely the consolidated untruth. On the one hand, the psychological

14

insight, especially the distinction between conscious and unconscious, is flattened out; on the other hand, society's moving forces are falsified into psychological powers, more precisely, into the powers of superficial ego-psychology.[13]

The precipitate 'socialization' of the unconscious thus revenges itself doubly: the severity of social repression is blurred (since its entire impact can be deciphered only from the stigmata of the unconscious *excluded* from the Social) and social relations themselves are surreptitiously transformed into psychic relations; in this way the two poles of the antagonism disappear: the radical heterogeneity of the unconscious as well as the reified, 'non-psychic' objectivity of social relations.[14]

This theoretical 'regression' of revisionism emerges most clearly through the relationship posited between theory and therapy. By putting theory at the service of therapy, revisionism obliterates their dialectical tension: in an alienated society, therapy is ultimately destined to fail, and the reasons for this failure are provided by theory itself. Therapeutic 'success' amounts to the 'normalization' of the patient, his adaptation to the 'normal' functioning of existing society, whereas the crucial achievement of psychoanalytic theory is precisely to explain how 'mental illness' results from the very structure of the existing social order; that is to say, individual 'madness' is based upon a certain 'discontent' that is endemic to civilization as such. Thus the subordination of theory to therapy requires the loss of the critical dimension of psychoanalysis:

> Psychoanalysis as individual therapy necessarily participates *within* the realm of social unfreedom, while psychoanalysis as theory is free to transcend and criticize this same realm. To take up only the first moment, psychoanalysis as therapy, is to blunt psychoanalysis as a critique of civilization, turning it into an instrument of individual adjustment and resignation. . . . *Psychoanalysis is a theory of an unfree society that necessitates psychoanalysis as a therapy.*[15]

So Jacoby formulates what amounts to the social-critical version of Freud's thesis on psychoanalysis as an 'impossible profession': therapy can succeed only in a society that has no need of it – that is, one that does not produce 'mental alienation'; or, to quote Freud: 'Psychoanalysis meets the optimum of favorable conditions where its practice is not needed, i.e., among the healthy.'[16] Here we have a special type of 'failed encounter': psychoanalytic therapy is necessary only where it is not possible, and possible only where it is no longer necessary.

'Repressive Desublimation'

The logic of this 'failed encounter' bears witness to the Frankfurt School's conception of psychoanalysis as a 'negative' theory: a theory of self-alienated, divided individuals, which implies as its inherent practical goal the achievement of a 'disalienated' condition in which individuals are undivided, no longer dominated by the alienated psychic substance (the 'unconscious') – a condition thereby rendering psychoanalysis itself superfluous. However, Freud continued to conceive of his own theory as 'positive', describing the unalterable condition of civilization. Because of this limitation – that is to say, because he comprehended 'repressive sublimation' (traumatic repression *qua* the underside of sublimation) as an anthropological constant – Freud could not foresee the unexpected, paradoxical condition actualized in our century: that of 'repressive desublimation', characteristic of 'post-liberal' societies in which 'the triumphant archaic urges, the victory of the Id over the Ego, live in harmony with the triumph of the society over the individual'.[17]

The Ego's relative autonomy was based on its role as the mediator between the Id (the non-sublimated life-substance of the drives) and the Superego (the agency of social 'repression', the representative of the demands of society). 'Repressive desublimation' succeeds in getting rid of this autonomous, mediating agency of 'synthesis' which is the Ego: through such 'desublimation' the Ego loses its relative autonomy and regresses towards the unconscious. However, this 'regressive', compulsive, blind, 'automatic' behaviour, which bears all the signs of the Id, far from liberating us from the pressures of the existing social order, adheres perfectly to the demands of the Superego, and is therefore already enlisted in the service of the social order. As a consequence, the forces of social 'repression' exert a direct control over drives.

The bourgeois liberal subject represses his unconscious urges by means of internalized prohibitions and, as a result, his self-control enables him to get hold of his libidinal 'spontaneity'. In post-liberal societies, however, the agency of social repression no longer acts in the guise of an internalized Law or Prohibition that requires renunciation and self-control; instead, it assumes the form of a hypnotic agency that imposes the attitude of 'yielding to temptation' – that is to say, its injunction amounts to a command: 'Enjoy yourself!'. Such an idiotic enjoyment is dictated by the social environment which includes the Anglo-Saxon psychoanalyst whose main goal is to render the patient capable of 'normal', 'healthy' pleasures. Society requires us to *fall asleep*, into a hypnotic trance, usually under the guise of just the opposite command: 'The Nazi battle cry of "Germany awake" hides its very opposite.'[18] Adorno interprets the formation of the 'masses' in the same sense of this 'regression' of the Ego towards automatic and compulsive behaviour:

To be sure, this process has a psychological dimension, but it also indicates a growing tendency towards the abolition of psychological motivation in the old, liberalistic sense. Such motivation is systematically controlled and absorbed by social mechanisms which are directed from above. When the leaders become conscious of mass psychology and take it into their own hands, it ceases to exist in a certain sense. This potentiality is contained in the basic construct of psychoanalysis inasmuch as for Freud the concept of psychology is essentially a negative one. He defines the realm of psychology by the supremacy of the unconscious and postulates that what is id should become ego.[19] The emancipation of man from the heteronomous rule of his unconscious would be tantamount to the abolition of his 'psychology'. Fascism furthers this abolition in the opposite sense through the perpetuation of dependence instead of the realization of potential freedom, through expropriation of the unconscious by social control instead of making the subjects conscious of their unconscious. For, while psychology always denotes some bondage of the individual, it also presupposes freedom in the sense of a certain self-sufficiency and autonomy of the individual. It is not accidental that the nineteenth century was the great era of psychological thought. In a thoroughly reified society, in which there are virtually no direct relationships between men, and in which each person has been reduced to a social atom, to a mere function of collectivity, the psychological processes, though they still persist in each individual, have ceased to appear as the determining forces of the social process. Thus, the psychology of the individual has lost what Hegel would have called substance. It is perhaps the greatest merit of Freud's book [*Group Psychology and the Analysis of the Ego*] that though he restricted himself to the field of individual psychology and wisely abstained from introducing sociological factors from outside, he nevertheless reached the turning point where psychology abdicates. The psychological 'impoverishment' of the subject that 'surrendered itself to the object' which 'it has substituted for its most important constituent,' that is, the super-ego, anticipates almost with clairvoyance the post-psychological de-individualized social atoms which form the fascist collectivities. In these social atoms the psychological dynamics of group formation have overreached themselves and are no longer a reality. The category of 'phoniness' applies to the leaders as well as to the act of identification on the part of the masses and their supposed frenzy and hysteria. Just as little as people believe in the depth of their hearts that the Jews are the devil, do they completely believe in their leader. They do not really identify themselves with him but act this identification, perform their own enthusiasm, and thus participate in their leader's performance. It is through this performance that they strike a balance between their continuously mobilized instinctual urges and the historical stage of enlightenment they have reached, and which cannot be revoked arbitrarily. It is probably the suspicion of this fictitiousness of their own 'group psychology' which makes fascist crowds so merciless and unapproachable. If they would stop to reason for a second, the whole performance would go to pieces, and they would be left to panic.[20]

This long passage offers a condensed version of the entire critical appropriation of psychoanalysis by the Frankfurt School. The notion of psychology at work in psychoanalysis is ultimately a negative one: the domain of the 'psychological' comprises all those factors which dominate the individual's 'inner life' behind his back, in the guise of an 'irrational', heteronomous force which eludes his conscious control. Consequently, the aim of the psychoanalytic process is that 'what is id should become ego' – that is, 'man should be emancipated from the heteronomous rule of his unconscious'. Such a free, autonomous subject would be, *stricto sensu*, a *subject without psychology* – in other words, psychoanalysis aims to 'de-psychologize' the subject.

It is against this background that we should measure the impact of 'repressive desublimation': in it, psychology is also surpassed, since subjects are deprived of the 'psychological' dimension in the sense of a wealth of 'natural needs', of spontaneous libidinal motivations. However, psychology is surpassed here not through a liberating reflection that enables the subject to appropriate his repressed content, but 'in the opposite sense': it is surpassed through a direct 'socialization' of the unconscious brought about by the 'short circuit' between the Id and the Superego at the expense of the Ego. The psychological dimension – that is, the libidinal life-substance – is thereby 'sublated' in the strict Hegelian sense: it is maintained, but deprived of its immediate character and thoroughly 'mediated', manipulated by the mechanisms of social domination.

As an example, let us take again the formation of the 'masses': in a first approach, we encounter here an exemplary case of the 'regression' of the autonomous Ego, which is suddenly seized by some force beyond its control and yields to its heteronomous hypnotic power. However, this appearance of 'spontaneity', of the explosion of a primordial irrational force that can be grasped only via a psychological analysis, should in no way obfuscate the crucial fact that the contemporary 'masses' are already an artificial formation, the result of an 'administered', directed process – in short, they are a 'post-psychological' phenomenon. The 'spontaneity', the 'fanaticism', the 'mass hysteria', are all ultimately fake. The general conclusion to be drawn from this account is that the 'object of psychoanalysis', its central topic, is a historically delimited entity, the 'monadological, relatively autonomous, individual, as the stage of the conflict between the drives and their prohibition'[21] – in short, the liberal bourgeois subject. The pre-bourgeois universe in which the individual is plunged into the social substance does not yet know this conflict; the contemporary, wholly socialized 'administered world' does not know it any more:

> The contemporary types are those in whom any Ego is absent; consequently, they do not act unconsciously in the proper meaning of this term, but simply mirror objective features. Together, they participate in this senseless ritual, following the compulsive rhythm of repetition, and grow poor affectively: the demolition of the Ego strengthens narcissism and its collective derivations.[22]

The last great act to be accomplished by psychoanalysis is therefore 'to arrive at the uncovering of the destructive forces which, in the midst of the destructive Universal, are at work in the Particular itself'.[23] Psychoanalysis must discern those subjective mechanisms (collective narcissism, etc.) which, in accordance with social coercion, work to demolish the 'monadological, relatively autonomous, individual' as the proper object of psychoanalysis. In other words, the last act of psychoanalytic theory is to articulate the conditions for its own obsolescence....

Something is amiss in this otherwise ingenious conception of 'repressive desublimation'. Adorno is compelled again and again to reduce totalitarian 'de-psychologization' to an attitude of conscious, or at least pre-conscious, 'selfish calculation' (manipulation, conformist adaptation), which is allegedly concealed beneath the façade of irrational seizure. This reduction has radical consequences for his approach to fascist ideology: Adorno refuses to treat fascism as an ideology in the proper sense of the term – that is, as 'rational legitimization of the existing order'. The so-called 'fascist ideology' no longer possesses the coherence of a rational construct that calls for conceptual analysis and ideologico-critical refutation. 'Fascist ideology' is not taken seriously even by its promoters; its status is purely instrumental, and ultimately relies on external coercion. Fascism no longer functions as a 'lie necessarily experienced as truth' – the sign of recognition of a true ideology.[24]

But is reducing 'fascist ideology' to conscious manipulation or conformist adaptation the only way to comprehend the de-psychologization at work in totalitarian ideological edifices? Lacan opens up the possibility of a different approach when, apropos of Clérambault's description of the psychotic phenomenon, he insists that we must always bear in mind its

> *ideationally neutral* nature, which in his language means that it's in total discord with the subject's mental state, that no mechanism of the affects adequately explains it, and which in ours means that it's structural ... the

nucleus of psychosis has to be linked to a relationship between the subject and the signifier in its most formal dimension, in its dimension as a pure signifier, and ... everything constructed around this consists only of affective reactions to the primary phenomenon, the relationship to the signifier.[25]

In this perspective, 'de-psychologization' means that the subject is confronted with an 'inert' signifying chain, one that does not seize him performatively, affecting his subjective position of enunciation: towards this chain the subject maintains a 'relation of exteriority'.[26] It is this very exteriority which, according to Lacan, defines the status of the superego: the superego is a Law in so far as it is not integrated into the subject's symbolic universe, in so far as it functions as an incomprehensible, nonsensical, traumatic injunction, incommensurable with the psychological wealth of the subject's affective attitudes, bearing witness to a kind of 'malevolent neutrality' directed towards the subject, indifferent to his empathies and fears. At this precise point, as the subject confronts the 'agency of the letter' in its original and radical *exteriority*, the signifier's nonsense at its purest, he encounters the superego command 'Enjoy!' which addresses the most *intimate* kernel of his being.

Suffice it to recall the unfortunate Schreber, the psychotic whose writings were analysed by Freud, the deluded judge who was constantly bombarded by divine 'voices' ordering him to enjoy (i.e. to change into a woman and copulate with God): the crucial feature of Schreber's God is that he is *totally unable to understand us living humans* – or, to quote Schreber himself: '... *in accordance with the Order of Things, God really knew nothing about living men* and did not need to know'.[27] This radical incommensurability between the psychotic God and man's inner life (in contrast to the 'normal' God who understands us better than we understand ourselves – that is, the God for whom 'our heart holds no secrets') is strictly correlative to his status as an agency that imposes enjoyment. In the domain of literature, the supreme example of this *short circuit between Law and enjoyment* is the obscene agency of Law in Kafka's great novels (which, for that very reason, announce the arrival of the totalitarian libidinal economy).[28] Therein consists the key to 'repressive desublimation', to this 'perverse reconciliation of the Id and the Super-Ego at the expense of the Ego': *'repressive desublimation' is a way – the only way open within the horizon of the Frankfurt School – to say that in 'totalitarianism', social Law assumes the features of a superego injunction.*

It is precisely the lack of the explicit concept of the superego that underlies Adorno's continuous reduction of the 'de-psychologization' of the fascist crowd to an effect of conscious manipulation. This insufficiency originates with Adorno's starting point, with his conception of psychoanalysis as a 'psychological' theory – that is, a theory whose object is the psychological individual: as soon as one accepts this notion, one cannot avoid concluding that the only thing psychoanalysis can do, faced with the passage from the 'psychological' individual of the liberal bourgeois society to the 'post-psychological' individual of the 'totalitarian' society, is to discern the contours of the process that leads to the demolition of its own object. Here, however, Lacan's 'return to Freud', based on the key role of the 'agency of the letter in the unconscious' – in other words, on the strictly *non-psychological* character of the unconscious – inverts the entire perspective: at the point where, according to Adorno, psychoanalysis reaches its limit and witnesses the demolition of its 'object' (the psychological individual), *at this very point the 'agency of the letter' emerges as such in 'historical reality' itself,* in the guise of the superego imperative at work in 'totalitarian' discourse.

This Lacanian inversion of Adorno's approach enables us to account for the so-called fascist 'aestheticization of the political': the accentuated 'theatricality' of the fascist ideological ritual reveals how fascism 'feigns', 'stages', the performative power of political discourse, transposing it into the modality of as-if. All the emphasis on the 'leader' and his 'escort', on 'mission' and the 'spirit of sacrifice', should not deceive us – such exaltations ultimately amount to a theatrical *simulation* of the pre-bourgeois discourse of the Master. Adorno is quite justified in highlighting this moment of 'simulation'. His error lies elsewhere: in perceiving this simulation as an effect of external coercion and/or pursuit of material gain ('cui bono?') – as if the mask of the 'totalitarian' ideological discourse conceals a 'normal', 'commonsensical' individual – that is, the good old 'utilitarian', 'egotist' subject of bourgeois individualism who simply pretends to be carried away by 'totalitarian' ideology out of fear or hopes for material profit. On the contrary, one must insist on the thoroughly 'serious' character of such feigning: it involves the 'non-integration of the subject into the register of the signifier', the 'external imitation' of the signifying game akin to the so-called *as if* phenomena characteristic of proto-psychotic states.[29]

More to the point, this 'inner distance' of the subject towards the 'totalitarian' discourse, far from enabling the subject to 'elude the madness' of the 'totalitarian' ideological spectacle, is the very factor on account of which the subject is effectively 'mad'. Now and then, Adorno himself has a presentiment of it – as, for example, when he implies that the subject 'beneath the mask' who 'feigns' his captivation must already be 'mad', 'hollow'. It is in order to escape this void that the subject is condemned to take refuge in the ceaseless ideological spectacle – if the 'show' were to stop for a moment, his entire universe would disintegrate....[30] In other words, 'madness' does not turn on effectively believing in the Jewish plot, in the charisma of the Leader, and so on –

such beliefs (in so far as they are repressed, that is, the unacknowledged fantasy-support of our universe of signification) form a constituent part of our ideological 'normality'. 'Madness', however, emerges in the *absence* of such engaging beliefs, in the fact that 'in the depth of their hearts, people *do not* believe that the Jews are the devil'. In short: madness emerges through the subject's 'simulation' and 'external imitation' of such beliefs; it thrives in that 'inner distance' maintained towards the ideological discourse which constitutes the subject's social-symbolic network.

Habermas: Psychoanalysis as Self-Reflection

Thus 'repressive desublimation' plays the role of the 'symptomatic' element that renders it possible to discern the fundamental antinomy in the Frankfurt School's appropriation of psychoanalysis. On the one hand, the notion of 'repressive desublimation' distils the Frankfurt School's critical attitude towards Freud by highlighting what had to remain 'unthinkable' for Freud: the uncanny 'reconciliation' of Id and Superego in 'totalitarian' societies. On the other hand, the self-cancelling, structurally ambiguous nature of this notion betrays the extent to which 'repressive desublimation' is a 'pseudo-concept' which signals the need to rearticulate the entire theoretical field.

How was this extreme tension resolved in further developments of the Frankfurt School? It was Jürgen Habermas who carried out the radical break in the relationship between the Frankfurt School and psycho-analysis. He begins by asking: 'What goes on in the psychoanalytic process?' – that is to say, he rehabilitates the psychoanalytic cure as the cornerstone of its theoretical edifice, in clear contrast to Adorno and Marcuse, for whom psychoanalytic treatment amounted to no more than a technique of social adaptation. This shift of emphasis tells of a more fundamental break: Adorno and Marcuse accept psychoanalytic theory as it is, since in the dialectical antagonism between theory and therapy, the truth for them resides on the side of theory. But according to Habermas, Freud's theory lagged behind psychoanalytic practice, mainly because Freud misrecognized the crucial dimension of psychoanalytic treatment: the self-reflective power of language. Consequently, Habermas accomplishes his own 'return to Freud' by reinterpreting Freud's entire theoretical framework from the perspective of language. His starting point is Dilthey's division of the 'elementary forms of comprehension' into linguistic elements, action patterns, and expressions:

In the normal case, these three categories of expressions are complementary, so that linguistic expressions 'fit' interactions and both language and action 'fit' experiential expressions; of course, their integration is imperfect, which makes possible the latitude necessary for indirect communications. In the limiting case, however, a language game can disintegrate to the point where the three categories of expressions no longer agree. Then actions and non-verbal expressions belie what is expressly stated. . . . The acting subject himself cannot observe the discrepancy; or, if he observes it, he cannot understand it, because he both expresses and misunderstands himself in this discrepancy. His self-understanding must keep to what is consciously intended, to linguistic expression – or at least to what can be verbalized.[31]

If, by means of an ironic tone or grimace, we let it be known that we do not take what we are asserting seriously, the gap between the content of our utterance and our true intention is still 'normal'; if, however, the refutation of what we are saying intervenes 'behind our back', in the guise of a 'spontaneous', unintended slip of the tongue, then we encounter a pathological case. Thus the criterion of 'normality' resides in the unity of (conscious) intention-of-signification that governs all three forms of expression. More precisely, since our conscious intention coincides with what can be expressed in language, 'normality' resides in the translatability of all our motives into intentions which can be expressed in public, intersubjectively recognized language. What causes pathological discrepancies is repressed desire: excluded from public communication, it finds an outlet in compulsive gestures and acts, as well as in distorted, 'private' language usage. Starting from these discrepancies, Habermas ultimately arrives at the ideological falsity of all hermeneutics that limits itself to the (conscious) intention-of-signification, abandoning errors and distortions of the interpreted text to philology: what hermeneutics cannot admit is that it is not sufficient to repair the mutilations and restore the 'original' text to its integrity, since 'mutilations have meaning *as such*':

> The omissions and distortions that it [psychoanalytic interpretation] rectifies have a systematic role and function. For the symbolic structures that psychoanalysis seeks to comprehend are corrupted by the impact of *internal conditions*.[32]

The standard hermeneutical attitude thus seems radically subverted: the true position of the speaking subject emerges precisely in the gaps in his self-comprehension, in the apparently 'meaningless' distortions of his text. But the reach of this subversion is strictly limited: Dilthey's standard model of the unity of language, action patterns and expressions retains its validity – not as a description of the *actual* functioning of communicative activities, but as a *practical-critical paradigm*, the norm by which we measure the 'pathology' of our actual communication. Dilthey's error was to use as his model for describing actual structures of signification that model which could be used only under conditions of a 'non-repressive' society, thus deafening himself to what is repressed by the actual discourse:

> In the methodically rigorous sense, 'wrong' behavior means *every deviation from the model of the language game of communicative action*, in which motives of action and linguistically expressed intentions coincide. In this model, split-off symbols and the need dispositions connected with them are not allowed. It is assumed either that they do not exist or, if they do, that they are without consequences on the level of public communication, habitual interaction, and observable expression. This model, however, could be generally applicable only under the conditions of a non-repressive society. Therefore deviations from it are the normal case under all known social conditions.[33]

This passage already suggests the link established by Habermas between psychoanalysis and the critique of ideology. What Freud baptized as the Superego emerges as the intrapsychic prolongation of social authority – that is, the pattern of knowing and desiring, of object-choices, and so on, sanctioned by society. In so far as this pattern is 'internalized' by the subject, the motives which come into conflict with it are 'repressed'; excommunicated from the domain of public communication, they assume a 'reified' existence in the guise of the Id, of an alien power in which the subject does not recognize himself. This defence of the subject against his own illicit motivations does not have the character of conscious self-control but is itself unconscious; on that account, the Superego resembles the Id, since the symbols of the Superego are 'sacralized', exempted from argumentative, rational communication.

This conception involves an entire 'pedagogy', a logic of the Ego's development up to its 'maturity'. In the (ontogenetically as well as philogenetically) inferior stages of its development, the Ego is not capable of controlling its drives in a rational, conscious way, so only an 'irrational'/'traumatic' agency of prohibition can induce it to renounce unrealizable surplus; with the gradual development of productive forces and forms of symbolic communication, the rational approach to renunciation becomes possible – that is to say, the subject can consciously undertake the necessary sacrifices.

Habermas's principal reproach against Freud is not that he set the barrier of repression 'too low', making it into a kind of anthropological constant instead of historicizing it; Habermas's reproach concerns instead the epistemological status of Freud's theory: the conceptual framework by means of which Freud endeavours to reflect his practice falls short of this practice. Psychoanalytic theory confers on the Ego the function of accommodating intelligently to reality, and regulating the drives – what is missing here is the specific act whose negative is the defence mechanisms: *self-reflection*. Psychoanalysis is neither a *comprehension* of the hidden meaning of symptoms nor an *explanation* of the causal chain which brought the symptom about: the act of self-reflection dialectically transcends this very duality of comprehension and causal explanation – how?

When libidinal motivations are prevented from emerging as conscious intentions, they assume the features of pseudo-natural causes – that is, of the Id *qua* blind force dominating the subject behind his back. The Id penetrates the texture of everyday language by distorting grammar and confounding the proper use of public language through false semantic identifications: in symptoms, the subject speaks a kind of 'private language' that is incomprehensible to his conscious Ego. In other words, symptoms are fragments of the public text chained to the symbols of illicit desires excluded from public communication:

> At the level of the public text, the suppressed symbol is objectively understandable through rules *resulting* from contingent circumstances of the individual's life history, but not connected with it according to intersubjectively *recognized* rules. That is why the symptomatic concealment of meaning and corresponding disturbance of interaction cannot at first be understood either by others or by the subject himself.[34]

Psychoanalytic interpretation unearths the idiosyncratic link between the fragments of public text and the symbols of illicit libidinal motivations; it retranslates these motivations into the language of intersubjective communication. The final stage of the psychoanalytic cure is reached when the subject recognizes himself, his own motivations, in the censured chapters of his self-expression, and is able to narrate the totality of his life story. In a first approach, psychoanalysis thus proceeds along the path of causal explanation: it brings to light the causal chain which, unbeknownst to the subject, produced the symptom. However – and herein resides the proper notion of self-reflection – *this very explanation of the causal chain cancels its efficacy.* An adequate interpretation does not only lead to the 'true knowledge' of the symptom, it simultaneously involves the symptom's dissolution, and thereby the 'reconciliation' of the subject with himself – the act of knowing is in itself an act of liberation from unconscious coercion. Consequently, Habermas can conceive of the unconscious according to the Hegelian model of self-alienation: in the unconscious, the subject's communication with himself is interrupted, and the psychoanalytic cure amounts to the subject's reconciliation with the Id, his alienated substance, his mis-recognized self-objectivization – that is to say, the cure amounts to the subject's deciphering the symptom as an expression of his own unac-knowledged motivations:

> For the insight to which analysis is to lead is indeed only this: that the I of the patient recognize itself in its other, represented by its illness, as in *its own* alienated *self* and identify with it.[35]

However, one must avoid yielding too readily to this apparent 'Hegelian-ism': already at work behind it is a kind of 'return to Kant'. The coincidence of true motivations with expressed meaning and the concomitant translation of all motivations into the language of public communication play the part of the Kantian regulative Idea approached in asymptotic movement. The repression of the symbols of illicit desires, the subject's interrupted communication with himself, the falsity of the ideological Universal which conceals a particular interest – all these occur because of *empirical* reasons which act *from outside* on the framework of language. To put it in Hegelese: the necessity of distortion is not inscribed into the very concept of communication but is due to the actual contingent circumstances of labour and domination which prevent the realization of the ideal – the relations of power and violence are not inherent to language.[36]

'The Object's Preponderance'

By obliterating the 'material weight' of the historical Real, by reducing it to a contingent force which, from outside, affects the neutral transcendental grid of language and prevents its 'normal' functioning, Habermas disfigures the psychoanalytic interpretative process. What gets lost in the process is Freud's distinction between the latent dream-thought and unconscious desire – that is, his insistence on how 'a normal train of thought' – normal and, as such, expressible in the language of public communication – 'is only submitted to the abnormal psychical treatment of the sort we have been describing' – to the dream work – 'if an unconscious wish, derived from infancy and in a state of repression, has been transferred on to it'.[37]

Habermas reduces the work of interpretation to retranslating the 'latent dream-thought' into the intersubjectively recognized language of public communication, without accounting for how this thought is 'pulled' into the unconscious only if some already unconscious wish finds an echo in it by means of a kind of transferential 'short circuit'.

And, as Freud put it, this already unconscious wish is 'primordially repressed': it constitutes a 'traumatic kernel' which has no 'original' in the language of intersubjective communication and which, for that reason, *for ever, constitutively, resists symbolization – that is, (re)translation into the language of intersubjective communication*. Here we confront the incommensurability between hermeneutics ('deep' as it may be) and psychoanalytic interpretation: Habermas can assert that distortions have meaning as such – what remains unthinkable for him is that *meaning as such results from a certain distortion* – that the emergence of meaning is based on a disavowal of some 'primordially repressed' traumatic kernel.

This traumatic kernel, this remainder which resists subjectivization-symbolization, is *stricto sensu* the *cause* of the subject. And it is with regard to this kernel that the unbridgeable gap separating Habermas from Adorno appears at its clearest: Habermas resuscitates the pseudo-Hegelian model of the subject's appropriation of the alienated-reified substantial content, whereas Adorno's late motif of the 'preponderance of the object' calls this very model into question by evoking a 'decentrement' which, far from bearing witness to the subject's alienation, outlines the dimension of possible 'reconciliation'. True, Habermas does resolve the tension detectable in late Adorno; however, he does so not by 'bringing to the concept' the 'unthought' of Adorno, but by changing the entire problematic so as simply to render invisible, flatten out, the tension at work in Adorno. How, then, on closer examination, *does* Lacan bring to the concept the unthought of Adorno (since, if we are to throw all our cards on the table, Lacan's achievement in this regard has been the underlying premiss of our reading of Adorno)?

Notes

1. It is clear, therefore, that what 'political correctness' is combating is simply *the manifestation of the other's desire*.

2. Russell Jacoby, *Social Amnesia: A Critique of Conformist Psychology from Adler to Laing*, Brighton: Harvester 1977.

3. Ibid., p. 31.

4. Ibid.

5. Jacoby quotes the following passage from a letter published by Jones which conceives of every inner compulsion as the internalization of an originally external pressure: 'every *internal* barrier of repression is the historical result of an *external* obstruction. Thus: the opposition is incorporated within [*Verinnerlichung der Widerstände*]; the history of mankind is deposited in the present-day inborn tendencies to repression' (ibid., p. 32).

6. Theodor W. Adorno, 'Zum Verhältnis von Soziologie und Psychologie', in *Gesellschaftstheorie und Kulturkritik*, Frankfurt: Suhrkamp 1975, p. 122.

7. Ibid., p. 131.

8. Ibid., p. 132.

9. Jacoby, *Social Amnesia*, pp. 27–8.

10. Adorno, 'Zum Verhältnis', p. 97.

11. Ibid., p. 106.

12. Ibid., p. 113.

13. Ibid., p. 110.

14. Freud himself did not succeed in escaping this 'short circuit' between libidinal life and social reality: the paradoxical reverse of his misrecognition of the social mediation of psychic content is his precipitate translation of the psychic content into alleged actual social events, as is the case with his postulate of the pre-historical fact of parricide – this postulate is possible only if one forgets the basic premiss of the psychoanalytic theory according to which 'social reality enters the unconscious only insofar as it is already "translated" into the language of the Id' (ibid., p. 112).

15. Jacoby, *Social Amnesia*, pp. 120, 122.

16. Ibid., p. 125.

17. Adorno, 'Zum Verhältnis', p. 133.

18. Theodor W. Adorno, 'Freudian Theory and the Pattern of Fascist Propaganda', in *The Culture Industry: Selected Essays on Mass Culture*, London: Routledge 1991, p. 132.

19. ... *daß, was Es war, Ich werden soll*: Adorno changes in a crucial way Freud's *wo es war, soll ich werden*, in which there is no mention of *quidditas*, of 'what is id', but only of a *place*, of 'where it was' – I should arrive at the place where it was.

20. Adorno, 'Freudian Theory', pp. 130–31.

21. Adorno, 'Zum Verhältnis', p. 134.

22. Ibid., p. 133.

23. Ibid.

24. See Theodor W. Adorno, 'Beitrag zur Ideologienlehre', in *Gesammelte Schriften: Ideologie*, Frankfurt: Suhrkamp 1972.

25. *The Seminar of Jacques Lacan. Book III: The Psychoses (1955–1956)*, New York: Norton 1993, p. 251.

26. Ibid.

27. Sigmund Freud, 'Psychoanalytic Notes on an Autobiographical Account of a Case of Paranoia (Schreber)', in *Case Histories* II, Harmondsworth: Penguin 1979, p. 156.

28. As to this notion of the superego in its connection with Kafka's universe, see Slavoj Žižek, *For They Know Not What They Do*, London: Verso 1991, pp. 236–41.

29. *The Seminar of Jacques Lacan. Book III*, p. 251.

30. In the case of Schreber, the corresponding phenomenon is his need for the constant accompaniment of the flux of God's speech: he 'no longer has the customary significant security, except through the accompaniment of a constant commentary on his gestures and acts' (ibid., p. 307). Some interpreters of Freud and critics of Lacan perceive Freud's text on Schreber as a patriarchal-reactionary dissimulation of the unbearable truth of Schreber's text: Schreber's desire to become 'a woman full of spirit [*geistreiches Weib*]' is to be taken as a presentiment of a non-patriarchal society – only a patriarchal perspective can reduce statements like this to the expression of 'repressed homosexuality' or 'failed paternity'. In opposition to such readings, it is worth recalling the fundamental structural homology between Schreber's 'visions' and Hitler's 'world-view' (the universal plot, the general cataclysm followed by a rebirth, etc.): in different circumstances, one could well imagine Schreber becoming a Hitler-like politician.

31. Jürgen Habermas, *Knowledge and Human Interest*, London: Heinemann 1972, pp. 217–18.

32. Ibid., p. 217.

33. Ibid., p. 226.

34. Ibid., p. 257.

35. Ibid., pp. 235–6.

36. The same also goes for sexuality, in contrast to Lacan, for whom sexual difference is the non-symbolizable Real which truncates the symbolic order from within; for that reason, the Lacanian subject of the signifier is always 'sexed', never neutral-asexual.

37. Sigmund Freud, *The Interpretation of Dreams*, Harmondsworth: Penguin 1977, p. 757.

2

Does the Subject Have a Cause?

Lacan: From Hermeneutics to the Cause

Lacan's opening gesture consisted of an unconditional espousal of hermeneutics: as early as his doctorial thesis from 1933, and especially in the *Discours de Rome*, he opposes determinism in the name of (psycho-analysis as) a hermeneutical approach: 'All analytic experience is an experience of signification.'[1] Here originates the great Lacanian motif of the *futur antérieur* of symbolization: a fact counts not as *factum brutum*, but only as it is always-already historicized. (What is at stake in the anal stage, for example, is not excretion as such but how the child makes sense of it: as a submission to the Other's – parent's – demand, as a triumph of his control, etc.). This Lacan can easily be translated into the later problematic of anti-psychiatry or existential psychoanalysis: Freudian clinical designations (hysteria, obsessional neurosis, perversion, etc.) are not 'objective' classifications stigmatizing the patient; instead, they aim at subjective attitudes, 'existential projects', which have grown out of the subject's concrete intersubjective situation and for which the subject, in his freedom, is ultimately responsible.

As early as the mid-1950s, however, this hermeneutical attitude was undermined by a worm of doubt. At the very least, the fact remains that Freud unambiguously resisted reducing psychoanalysis to hermeneutics: his interpretation of dreams took shape through his break with the traditional inquiry into their meaning. This resistance of Freud, his persistent quest for a cause (in trauma), cannot be dismissed as a naturalist-determinist prejudice. Likewise, Lacan's similar shift away from hermeneutics involves no regression into naturalism but, rather, renders visible the 'ex-timate', inherent decentrement of the field of signification – that is, the Cause at work in the midst of this very field. This shift occurs in two steps. First, Lacan embraces structuralism: the decentred cause of signification is identified as the signifying structure. What is at stake in this first shift from hermeneutics to structuralism, therefore, is precisely the question of cause. As we move *from signification to its cause*, signification is conceived of as the *effect*-of-sense: it is the imaginary experience-of-meaning whose inherent constituent is the misrecognition of its determining *cause*, the formal mechanism of the signifying structure itself.

This shift from signification to the signifying cause (correlative to the notion of signification as an effect) does not reduce signification to a product of positive determinism – that is to say, this is not a step from hermeneutics to natural sciences. What forestalls this reduction is the gap that separates the Symbolic from the Real. Thus, Lacan's next step involves precisely the insight into *how this gap between the Real and the Symbolic affects the symbolic order itself*: it functions as the *inherent* limitation of this order. The symbolic order is 'barred', the signifying chain is inherently inconsistent, 'non-all', structured around a hole. This inherent non-symbolizable reef maintains the gap between the Symbolic and the Real – that is, it prevents the Symbolic from 'falling into' the Real – and, again, what is ultimately at stake in this decentrement of the Real with regard to the Symbolic is the Cause: the Real is the absent Cause of the Symbolic. The Freudian and Lacanian name for this cause is, of course, *trauma*. In this sense, Lacan's theoretical enterprise already lies 'beyond hermeneutics and structuralism' (the subtitle of Dreyfus and Rabinow's book on Foucault).

The relationship between the cause and the law – the law of causality, of symbolic determination – is therefore an antagonistic one: 'Cause is to be distinguished from that which is determinate in a chain, in other words the *law* ... there is cause only in something that doesn't work.'[2] The Cause *qua* the Real intervenes where symbolic determination stumbles, misfires – that is, where a signifier falls out. For that reason, the Cause *qua* the Real can never effectuate its causal power in a direct way, as such, but must always operate intermediately, under the guise of disturbances within the symbolic order. Suffice it to recall slips of the tongue when the *automaton* of the signifying chain is, for a brief moment, disrupted by the intervention of some traumatic memory. However, the fact that the Real operates and is accessible only through the Symbolic does not authorize us to conceive of it as a factor immanent to the Symbolic: the Real is precisely that which resists and eludes the grasp of the Symbolic and, consequently, that which is detectable within the Symbolic only under the guise of its disturbances.

In short, the Real is the absent Cause which perturbs the causality of the symbolic law. On that account, the structure of overdetermination is irreducible: the Cause exercises its influence only as redoubled, through a certain discrepancy or time-lag – that is, if the 'original' trauma of the Real is to become effective, it must hook on to, find an echo in, some present deadlock. Recall Freud's crucial statement on how 'a normal train of thought' – expressing a present deadlock – 'is only submitted to the abnormal psychical treatment of the sort we have been describing' – to the dream work – 'if an unconscious wish, derived from infancy and in a state of repression' – that is, a desire concomitant to the 'original' trauma – 'has been transferred on to it'.[3] Overdetermination means that this statement must also be read in the opposite direction: 'An unconscious wish, derived from infancy and in a state of repression, can only exert its influence if it is transferred on to a normal train of thought.'[4]

Consequently, a certain radical ambiguity pertains to the Cause: the Cause is real, the presupposed reef which resists symbolization and disturbs the course of its *automaton*, yet the Cause is simultaneously the retroactive product of its own effects. In the case of the Wolf Man, Freud's most famous patient, the Cause, of course, was the traumatic scene of the parental *coitus a tergo* – this scene was the non-symbolizable kernel around which all later successive symbolizations whirled. This Cause, however, not only exerted its efficiency after a certain time-lag, it literally *became* trauma – that is, Cause – through delay: when the Wolf Man, at the age of two, witnessed the *coitus a tergo*, nothing traumatic marked this scene; the scene acquired traumatic features only in retrospect, with the later development of the child's infantile sexual theories, when it become impossible to integrate the scene within the newly emerged horizon of narrativization–historicization–symbolization.

Herein lies the trauma's vicious cycle: the trauma is the Cause which perturbs the smooth engine of symbolization and throws it off balance; it gives rise to an indelible inconsistency in the symbolic field; but for all that, the trauma has no existence of its own prior to symbolization; it remains an anamorphic entity that gains its consistency only in retrospect, viewed from within the symbolic horizon – it acquires its consistency from the structural necessity of the inconsistency of the symbolic field. As soon as we obliterate this retrospective character of the trauma and 'substantialize' it into a positive entity, one that can be isolated as a cause preceding its symbolic effects, we regress to common linear determinism. Therefore, in order to apprehend this paradox of the traumatic object-cause (the Lacanian *objet petit a*), a topological model is needed in which *the limit that separates Inside from Outside coincides with the internal limit.* Viewed from within the symbolic order, the object appears as its irreducible/constitutive Outside, as a reef that bends the symbolic space, disturbs the symbolic circuit; as a trauma that cannot be integrated into it, a foreign body that prevents the symbolic order from fully constituting itself. However, the moment we 'step out' in order to grasp the trauma as it is in itself and not through its distorted reflections within the symbolic space, the traumatic object evaporates into nothingness.[5]

This paradox of trauma *qua* cause that does not pre-exist its effects but is itself retroactively 'posited' by them involves a kind of temporal loop: *it is through its 'repetition', through its echoes within the signifying structure, that the cause retroactively becomes what it always-already was.* In other words, a direct approach necessarily fails: if we try to grasp the trauma directly, irrespective of its later effects, we are left with a meaningless *factum brutum* – in the case of the Wolf Man, with the fact of the parental *coitus a tergo*, which is not a cause at all, since it involves no direct psychic efficiency. It is only through its echoes within the symbolic structure that the *factum brutum* of the parental *coitus a tergo* retroactively acquires its traumatic character and becomes the Cause.

This is what Lacan has in mind when he speaks of the signifier's *synchrony* as opposed to simple atemporal simultaneity: synchrony designates such a paradoxical synchronization, coincidence, of present and past – that is, such a temporal loop where, by progressing forward, we return to where we always-already were. Herein resides the sense of Lacan's obsession with topological models of 'curved' space in the 1960s and 1970s (Moebius band, Klein's bottle, inner eight, etc.): what all these models have in common is the fact that they cannot be seized 'at a glance', 'in one view' – they all involve a kind of logical temporality – that is, we must first let ourselves be caught in a trap, become the victim of an optical illusion, in order to reach the turning point at which, all of a sudden, the entire perspective shifts and we discover that we are already 'on the other side', on another surface. In the case of the Moebius band, for example, 'synchrony' occurs when, after passing through the whole circle, we find ourselves at the same point, yet on the opposite surface. It is impossible to miss the Hegelian overtones of this paradox: does not this repetition of the same, this return to the same, which brings about the change of the surface, offer a perfect illustration of Hegel's thesis on identity as absolute contradiction? Moreover, does not Hegel himself assert that, through the dialectical process, the thing *becomes what it is*?

Such a 'curved' surface-structure is the structure of the subject: what we call 'subject' can emerge only within the structure of overdetermination – that is, in this vicious cycle where the Cause itself is (presup)posed by its effects. The subject is strictly correlative to this real *qua* Cause: $ – a. In order to grasp the constitutive paradox of the subject, therefore, we must move beyond the standard opposition of 'subjective' and 'objective', the order of 'appearances' (of what is 'only for the subject') and the 'In-itself'. Likewise, we must reject the concomitant notion of the subject as the agency that 'subjectivizes', moulds and makes sense of the inert-senseless In-itself. The *objet a* as cause is an In-itself that resists

32

subjectivization-symbolization, yet far from being 'independent of the subject', it is *stricto sensu* the subject's shadow among the objects, a kind of stand-in for the subject, a pure semblance lacking any consistency of its own.

In other words, if the subject is to emerge, he must set himself against a paradoxical object that is real, that cannot be subjectivized. Such an object remains an 'absolute non-subject' whose very presence involves *aphanisis*, the erasure of the subject; yet as such this presence is the subject himself in his oppositional determination, the negative of the subject, a piece of flesh that the subject has to lose if he is to emerge as the void of the distance towards every objectivity. This uncanny object is the subject itself in the mode of objectivity, an object which is the subject's absolute otherness precisely in so far as it is closer to the subject than anything the subject can set against itself in the domain of objectivity.[6] This is what the Kojèvean quasi-Hegelian negative ontology of the subject *qua* negativity, nothing, a hole in the positivity of the real, and so on, fails to see: this void of subjectivity is strictly correlative to the emergence, in the Real itself, of a stain which 'is' the subject. (In the domain of philosophy, perhaps the only concept that corresponds to this uncanny object is Kant's transcendental object: noumenal 'In-itself', an absolute presupposition, yet simultaneously pure positedness – that is, the only object thoroughly posited by the subject, and not – as is the case with ordinary phenomenal objects – some transcendentally moulded stuff in whose guise the In-itself affects the passive subject.[7])

We can see, now, how Lacanian theory surmounts the antagonism of explanation and comprehension, of signification and determinism: the traumatic Real is *stricto sensu* the cause of the subject – not the initial impetus in the linear chain of causes that brings about the subject, but, on the contrary, the missing link in the chain – that is, the cause as remainder, as 'the object that cannot be swallowed, as it were, which remains stuck in the gullet of the signifier'.[8] As such, it is correlative to the subject *qua* break in the chain of the signifying causality, hole in the signifying network: 'the subject sees himself caused as a lack by *a*'.[9] This Lacanian concept of the subject as $, correlative to *a*, also elucidates Adorno's foreboding of a subject paradoxically concomitant to a 'preponderance of the object' – this object can only be the *objet petit a*.

Between Substance and Subject

How, then, in the light of this Lacanian concept of the subject, are we to comprehend Hegel's proposition on substance as subject? In the classic Frankfurt School, as well as in Habermas, the motif of 'substance as subject' involves the traditional notion of disalienation: 'repression' designates the subject's self-alienation, and by accomplishing the gesture of disalienation the subject recognizes in the alienated substance, in this false appearance of a foreign power, the reified result of his own activity. In short, substance becomes subject when the subject appropriates the alienated substantial content. 'Hegelian' as it may appear, this conception was never really Hegel's own, and it is precisely Lacan's notion of the subject which enables us to bypass this traditional 'Hegelianism'; or, to put it in the language of the triad of positing–external–determining reflection: the Frankfurt School's Hegelianism surmounts the external reflection by way of returning to the positing reflection, to the notion of the subject who posits the entire substantial content, whereas Hegel directly opposes such a resolution. How?

Let us tackle the problem at the precise point of the passage of substance into subject; this point lies at the end of the 'logic of essence' where, with the shift of absolute necessity into freedom, objective logic passes into subjective logic. In the terms of the last, third part of Hegel's logic of essence ('Actuality'), the problem of 'substance as subject' is set out in the following terms: how can we formulate a contingency that would not collapse into necessity?[10] That is to say, the abstract, immediate setting of necessity against contingency leads to their abstract identity – that is, to the impossibility of their conceptual differentiation:

• The first attempt to differentiate contingency and necessity, '*formal* actuality, possibility and necessity', defines categories in a purely formal-logical way, without any determination-of-content (contingent is an actual entity whose opposite is also possible; necessary is an actual entity whose opposite is inherently impossible; possible is an entity which is inherently non-contradictory); the dialectical analysis of these notions leads to the empty tautology according to which whatever exists exists necessarily since, by the mere fact of its existence, its opposite is no longer possible. In this way, the thought becomes reduced to a formal assertion of the necessity of the most trivial empirical reality.

• In the second attempt, '*real* actuality, possibility and necessity', all distinctions again collapse into necessity. Here, one endeavours to articulate the relationship between possibility and actuality in a more concrete, content-related way: as the relationship between a determinate state of things and the conditions of its possibility – that is, those circumstances that must have been present when this particular state of things was realized. At this level, possibility does not designate a simple formal non-contradiction; it is real, it equals the totality of real conditions. However, a closer analysis again reveals the inherent contradiction of the category of real possibility: as soon as the possibility in question is truly real – that is, as soon as *all* conditions of a thing are present – we are no longer dealing with possibility but with necessity; a thing necessarily occurs. If, on the contrary, all conditions are not present, the possibility in question is simply not yet real.

• The third attempt, *absolute* necessity, corresponds to the standard notion of the dialectical synthesis of necessity and contingency – that is, of a necessity that asserts itself through the interplay of contingencies. This necessity encompasses its otherness, it 'remains with itself in its otherness', it contains contingency as its ideal, sublated moment – herein lies its 'absolute' character. In other words, far from being a process in which 'everything is governed by absolute necessity' without even the slightest element of contingency, absolute necessity is a process whose very necessity realizes itself not *in opposition to* contingency but *in the form of* contingency. We could invoke to infinity examples of this necessity *qua* totality of the process that dominates the multitude of its contingent moments. Suffice it to mention the classic Marxist example: the necessity of the shift of the French Revolution into Bonapartism, which was realized in the contingent person of Napoleon.

A better example of absolute necessity than this unfortunate Marxist reference is Marx's case of the capitalist system as a totality: the capitalist system is an 'absolute necessity' in so far as it reproduces itself, its notional structure, through a set of external, contingent circumstances. These contingent circumstances exhibit the structure of real necessity broadly corresponding to what we usually conceive of as mechanical necessity – that is, a necessity in which the causal chain is linear, running from the circumstances or conditions of a thing to the thing itself as the necessary effect of these same circumstances or conditions. What eludes us when we observe phenomena from the point of view of real necessity is the living totality that reproduces itself through the interplay of contingent linear necessities.

For each individual act that pertains to the capitalist system, a set of external causes can be found which thoroughly explain the act's occurrence (why gold was found in a certain place, why some capitalist introduced the first weaving machine, etc., *ad infinitum*). Yet this 'bad infinity' of moments whose occurrence can be explained by the categories of real necessity is in its entirety contingent, since it does not provide an answer to the crucial question: how does the capitalist system *qua* living totality reproduce itself through this network of indifferent, external circumstances – indifferent in the precise sense that their connection with the capitalist system is contingent and not comprised in the very notion of capitalism? The absolute necessity *qua* living totality that reproduces itself through the interplay of indifferent circumstances contains the moment of *teleology*, but not in the usual meaning of the term. In order to explain any particular phenomenon, we need not have recourse to its alleged external aims; every phenomenon, taken apart, can be explained via real necessity. The true enigma, however, is how the totality makes use of the previously given contingent circumstances for its reproduction. Here Marx speaks the language of Hegelian absolute necessity: he points out that capitalism is indifferent to its empirical genesis (was it founded on robbery? etc.) – once the system achieves its balance and starts to reproduce itself, it posits its presupposed external conditions as its inherent moments.

This, however, is not Hegel's last word. The dialectical synthesis of necessity and contingency cannot be reduced to the preservation-sublation of contingency as a subordinated, partial moment of global necessity – the acme of the dialectic of necessity and contingency arrives in the assertion of the contingent character of necessity as such. How are we to conceive of this assertion? Its elementary matrix is provided by *narrativization*, that mode in which the contingency of past events becomes transposed into a homogeneous symbolic structure. If, for example, we are Marxists, the entire past is perceived as one long narrative whose constant theme is the class struggle and whose plot strives towards that classless society which resolves social antagonisms; if we are liberals, the past tells the story of the gradual emancipation of the individual from the constraints of collectivity and Fate, and so on. And it is *here* that freedom and the subject intervene: freedom is *stricto sensu* the contingency of necessity – that is, it is contained in the initial 'if . . .', in the (contingent) choice of the modality by means of which we symbolize the contingent real or impose some narrative necessity upon it. 'Substance as subject' means that the very necessity that sublates contingency by positing it as its ideal moment is itself contingent.[11]

Let us explain this passage in a more immanent way. Absolute necessity as *causa sui* is an inherently contradictory notion; its contradiction is explicated, posited as such, when the notion of substance (synonymous with Spinozean absolute necessity) splits into active substance (cause) and passive substance (effect). This opposition is then surmounted by the category of *reciprocity*, wherein the cause which determines its effect is itself determined by the effect – thereby, we pass from substance to subject:

> This infinite reflection-into-self /reciprocity/, namely, that being is in and for itself only insofar as it is posited, is the *consummation of substance*. But this consummation is no longer substance itself but something higher, the *concept*, the *subject*.[12]

This category of reciprocity, however, is more intricate than it may seem: in order to comprehend it adequately (i.e. in order to avoid the usual platitudes about the moments of a living totality that reciprocally condition themselves) we must return to the relationship between $ and *a*. The *a* is an object which is in-itself only in so far as it is posited; as the subject's cause, it is entirely posited by the subject. In other words, 'reciprocity' designates that same vicious cycle of the real Cause and its signifying effects out of which the subject emerges – that is, that cycle in which the symbolic network of effects retroactively posits its traumatic Cause. Thus we arrive at the most concise definition of the subject: the subject is an effect that entirely posits its own cause. Hegel says the same thing when he concludes that absolute necessity

> is a relation because it is a distinguishing whose moments are themselves its whole totality, and therefore absolutely subsist, but in such a manner that there is only one subsistence and the difference is only the *Schein* of the expository process, and this [*Schein*] is the absolute itself.[13]

The vertiginous reversal is brought about by the last clause of the last sentence. That is to say, had the sentence ended *without* 'and this is the absolute itself', we would be left with the traditional definition of the substance as absolute: each of its moments (attributes) is in itself the whole totality of the substance, it 'subsists absolutely', so that there is only one subsistence, and difference concerns only the appearance. (In Spinoza, for example, every attribute expresses the substance in its entirety – that is, the totality of its determinations. The chair and the notion of the chair are not two different entities, but one and the same entity expressed in two attributes, that is, in two modalities of the 'absolutely same subsistence'.) However – and here we encounter the Hegelian passage from substance to subject – the 'absolute' is not this self-identical 'absolute subsistence' that remains the same in all attributes, as a kind of kernel of the Real. If we accept such a notion of the absolute, the moment of difference (the differentiation of the absolute's content into a multitude of particular determinations) concerns only the 'expository process', *Darstellungsweise*, the way we as finite subjects, from our position of external reflection, conceive of the absolute, not the absolute-in-itself. The 'substance as subject', on the contrary, means precisely that the 'expository process' – the way we, from our position of external reflection, conceive of the absolute – is *the inherent determination of the absolute itself*.[14]

The Syllogism of Christianity

We can now see how the reversal of absolute necessity into freedom, of substance into subject, involves a purely formal conversion: at the level of substance, the absolute is a subsistence which remains the same through all its moments; at the level of subject, the absolute is this very *Schein* of the differentiation of moments, each of them containing in itself the totality of substance. The tension between external and positing reflection, between 'substance' and 'subject', appears in its purest apropos the paradox of *social Cause*, which is the product of the subject's belief in itself. To declare 'I believe in ... (Communism, freedom, nation)' means – what? It attests to my belief that I am not alone; others exist who also believe in the same Cause. As to its inherent semantic structure, the proposition 'I believe in ...' is therefore reflexive – that is, self-referential; its express form (the form of an immediate relationship of the subject to the Cause) should not deceive us: to believe in a social Cause ultimately means *to believe in belief (of the others) itself*. Here is a characteristic passage from Hegel's *Phenomenology*:

> ... the absolute being of faith is essentially not the abstract being, the Beyond of believing consciousness. Rather it is the *Geist* of the community, the unity of the abstract being and self-consciousness. That this *Geist* is the *Geist* of the community depends essentially on the doing of the community. For this *Geist* exists only through the productive action of consciousness – or rather, it is not without having been brought forth by consciousness. For although such doing is essential, it is nevertheless not the sole essential ground of that being, but merely one moment. At the same time, the being [of faith] exists in and for itself.[15]

This is how we are to read Hegel's proposition that 'being is in and for itself only insofar as it is posited': not as a subjectivist platitude according to which every being is already subjectively posited, but as the paradox of an object which is *posited* precisely as *existing in and for itself*. (The key to this paradox turns on how the gesture of subjectivization-positing, in its most fundamental dimension, consists of a *purely formal gesture of conceiving as the result of our positing something which occurs inevitably, notwithstanding our activity*.[16]) The social Cause, the object of Faith, is produced by the community's labour in its very capacity as the presupposed Ground that exists in and for itself. Hegel asserts the same paradox with regard to the relationship between knowledge and truth: the subject not only passively mirrors truth, he 'posits' it by means of his cognitive activity, yet he posits it as 'the true existing in and for itself': 'The concept, to be sure, produces the truth – for such is subjective freedom – but at the same time it recognizes this truth not as something produced, but as the true existing in and for itself.'[17]

In this precise sense, the 'death of God' designates for Hegel the death of the transcendent Beyond that exists in itself: the outcome of this death is God *qua* Holy Spirit – that is, the product of the labour of the community of believers. The relationship between cause and effect is dialectically reflected here. On the one hand, the Cause is unambiguously the product of the subjects' activity; it is 'alive' only in so far as it is continually resuscitated by the believers' passion. On the other hand, these same believers experience the Cause as the Absolute, as what sets their lives in motion – in short: as the Cause of their activity; by the same token, they experience themselves as mere transient accidents of their Cause. Subjects therefore posit the Cause, yet they posit it not as something subordinated to them but as their absolute Cause. What we encounter here is again the paradoxical temporal loop of the subject: the Cause is posited, but it is posited as what it 'always-already was'.

How, precisely, are we to grasp this dialectical unity of God *qua* substantial Ground of transient individuals and of these same individuals *qua* subjects whose activity animates God? The 'positing reflection', which conceives of religious content as something produced by the subjects, and the 'external reflection', which conceives of subjects as passing moments of the religious Substance-God, are both in themselves the whole totality: the *entire* religious content is posited by the subjects, and the subjects are *entirely* moments of the religious Substance which exists in-itself. For that reason, the 'dialectical synthesis' of the two moments – the 'determining reflection' – does not amount to a compromise that concedes to each of the two extremes its partial justification ('religious content is *in part* produced by men and *in part* exists in-itself'). Instead, it involves the absolute mediation of both sides in the person of Christ, who is simultaneously the representative of God among human subjects and the subject who passes into God. In Christianity, the only identity of man and God is the identity in Christ – in clear contrast to the pre-Christian attitude, which conceives of such an identity as the asymptotic point of man's infinite approach to God by means of his spiritual purification. In the language of Hegelian speculation, this intermediary role of Christ means that Christianity has the structure of a syllogism: the Christian triad of Doctrine, Faith and Ritual is structured according to the triad of qualitative syllogism, syllogism of reflection, and syllogism of necessity.[18]

The paradigmatic matrix of the first syllogism is S–P–U: the ascension from the singular to the universal, with the particular as the middle term that disappears in the conclusion (Socrates is a man; man is mortal; therefore, Socrates is mortal). The nature of the second syllogism is inductive – that is, its matrix is P–S–U: the singular is the middle term which enables us to connect the particular and the universal (this swan is white; that swan is white, etc.; therefore, swan as such is white). Finally, the third syllogism is S–U–P – that is, its middle term is the universal which mediates between the singular and the particular – for example, in the case of the disjunctive syllogism 'Rational beings are either men or angels; Socrates, who is a rational being, is a man; therefore, he is not an angel'.[19] – How is this syllogistic trinity linked to Christianity? The answer is provided by the Christian triad of Doctrine, Faith and Ritual:

• The content of Christian *Doctrine* is Christ's ascension through his death, which means that the role of the middle term is played by death *qua* negativity which is the way of all flesh. Death denotes here the moment of judgement in the judicial sense – the sentencing of Christ to death – as well as in the logical sense – the distinguishing of subject and predicate, of the perishable individual and the perennial Universal. At this level, therefore, the syllogism is as follows: 'Christ, this individual, is exposed to death, to the judgement that awaits all particular living beings; but he rises from the dead and ascends into Heaven – that is, is united with the imperishable Universal.' In this sense, one could say that the death of Christ in the Doctrine is 'objective', its subject matter, and not yet existentially experienced. On this account, we remain within the abstract opposition of perishable finitude and transcendent Infinity: death is still experienced as the force of negativity that affects a particular, finite being; it is not yet experienced as the simultaneous death of the abstract Beyond itself.

• The content of Christian *Faith* is salvation, accomplished by Christ when he took upon himself the sins of humanity and expired on the Cross as a common mortal – salvation thus involves the identity of man and God. This identity, which in the Doctrine was a mere object of knowledge, occurs in Faith as an existential experience. What does this mean with regard to the structure of the syllogism? How do I, a finite mortal, concretely experience my *identity* with God? I experience it in my own radical despair, which – paradoxically – involves a *loss* of faith: when, apparently forsaken by God, I am driven to despair, thrown into absolute solitude, I can identify with Christ on the Cross ('Father, why hast Thou forsaken me?'). In the identity of man and God, my personal experience of being abandoned by God thus overlaps with the despair of Christ himself at being abandoned by the divine Father, and it is in this sense that we are dealing with the syllogism of analogy/induction: the imposed analogy is drawn between my own miserable position and the position of Christ on the Cross. Thus the identity of man and God in Faith is not 'immediate', it consists of the very *identity of the two splittings*. So the difference between this experience of Faith and Doctrine is double: here the death of Christ is not merely 'objective' but also 'subjective', involving my intimate experience of despair; on that account, I find myself absolutely alone, I 'contract' into the night of the pure I in which all reality disintegrates – what expires on the Cross is thus not only the terrestrial representative of God (as it still seemed in the first syllogism of the Doctrine) but God himself, namely the God of Beyond, God as the transcendent Substance, as the divine Reason which guarantees that our lives have Meaning.

• The content of the *Ritual*, finally, is the Holy Spirit as the positive unity of man and God: the God who expired on the Cross is resurrected in the guise of the Spirit of the religious community. He is no longer the Father who, safe in His Beyond, regulates our fate, but the work of us all, members of the community, since he is present in the ritual performed by us. The structure of the syllogism here is S–U–P: the Universal, the Holy Spirit, mediates between us as particular humans, and Christ as the singular individual – in the ritual of the Christian community, the resurrected Christ is again here, alive among us believers.

Why Isn't Hegel a Humanist Atheist?

The crucial feature not to be missed here is the abyss that continues to separate Hegel from humanist atheism according to which God is a product of the collective imagination of the people. That is to say, at first glance it may appear that Hegel interprets the philosophical content of Christianity as positing just such a 'death of God': do not the death of God on the Cross, and his later resurrection in the spirit of the religious community, amount to the fact that God passes over, ceases to exist as the transcendent Beyond which dominates the lives of men (and this, precisely, is what the word 'God' means in the common religious use), in order to be restored to life in the guise of the spirit of community – that is to say, as the result-product of the communal activity of men?

Why does Hegel resist such a reading? This resistance by no means attests to Hegel's inconsequence, due to his placating attitude towards traditional theology or even to his political conformism; rather, it results from Hegel's having thought out all the consequences of the 'death of

God' – that is to say, the consequences of reducing all objective content to the pure I. Conceived this way, the 'death of God' can no longer appear as a liberating experience, as the retreat of the Beyond which sets man free, opening up to him the domain of terrestrial activity as the field in which he is to affirm his creative subjectivity; instead the 'death of God' involves the loss of the consistent 'terrestrial' reality itself. Far from heralding the triumph of man's autonomous creative capacity, the 'death of God' is more akin to what the great texts of mysticism usually designate as the 'night of the world': the dissolution of (symbolically constituted) reality.

In Lacanian terms, we are dealing with the suspension of the big Other, which guarantees the subject's access to reality: in the experience of the death of God, we stumble upon the fact that 'the big Other doesn't exist [*l'Autre n'existe pas*]' (Lacan).[20] In the Holy Spirit, the big Other is then posited as a symbolic, de-substantialized fiction – that is, as an entity that does not exist as an in-itself, but only in so far as it is animated by the 'work of each and all', that is to say, in the guise of a spiritual substance. Why, then, is this spiritual substance not comprehended as the product of the collective subject? Why is the place of the Holy Spirit irreducibly Other with regard to the subject? The answer is provided by invoking the Lacanian concept of the big Other.

What is the big Other? Let us recall the scene from Act II of Mozart's *Così fan tutte* in which Don Alfonso and Despina bring the two couples together: they overcome the couples' reticence by literally conversing in their place (Alfonso addresses the ladies on behalf of the two 'Albanians' – 'Se voi non parlate, per voi parlero ...', and Despina delivers the ladies' affirmative answer – 'Per voi la risposta a loro daro ...'). The comical, caricatural nature of this dialogue should not deceive us for a moment: things are for real, 'everything is decided' in this externalized form. It is precisely through representatives that the two new amorous couples are constituted, and all that follows (the explicit acknowledgement of love) is just a matter of execution. For this reason, once the couples join hands, Despina and Alfonso can quickly withdraw to let things take their own course; their mediatory job is done....[21]

In the totally different domain of crime novels, Ruth Rendell exercises the extraordinary power to make some material network function as a metaphor of the big Other. In *King Solomon's Carpet*, for example, this metaphor is the network of the London Underground. Each of the novel's principal protagonists is caught in a closed psychotic universe, lacking any proper communication with fellow-creatures and interpreting contingent accidents as meaningful 'answers of the real' – that is, as confirmations of his or her paranoiac forebodings. For all that, it seems as if their encounters are controlled by an invisible hand, as if they are all part of some hidden scheme materialized in the network of underground tunnels and trains, this nocturnal, subterranean Other Place (the metaphor of the Unconscious) which redoubles the 'daily world' of the chaotic streets of London.[22]

Here we confront the decentrement of the Other with regard to the subject, on account of which the subject – as soon as he returns from the 'night of the world', from the absolute negativity of I = I, into the 'daily' world of *logos* – is caught in a network whose effects a priori elude his grasp. This is why self-consciousness is strictly correlative to the Unconscious in the Freudian sense of the term, which is akin to the Kantian infinite judgement: when I assert about a thought that 'it *is* unconscious', this is quite different from asserting that such a thought '*is not* conscious'. In the latter case – when I negate the predicate 'conscious' – the (logical) subject is simply located in the domain of the non-psychic (of biology, and so on – in short, in the vast domain of all that goes on in our body beyond the reach of our consciousness). However, when I affirm a non-predicate and assert that the thought is unconscious, I thereby open up a third, uncanny domain that subverts the very distinction between psychic-conscious and somatic, a domain that has no place in the ontological-phenomenological distinction between psychic and somatic, and whose status is for that reason, as Lacan puts it in *Seminar XI*, 'pre-ontological'.[23]

The Enigma of 'Mechanical Memory'

Is the Lacanian big Other *qua* decentred order of the signifier not defined, however, by the primacy of the signifier's nonsense over the dimension of expression – where is *this* to be found in Hegel? The biggest surprise that awaits us in the paragraphs on language in Hegel's *Encyclopaedia* (paras 451–64[24]) is the sudden and unexpected appearance of the so-called 'Mechanical Memory' *after* the fully accomplished 'sublation' of the language-sign in its spiritual content.[25]

Hegel develops his theory of language in 'Representation', Section 2 of 'Psychology', which delineates the contours of the transition from 'Intuition' to 'Thinking' – that is to say, the process of the subject's gradual deliverance from externally found and imposed content, provided by the senses, through its internalization and universalization. As usual with Hegel, the process occurs in three moments. First, in 'Recollection', an intuition is torn out of the external causal spatiotemporal context and brought within the subject's own inner space and time; in this way, it is at his disposal as a contingent element that can be freely recalled at any time. Once intuition is transposed within Intelligence, it comes under its power – Intelligence may do with it as it pleases: it can decompose an intuition into its ingredients and then recombine them in a different, 'unnatural' Whole; it can compare it with other intuitions and set out common markers; all this is the work of 'Imagination' which gradually leads to the Symbol.

First, a particular image stands for some more complex network of representations, or for some universal feature (the image of a beard, for example, can recall to one's mind virile masculinity, authority, etc.). This universal feature, however, is still tainted with the particular sensible image that stands for it – we reach true universality only when every resemblance between the universal feature and the image that represents it is abolished. In this way, we arrive at *Word*: at an external, arbitrary sign whose link with its meaning is wholly arbitrary. It is only this abasement of sign to a pure indifferent externality that enables meaning to free itself of sensible intuition, and thus to purify itself into true universality. In this way, the sign (word) is posited in its truth: as the pure movement of self-sublation, as an entity that attains its truth by obliterating itself in the face of its meaning.

'Verbal Memory' then internalizes and universalizes the very external sign that signifies a universal feature. The result at which we thus arrive is a 'representational language' composed of signs which are the unity of two ingredients: on the one hand, the universalized name, mental sound, a type recognized as the same in different utterances; on the other hand, its meaning, some universal representation. Names in 'representational language' possess a fixed universal content determined not by their relationship to other names but by their relationship to represented reality. What we are dealing with here is the standard notion of language as a collection of signs with a fixed universal meaning that mirrors reality, the notion which involves the triad of sign itself *qua* body, signified content in the subject's mind, and reality that signs refer to ... a simple pre-theoretical sensitivity tells us that something is missing here, that this is not yet a true, living language. What is missing are chiefly two things: on the one hand, the syntactic and semantic relations between signs themselves – that is, the *self-referential circularity* on account of which one can always say that the meaning of a word is a series of other words (asked 'What is a camel?', one usually answers with a series of words: 'A four-footed mammal resembling a horse, yet with a high hump on its back', etc.); on the other hand, the *relationship to the speaking subject* – it is not clear how the speaker himself is inscribed in 'representational language' as the mirroring of the three levels of signs, mental ideas, and reality.

In Hegelese, the fatal weakness of representational language resides precisely in its representational character: in the fact that it remains stuck at the level of *Vorstellung*, of the external, finite representation that refers to some transcendent, external content. To put it in contemporary terms: representational language is the self-effacing medium of representing-transmitting some universal notional Content that remains external to this medium: the medium itself functions as an indifferent means of transmitting an independent content. What is missing here is a word that would not merely represent its external content but would also constitute it, bring it forth – a word through which this signified content would become what it is – in short, a 'performative'.

How, then, do we progress from here to a speech that acts as the adequate medium of infinite thought? At this point we come across a surprise that causes much embarrassment to the interpreters of Hegel: between the 'Verbal Memory' that warrants the concrete unity of meaning and expression, and the 'Thought' proper, Hegel somewhat mysteriously interposes 'Mechanical Memory', a recitation by heart of the series of words in which one attaches no meaning to one's words – in short, an 'abandoning of the spirit [*Geistesverlassen*]' – as the very transition to the activity of thinking. Having exposed how the sign remains within the confines of representation – that is, of the external synthesis of meaning and expression – Hegel does not dismantle the 'false' unity of sign by casting off its external side – expression as the external medium of the designated content; on the contrary, he discards, sacrifices, the inner content itself. The outcome of such a radical reduction is that within the space of language we 'regress' to the level of Being, the poorest category: Hegel refers to the Intelligence in Mechanical Memory as 'Being, the universal space of names as such, i.e., of senseless words' (para. 463) which in a way disappear even before they fully arise; of 'articulated tones' as 'transient, disappearing, completely ideal realizations which follow forth in an element which offers no resistance' (para. 444).

What we have here are no longer representational words as universal types of the fixed connection of an expression with its meaning (the word 'horse' always means . . .) but a pure becoming, a flux of senseless individuality of utterances – the only thing that unites them is the 'empty connective band' of Intelligence itself. At this level, the meaning of a name can reside only in the fact that it follows on and/or triggers other such names. *It is only here that the true, concrete negativity of the linguistic sign emerges*: for this negativity to emerge, it is not sufficient for the word to be reduced to the pure flux of self-obliteration – its Beyond itself, meaning, has to be 'flattened', it has to lose all its positive content, so that the only thing which remains is the empty negativity that 'is' the subject.

The Christological connotation of this sacrificing of the

representational-objective meaning is unmistakeable: the reduction of the word to the pure flux of becoming is not the word's self-obliteration in the face of its Meaning but the death of this Meaning itself – as with Christ, whose death on the Cross is not the passing of God's terrestrial representative but the death of the God of Beyond Himself. Therein resides Hegel's properly dialectical insight: the stumbling block to the true-infinite activity of Thought in the representational name is not its external sight but the very fixed universality of its inner meaning.

The voidance that occurs here is double. First, the entire objective-representational content is evacuated, so that the only thing that remains is the void of Intelligence (subject) itself – in Lacanese, from *sign*, which represents something (a positive content) for someone, we pass to *signifier*, which represents the subject itself for other signifiers. With the same gesture, however, the subject (S) itself ceases to be the fullness of the experienced inner content, of meaning, and is 'barred', hollowed out, reduced to $ – or, as Hegel puts it, the job of Mechanical Memory is 'to flatten the ground of interiority to pure Being, to pure space ... without opposition from a subjective interiority' (para. 464).[26] It is only this 'flattening', this reduction to Being, to the new immediacy of the word, that opens up the *performative* dimension – why? Let us approach this crucial point via a passage from *Jenaer Realphilosophie*, in which Hegel describes how

> to the question 'What is this?' we usually answer, 'it is a lion, donkey,' etc. It is – that means that it is not a yellow thing that has feet, etc., something independent on its own, but a name, a tone of my voice – something completely different from what it is in the intuition. And that is [its] true Being.[27]

Hegel draws our attention to the paradox of naming, so obvious that it is generally passed over in silence: when I say 'This is an elephant', what I literally, at the most elementary, immediate level, claim is that this gigantic creature with a trunk, and so on, really is a sound in my mouth, the eight letters I have just pronounced. In his *Seminar I*, on Freud's technical writings, Lacan plays on the same paradox: once the word 'elephant' is pronounced, the elephant is here in all his massive presence – although he is nowhere to be seen in reality, his notion is rendered present. Here we encounter the unexpected Stoic aspect of Hegel (and Lacan): Stoic logic liked to point out how, when you pronounce the word 'carriage', a carriage effectively runs through your mouth.

What Hegel has in mind, however, is something else: the simple, apparently symmetrical inversion of 'an elephant is ... /a four-footed mammal with a trunk/' into 'this is an elephant' involves the reversal of a representational constative into a performative. That is, when I say 'an elephant is ... /a four-footed mammal with a trunk/' , I treat 'elephant' as a representational name, and point out the external content it designates. When I say 'this is an elephant', however, I thereby confer upon an object its symbolic identity; I add to the bundle of real properties a symbolic unifying feature that changes this bundle into One, a self-identical object. The paradox of symbolization resides in the fact that the object is constituted as One through a feature that is radically external to the object itself, to its reality; through a name that bears no resemblance to the object. The object becomes One through the appendage of some completely null, self-obliterating Being, *le peu de réalité* of a couple of sounds – the fly that makes the elephant – as with the Monarch, this imbecile contingent body of an individual that does not merely 'represent' the State *qua* rational totality but constitutes it, renders it effective. This performative dimension, by means of which the signifier is inscribed into the signified content itself as its constituent (or, as Lacan puts it, by means of which the signifier 'falls into the signified'), is what is lacking in the representational name.

Hegel's Logic of the Signifier

From what we have just said, it is not difficult to ascertain how the Hegelian duality of 'representational names' and 'names as such' that emerge in Mechanical Memory corresponds perfectly to the Lacanian opposition of *sign* and *signifier*. The sign is defined by a fixed relationship between the signifier and the signified represented by the signifier – its *signification* – whereas the signifier, through its incessant sliding, refer-ring to the other signifiers in the chain, brings forth the effect-of-*sense*. The sign is a body related to other bodies, the signifier is a pure flux, 'event'; the sign refers to the substantial fullness of things, the signifier refers to the subject *qua* the void of negativity that mediates the self-relating of the signifying chain ('a signifier represents the subject for other signifiers'). Hegel as a Deleuzian – although a stronger contrast seems unthinkable, we do encounter in Hegel's 'Mechanical Memory' the notion of Sense *qua* pure Event later articulated by Deleuze in *The Logic of Sense*. ... The proof that Hegel's dialectic truly is the logic of the signifier *avant la lettre* is provided by John McCumber who, in *The Company of Words*,[28] proposes a provocative and perspicacious reading of the Hegelian dialectical process as a self-relating operation with symbolic 'markers' (Hegel's German term is *Merkmal*; its French equivalent would be *le trait signifiant*, the signifying feature). We arrive at the starting point of the process, the 'thesis', through the operation of 'immediation-abbreviation': a series of markers, $M_1 \ldots M_J$, is abbreviated in the marker M_K whose content (i.e. what this marker designates) is this very series:

(1) $(M_1 \ldots M_J) - M_K$

What then follows is the inverse operation of 'explication' in which the series $M_1 \ldots M_J$ explicates the M_K:

(2) $M_K - (M_1 \ldots M_J)$

What occurs now is yet another reversal – and the crucial point not to be missed here is that this additional reversal does not bring us back to our starting point, to (1) (or, in Hegelese, that 'negation of negation' does not entail a return to the initial position):

(3) $(M_1 \ldots M_J) / M_K$

In order to indicate this shift from (1), McCumber uses a different symbol, / instead of – ; he determines / as the 'synthesis' in which explication and abbreviation occur simultaneously. What can this mean? In (3), the marker M_K is *stricto sensu* 'reflexive': it no longer stands for immediation that is abstractly opposed to explication, since *it explicates the very series that explicated M_K itself in (2)*. In order to explain this 'reflexivity', let us resort to the logic of anti-Semitism. First, the series of markers that designate real properties are abbreviated-immediated in the marker 'Jew':

(1)   (avaricious, profiteering, plotting, dirty...) – Jew

We then reverse the order and 'explicate' the marker 'Jew' with the series (avaricious, profiteering, plotting, dirty...) – that is, this series now provides the answer to the question 'What does "Jew" mean?':

(2)   Jew – (avaricious, profiteering, plotting, dirty...)

Finally, we reverse the order again and posit 'Jew' as the reflexive abbreviation of the series:

(3)   (avaricious, profiteering, plotting, dirty...) / Jew

In what, precisely, resides the difference between (1) and (3)? In (3), 'Jew' *explicates the very preceding series it immediates-abbreviates*: in it, abbreviation and explication dialectically coincide. That is to say, within the discursive space of anti-Semitism, a collection of individuals not only pass for Jews because they display the series of properties (avaricious, profiteering, plotting, dirty...), *they have this series of properties BECAUSE THEY ARE JEWS*. This becomes clear if we translate abbreviation in (1) as

(1)   (profiteering, plotting . . .) *is called* Jewish

and explication in (2) as

(2)   X is Jewish *because he is* (profiteering, plotting . . .)

In this perspective, the uniqueness of (3) is that it returns to (1) *while maintaining the copulative of (2)*:

(3)   X is (profiteering, plotting . . .) *because he is* Jewish

In short, 'Jew' designates here the hidden ground of the phenomenal series of actual properties (avaricious, profiteering, plotting, dirty . . .). What thus occurs is a kind of 'transubstantiation': 'Jew' starts to function as the marker of the hidden ground, the mysterious *je ne sais quoi*, that accounts for the 'Jewishness' of the Jews. (*Cognoscenti* of Marx, of course, will immediately realize how these inversions are homologous to the development of the form of commodity in Chapter 1 of *Capital*: the simple inversion of the 'developed' form into the form of 'general equivalent' brings forth a new entity, the general equivalent itself as the exception constitutive of the totality.[29])

Our ultimate point is therefore a rather technical one: McCumber's formulas gain considerable clarity and power of insight if we replace the series of markers $M_1 \ldots M_J$ with Lacan's mathem S_2, the signifier of the chain of knowledge, and M_K, the abbreviation of the series $M_1 \ldots M_J$, with S_1, the Master-Signifier. Let us elucidate this point via an example that is structurally homologous to that of anti-Semitism, the Polish anti-Socialist cynical witticism: 'True, we don't have enough food, electricity, flats, books, freedom, but what does it matter in the end, since we do have Socialism!' The underlying Hegelian logic here is as follows: first, socialism is posited as the simple abbreviation of a series of markers that designate effective qualities ('When we have enough food, electricity, flats, books, freedom . . ., we have socialism'); one then inverts the relationship and refers to this series of markers in order to 'explicate' socialism ('socialism means enough food, electricity, flats, books, freedom . . .'); when we perform another inversion, however, we are not thrown back to our starting point, since 'socialism' now changes into 'Socialism', the Master-Signifier – that is, no longer a simple abbreviation that designates a series of markers but the name of the hidden ground of this series of markers that act as so many expressions-effects of this ground. And since 'Socialism' is now the Cause expressed in the series of phenomenal markers, one can ultimately say 'What does it matter if all these markers disappear – they are not what our struggle is really about! The main thing is that we still have Socialism!' . . .

To summarize: in (1), the marker of abbreviation-immediation is a simple *sign*, an external designation of the given series; whereas in (3), this marker is a *signifier* that performatively establishes the series in its totality. In (1), we are victims of the illusion that the complete series is an In-itself that persists independently of its sign; whereas in (3), it becomes clear that the series is completed, constituted, only through the reflexive marker that supplements it – that is, in (3), the sign is *comprised within the 'thing itself' as its inherent constituent*; the distance that keeps the sign and the designated content apart disappears.

Back to the relationship between Lacan and the Frankfurt School: is not the Lacanian solution (*objet petit a* as the cause of the subject) ideological, however, in the precise sense this term acquires in the Frankfurt School – that is to say, does it not repeat the gesture of psychoanalytic 'revisionism' repudiated by Adorno, that of providing a new, 'better' theory which obliterates the inconsistencies of the previous theory, leaving out of consideration the social antagonisms that were the 'absent cause' of these inconsistencies? What is needed if we are to answer this reproach is a closer look into the paradoxes of the concept of the superego, the concept which, as we saw at the end of Chapter 1, condenses the problem of the relationship between Lacan and the heritage of the Frankfurt School.

Notes

1. *The Seminar of Jacques Lacan. Book II: The Ego in Freud's Theory and in the Technique of Psychoanalysis (1954–55)*, New York: Norton 1991, p. 325.
2. Jacques Lacan, *The Four Fundamental Concepts of Psycho-Analysis*, London: Hogarth Press 1977, p. 22.
3. Sigmund Freud, *The Interpretation of Dreams*, Harmondsworth: Penguin 1977, p. 757.
4. In this sense, the status of freedom in Kant is also real: freedom is the causality of the moral Law as the paradoxical object ('voice of duty') which suspends the phenomenal causal chain.
5. For a detailed account of the ex-timate, 'uncanny', status of *objet petit a*, see Mladen Dolar, '"I shall be with you on your wedding night": Lacan and the Uncanny', *October* 58 (Cambridge, MA: MIT Press 1992), pp. 5–23.
6. The paradox of this object – of *objet petit a* – is that, although imaginary, it occupies the place of the Real – that is, it is a non-specularizable object, an object that has no specular image and which, as such, precludes any relationship of empathy, of sympathetic recognition. In the course of psychoanalysis, the analysand has to reach the point at which he experiences his impossible identity with this absolute otherness – 'Thou art that!'. The fact that Lacan's concepts are part of the accepted *doxa* today tends to make us insensitive to how astonishing is the sign of equation between *plus-de-jouir* and *objet a*: between the surplus of enjoyment over any positive object and, again, an object. That is to say, *a* stands precisely for an 'impossible' object that gives body to what can never become a positive object. On account of this feature, the abyss that separates Lacan from the line of thought that runs from Bergson to Deleuze is unbridgeable: *objet a* means that libido has to be

apprehended not as a reservoir of free-floating energy but as an object, an 'incorporeal *organ*' ('lamella'). We are dealing here with a *cause*: desire (i.e. subject) has a cause precisely in so far as surplus-enjoyment is an object.

7. The true reach of the Kantian revolution is condensed in the notion of transcendental schematism, which is more paradoxical than it may appear: it means the exact opposite of what it seems to mean. It does *not* mean that since pure notions are alien to temporal, finite, sensible experience, a mediator has to intervene between the intellectual framework of a priori notions and the objects of sensible intuition. On the contrary, it means that *time* (since schematism concerns precisely the relationship to time: it relates notions to time *qua* form of pure intuition) is the *insurmountable horizon of the legitimate use of pure notions themselves*: these notions can be applied only to the objects of temporal, finite, sensible experience. Herein lies Kant's break with traditional metaphysics: the Finite is not simply a deficient mode of the Infinite which persists in itself outside time; *it simultaneously involves its own version of the noumenal Infinite*. That is why the Kantian duality of noumena and phenomena does not coincide with the traditional metaphysical dualism of essence-substance and appearance: with regard to this dualism, Kant introduces a supplementary splitting, the splitting between the noumenal In-itself and – not the phenomenal, but *the way this In-itself appears within the phenomenal field*. From our perspective – from the perspective of finite mortals whose experience is limited to temporal sensible objects – the noumenal sphere appears in the guise of freedom, of the kingdom of ethical ends, and so on. If, however, we were to have direct access to the noumenal sphere, bypassing the phenomenal level, the noumenal sphere would lose these very characteristics of freedom, and so on – the subject would be able to discern his inclusion in the noumenal causal mechanism. This *splitting of the noumenal itself* into the In-itself and the way this In-itself appears to us finite subjects means that 'substance became subject'.

8. Lacan, *The Four Fundamental Concepts of Psycho-Analysis*, p. 270.

9. Ibid.

10. In this paradox it is easy to discern Hegel's typical approach: the problem is not how to prove, via dialectical sophistry, the ultimate identity of the opposites, necessity and contingency (as the common notion of 'Hegelianism' leads us to expect) but, on the contrary, *how to tell one from the other on a strict conceptual level*; Hegel's solution, of course, is that the only way to differentiate them is to define the necessity of contingency itself.

11. Here Hegel is far more subversive than those of his critics – Schelling, for example – who reproach him for 'sublating' contingency in the all-comprehensive necessity of the Notion. Schelling limits the reach of notional deduction to the a priori ideal structure of the possibility of a thing – the actualization of this possibility depends on the contingency of the real ground of being, the 'irrational' Will. According to Schelling, Hegel's error resides in his endeavour to deduce the contingent fact of existence from the notion: the pure notion of a thing can deliver only *what* this thing is, never the *fact that* it is. It is Schelling himself, however, who thereby excludes contingency from the domain of notion: this domain is exclusively that of necessity – that is to say, what remains unthinkable for Schelling is *a contingency that pertains to the notion itself*.

The relationship between Schelling and Hegel can also be conceived of as the relationship between the two aspects of the Lacanian Real: pure contingency of the 'irrational', pre-logical chaos, *and* a meaningless logical construct. Hegel's logic ('God prior to the creation of the universe') endeavours to accomplish what Lacan later had in mind with 'mathems': it does not provide any kind of 'horizon of meaning', it simply renders the empty, meaningless frame later filled out by some symbolic content (the subject matter of the Philosophy of Spirit). In this respect, Hegel's logic is the very opposite of Schelling's philosophy in which the Real is the domain of the divine drives (see Chapter 5 below). It is easy to conceive of Schelling as the forerunner of the late Lacan, and to establish a link between Schelling's critique of idealism (reproaching it for not taking into account the Real in God) and Lacan's insistence of the Real as that which resists symbolization, symbolic integration-mediation; however, such a hasty reduction of the Real to the abyss of 'irrational' drives misses Lacan's crucial point that the Real is at the same time a 'mathem', a purely logical formation to which nothing corresponds in 'reality'.

12. *Hegel's Science of Logic*, Atlantic Highlands, NJ: Humanities Press International 1989, p. 580.

13. Ibid., p. 554.

14. In so far as the subject *qua* absolute is this *Schein* itself – that is to say, in so far as the status of the subject is essentially *superficial*, that of a 'spectral' surface – the Hegelian opposition substance/subject subverts the standard metaphysical duality of essence and appearance and is, as such, close to the Deleuzian opposition between the impenetrable bodily depth and the surface event. On this unexpected link between Hegel and Deleuze, see the final part of this chapter.

15. G.W.F. Hegel, *Phenomenology of Spirit*, Oxford: Oxford University Press 1977, p. 391.

16. For a more detailed examination of this paradox, see Chapter 6 of Slavoj Žižek, *The Sublime Object of Ideology*, London: Verso 1989. The opposite also holds: the fact that something appears to us as a raw, meaningless, unjustified state of things is also a result of our 'positing'. Suffice it to recall the early bourgeois opposition to feudal repression. One of the standard motifs of the early bourgeois melodrama (Richardson's *Clarissa*, for example) is the desperate struggle of the bourgeois girl against the intrigues of the feudal debauchee who poses a threat to her virtue. What is crucial here is the symbolic mutation by way of which the subject experiences as an unbearable pressure upon her free individuality what was previously simply the social framework in which she was embedded. It is not enough to say that the individual 'becomes aware of' the (feudal) repression: what gets lost in this formulation is the performative dimension – that is, the fact that through the act of 'awareness' the subject *posits* social conditions as exerting an unbearable pressure upon her free individuality, thereby *constituting* herself as a 'free individual'.

17. G.W.F. Hegel, *Lectures on the Philosophy of Religion*, vol. III, Berkeley: University of California Press 1985, p. 345.

18. On this syllogistic structure of Christianity, see John W. Burbidge, 'The Syllogisms of Revealed Religion', in *Hegel on Logic and Religion*, Albany, NY: SUNY Press 1992.

19. Hegel's logic of syllogism is therefore based on the structure of the 'vanishing mediator': what vanishes in the conclusion of the syllogism is the third element which, by way of its mediatory role, enables the final unification (copulation) of subject and predicate. (Hegel differentiates the three basic types of syllogism precisely with regard to the nature of this 'vanishing mediator': particular, singular, or universal.)

One is tempted to account for Lacan's 'impossibility of sexual relationship' in terms of this syllogistic structure: contrary to immediate appearance, the sexual relationship does not possess the structure of judgement, of the copulation between the two subjects involved, but that of syllogism. That is to say, the sexual relationship is doomed to fail, since in it a man does not relate directly to a woman – his relating to a woman is always mediated by a third term, the *objet a*: John desires *a*, his object-cause of desire; John presupposes that Mary possesses, has in herself, *a*; John desires Mary. The problem, however, is that this *a* is irreducibly decentred with regard to the subject to whom it is attributed: between the *a* – that is, the fantasy in the guise of which the subject structures his relationship towards *a* – and the concrete woman, the real kernel of her being beyond fantasy, the abyss remains uncrossable. *Vulgari eloquentia*: a man thinks he is fucking a woman, but what he is actually fucking is the fantasy attached to this woman.

20. The recent ecological crisis offers, perhaps, the most stringent experience of $ *qua* empty, substanceless subjectivity. In it, the very ground of our daily life is threatened, the circuit of the Real which 'always returns to its place' is perturbed: all of a sudden, the most basic pattern and support of our being – water and air, the rhythm of the seasons of the year, and so on, this natural ground of our social activity – appears as something *contingent* and unreliable. The Enlightenment vision of man's complete domination over nature and its exploitation thus arrives at its truth in an inverted form: we cannot fully *dominate* nature; what we can do is *disrupt* it. It is only here that 'substance becomes subject': the subject is bereft of the most fundamental 'substantial' support in nature as that which always finds its balance and follows its path notwithstanding the perturbations of social life. The usual reaction to the ecological crisis – the desperate endeavours to find a way back to the 'natural balance' – is therefore simply a mode of eluding the true dimension of this crisis: the only way to confront its full extent is to assume fully the

experience of radical contingency that it involves.

21. At a deeper level, one would have to focus on the enigmatic relationship between Despina and Alfonso: by pretending to play the mediatory role between the other two couples, do they not actually declare love *to each other*? In short, does not the 'truth' of *Così fan tutte* reside in the fact that its truly amorous couple, hindered in the acknowledgement of love, is the couple Despina and Alfonso? Do they not stage the farce with the other two intermingled couples in order to resolve the tension of their own relationship? This is the insight on which Peter Sellars's great production of the opera is based.

22. A further example of this 'subterranean' character of the big Other is provided by Miloš Forman's American films. Although most of them are set in America, one cannot avoid the impression that, in a sense, his American films remain Czech: their implicit 'spiritual substance', their elusive 'mood', is Czech. The problem we confront here is how it was possible for the specific universe of late Czech Socialism to contain a universal dimension which enabled it to function as the matrix for the (quite convincing) portrayal of modern American life. Among numerous similar examples, suffice it to mention the TV movie on Stalin with Robert Duvall: it soon becomes clear that its hidden reference is Mafia-sagas *à la Godfather*. What we are actually watching is a movie about the power struggle in a Mafia family, with Lenin as the aged and mortally ill *Don*, Stalin and Trotsky as the two *consiglieri* fighting for his legacy, and so on.

23. Moreover, this assertion of the 'pre-ontological' status of the unconscious is inherently ambiguous: it can also be understood (and it was understood by Lacan in his first two *Seminars*) phenomenologically, as designating that the unconscious *is* not, but persists only in the *futur antérieur* of a 'will have been' – it does not exist as some positive entity; its only consistency is that of a hypothesis retroactively confirmed by the interpretative construct which afterwards confers sense upon the fragmentary traces by way of providing their context of signification. Only the reading of the 'pre-ontological' status of the unconscious against the background of the Kantian infinite judgement enables us to avoid this phenomenological trap, and to confer upon the unconscious a status that eludes the standard phenomenological–ontological distinctions.

24. See *Hegel's Philosophy of Mind*, Oxford: Clarendon Press 1992.

25. We are relying here on the excellent, though somewhat one-sided, reconstruction of Hegel's line of argumentation in Chapter 7 ('Hegelian Words: Analysis') of John McCumber, *The Company of Words: Hegel, Language, and Systematic Philosophy*, Evanston, IL: Northwestern University Press 1993.

26. This is what seems to elude the Derridean reading that conceives of 'Mechanical Memory' as a kind of 'vanishing mediator', an externalization that is subsequently self-sublated in the Inwardness of the Spirit: by obliterating the entire representational inner content, 'Mechanical Memory' opens up and maintains the absolute Void as the medium of the Spirit, as the space filled out by the spiritual content. In short, by performing the radical obliteration of the entire *enunciated* representational content, 'Mechanical Memory' makes room for the *subject of enunciation*. What is crucial here is the co-dependence of the reduction of the sign to the senseless externality of the signifier and the emergence of the 'barred' subject *qua* pure void ($): here Hegel is unexpectedly close to Althusser, who also articulates the co-dependence of Ideological State Apparatuses (ideological practice *qua* pure externality of a 'mechanical' ritual) and the process of subjectivization. The problem with Althusser, however, is that he lacks the concept of the subject of the signifier ($): since he reduces the subject to imaginary recognition in the ideological Sense, he fails to notice the correlation between the emergence of the subject and the radical loss of sense in the senseless ritual. At a somewhat different level, the same paradox defines the status of woman in Weininger (see Chapter 6 below): woman is the subject *par excellence* precisely in so far as the feminine position involves the evacuation of the entire spiritual content – this voidance confronts us with the subject *qua* empty container of sense....

27. G.W.F. Hegel, *Jenaer Realphilosophie*, Hamburg: Meiner 1931, p. 183.

28. See McCumber, *The Company of Words*, pp. 130–43.

29. See Chapter 1 of Slavoj Žižek, *For They Know Not What They Do*, London: Verso 1991.

3

Superego by Default

A Law that Enjoys Itself

The proper way to approach the theme 'psychoanalysis and Law' is to ask: what kind of Law is the object of psychoanalysis? The answer is, of course: *superego*. Superego emerges where the Law – the public Law, the Law articulated in the public discourse – fails; at this point of failure, the public Law is compelled to search for support in an *illegal* enjoyment.

Superego is the obscene 'nightly' law that necessarily redoubles and accompanies, as its shadow, the 'public' Law. This inherent and constitutive splitting in the Law is the subject of Rob Reiner's film *A Few Good Men*, the court-martial drama about two Marines accused of murdering one of their fellow-soldiers. The military prosecutor claims that the two Marines' act was a deliberate murder, whereas the defence succeeds in proving that the defendants simply followed the so-called 'Code Red', which authorizes the clandestine night-time beating of a fellow-soldier who, in the opinion of his peers or the superior officer, has broken the ethical code of the Marines.

The function of this 'Code Red' is extremely interesting: it condones an act of transgression – illegal punishment of a fellow-soldier – yet at the same time it reaffirms the cohesion of the group – it calls for an act of supreme identification with group values. Such a code must remain under cover of night, unacknowledged, unutterable – in public, everybody pretends to know nothing about it, or even actively denies its existence. It represents the 'spirit of community' at its purest, exerting the strongest pressure on the individual to comply with its mandate of group identification. Yet, simultaneously, it violates the explicit rules of community life. (The plight of the two accused soldiers is that they are unable to grasp this exclusion of 'Code Red' from the 'big Other', the domain of the public Law: they desperately ask themselves 'What did we do wrong?', since they simply followed the order of the superior officer.) Where does this splitting of the law into the written public Law and its underside, the 'unwritten', obscene secret code, come from? From the incomplete, 'non-all' character of the public Law: explicit, public rules do not suffice, so they have to be supplemented by a clandestine 'unwritten' code aimed at those who, although they violate no public rules, maintain a kind of inner distance and do not truly identify with the 'spirit of community'.[1]

Sadism thus relies on the splitting of the field of the Law into Law *qua* 'Ego-Ideal' – that is, a symbolic order which regulates social life and maintains social peace – and its obscene, superegotistical inverse. As numerous analyses from Bakhtin onwards have shown, periodic trans- gressions of the public law are inherent to the social order; they function as a condition of the latter's stability. (Bakhtin's mistake – or, rather, that of some of his followers – was to present an idealized image of these 'transgressions', while passing in silence over lynching parties, and so on, as the crucial form of the 'carnivalesque suspension of social hierarchy'.) What 'holds together' a community most deeply is not so much identification with the Law that regulates the community's 'normal' everyday circuit, but rather *identification with a specific form of transgression of the Law, of the Law's suspension* (in psychoanalytic terms, with a specific form of *enjoyment*).

Let us return to those small-town white communities in the American South of the 1920s, where the reign of the official, public Law is accompanied by its shadowy double, the nightly terror of Ku Klux Klan, with its lynchings of powerless blacks: a (white) man is easily forgiven minor infractions of the Law, especially when they can be justified by a 'code of honour'; the community still recognizes him as 'one of us'. Yet he will be effectively excommunicated, perceived as 'not one of us', the moment he disowns the specific form of *transgression* that pertains to this community – say, the moment he refuses to partake in the ritual lynchings by the Klan, or even reports them to the Law (which, of course, does not want to hear about them, since they exemplify its own hidden underside). The Nazi community relied on the same solidarity-in-guilt induced by participation in a common transgression: it ostracized those who were not ready to take on the dark side of the idyllic *Volksge- meinschaft*: the night pogroms, the beatings of political opponents – in short, all that 'everybody knew, yet did not want to speak about aloud'.[2]

When, as a consequence of the bourgeois egalitarian ideology's rise to power, the public space loses its direct patriarchal character, the relationship between the public Law and its obscene superego underside also undergoes a radical change. In traditional patriarchal society, the inherent transgression of the Law assumes the form of a carnivalesque reversal of authority: the King becomes a beggar, madness poses as wisdom, and so forth. An exemplary case of this reversal is a custom practised in the villages of northern Greece up to the middle of this century: for one day, the women took over – the men had to stay at home and look after the children, while the women gathered in the local inn, drank to excess and organized mock trials of men.... What breaks out in this carnivalesque transgression-suspension of the ruling patriarchal Law is, therefore, the fantasy of feminine power. When Lacan draws attention to the fact that one term for 'wife' in everyday French is *la bourgeoise* – that is, the one who, beneath the semblance of male domination, actually pulls the strings – this can by no means be reduced to a version of the standard male-chauvinist wisecracking on how, after all, patriarchal domination is not so bad for women, since – at least in the close circle of the family – they run the show.

The problem goes deeper: one of the consequences of the fact that Master is always an impostor is the duplication of the Master – the agency of the Master is always perceived as a semblance concealing another, 'true' Master. Suffice it to recall Adorno's anecdote in *Minima Moralia* about a wife who apparently subordinates herself to her husband and, when they are about to leave a party, obediently holds his coat, yet while she is doing this, she exchanges ironic patronizing glances behind his back with fellow-guests which deliver the message 'Poor weakling, let him think he is the master!'. The opposition of male and female power is thus perceived as the opposition of semblance and actual power: man is an impostor, condemned to perform empty symbolic gestures, whereas the actual responsibility falls to women. The point not to be missed here, however, is that this spectre of woman's power structurally depends on male domination: it remains its shadowy double, its retroactive effect and, as such, its inherent moment. For that reason, the idea of bringing the shadowy woman's power to light and acknowledging its central position publicly is the most subtle way of succumbing to the patriarchal trap.

However, once the public Law casts off its direct patriarchal dress and presents itself as neutral-egalitarian, the character of its obscene double also undergoes a radical shift: what now erupts in the carnivalesque suspension of the 'egalitarian' public Law is precisely the authoritarian-patriarchal logic that continues to determine our attitudes, although its direct public expression is no longer permitted. 'Carnival' thus becomes the outlet for the repressed social *jouissance*: Jew-baiting riots, gang-rapes....

In so far as the superego designates the intrusion of enjoyment into the field of ideology, we can also say that the opposition of symbolic Law and superego points towards the tension between ideological meaning and enjoyment: symbolic Law guarantees meaning, whereas superego provides enjoyment which serves as the unacknowledged support of meaning. Today, in the so-called 'post-ideological' era, it is crucial to avoid confounding fantasy that supports an ideological edifice with ideological meaning – how, otherwise, are we to account for the paradoxical alliance of post-Communism and Fascist nationalism (in Serbia, Russia, etc.)? At the level of meaning, their relationship is one of mutual exclusion; yet they share a common phantasmic support (when Communism was the discourse of power, it played deftly with nationalist fantasies – from Stalin to Ceauşescu). Consequently, there is also no incompatibility between the 'postmodern' cynical attitude of non-identification, of distance towards every ideology, and the nationalist obsession with the ethnic Thing. The Thing is the substance of enjoyment: according to Lacan, the cynic is a person who believes only in enjoyment – and is not the clearest example of it precisely the cynic obsessed with the national Thing?

The difference between Law and superego also coincides with that between writing and voice. Public Law is essentially *written* – precisely and only because 'it is written', our ignorance of Law cannot serve as an excuse; it does not exculpate us in the eyes of the Law. The status of the superego, in contrast, is that of a traumatic *voice*, an intruder persecuting us and disturbing our psychic balance. Here the standard Derridean relationship between voice and writing is inverted: it is the voice that supplements the writing, functioning as a non-transparent stain that truncates the field of Law, while being necessary for its completion.

Another facet of this obscene underside of the Law is exhibited by the custom of the power elite in the USA. A rumour is rife that every year, the entire power elite (top politicians, managers, military, journalists, the wealthiest ...) gather for a week in a closed resort south of San Francisco in order to 'socialize'. What they actually do there is, for the most part, to indulge in obscene games that suspend the dignity of social rituals – hard drinking, dancing and singing vulgar songs in women's clothes, telling 'dirty' stories....

The Split Subject of Interpellation

We could also say that this nightly, obscene law consists of *proton pseudos*, the primordial lie that founds a community. That is to say, identification with community is ultimately always based upon some shared guilt or, more precisely, upon the *fetishistic disavowal of this guilt*. When, for example, a Communist in the Soviet Union of the 1930s answers the reproach that the Communist regime is terroristic beyond compare, that thousands are condemned and shot without proven guilt, that the whole of agriculture is in ruins, the actual strategy of his response consists not in a direct denial of these facts but, rather, in claiming that the authors of these reproaches 'are unable to penetrate the essence of what is going on' and to perceive the emergence of a New Man, of classless solidarity – a Communist knows very well that millions are dying in the camps, yet this knowledge only confirms his belief that the sublime 'true People' happily and enthusiastically builds Socialism.... The more reality is miserable and depressive, the more a true Stalinist Communist clings to his fetish.

Every allegiance to some community eventually involves such a fetish, which functions as the disavowal of its founding crime: is not 'America' the fetish of an infinitely open space enabling every individual to pursue happiness in his or her own way? The nature of this solidarity-in-guilt can also be much more specific; when, for example, the Leader is caught with his pants down, the solidarity of the group is strengthened by the subjects' common disavowal of the misfortune that laid bare the Leader's failure or impotence – a shared lie is an incomparably more effective bond for a group than the truth. Perhaps one should reread Hans Christian Andersen's 'The Emperor's New Clothes' along these lines: of course everybody knew that the emperor was naked, yet it was precisely the disavowal of this fact that held the subjects together – by stating this reality, the unfortunate child effectively dissolved the social link.

This paradox of solidarity-in-guilt, however, is far from holding true only for totalitarian communities – suffice it to recall today's 'progressive' cultural critique communities: is not their founding gesture a fetishizing elevation of an author (typical candidates: Alfred Hitchcock, Jane Austen, Virginia Woolf ...) all of whose 'politically incorrect' misdeeds are pardoned in advance or reinterpreted as subversive-progressive in an unheard-of, hidden way.... The community's enjoyment is provided by this very collective disavowal – for example, by our insistence on the 'progressive' character of Hitchcock, which suspends the symbolic efficiency of what obviously does not enter this frame.

In this respect, we are ultimately doing the same thing as the Western Stalinist Communist who, in the 1930s, faithfully followed the reversals of the Party line and first saw the main enemy in Fascism, then changed into an engaged pacifist enthusiastically supporting the Soviet–German pact and warning against English or French militarism, and ended by calling for a common front of all 'progressive' forces, Communists and bourgeois democrats, against Fascism – far from putting him to much trouble, these reversals only confirmed him in his Communist creed. Or – as Jean-Claude Milner put it[3] – perhaps the principal function of the Master is to set down the lie that can sustain group solidarity: to surprise the subjects with statements that manifestly contradict facts, to claim again and again that 'black is white'. . . . Consequently, it is not sufficient to say 'My country, right or wrong!' – my country is truly mine only in so far as, at a certain crucial point, it *is* wrong.

This tension between the public Law and its obscene superego underside also enables us to approach Althusser's notion of ideological interpellation in a new way. The Althusserian theory of 'Ideological State Apparatuses' and ideological interpellation is more complex than it may appear: when Althusser repeats, after Pascal, 'Act as if you believe, pray, kneel down, and you shall believe, faith will arrive by itself', he delineates an intricate reflexive mechanism of retroactive 'autopoetic' foundation that far exceeds the reductionist assertion of inner belief's dependence on external behaviour. That is to say, the implicit logic of his argument is: kneel down and *you shall believe that you knelt down because of your belief* – that is, that your following the ritual is an expression/effect of your inner belief. In short, the 'external' ritual performatively generates its own ideological foundation. Herein resides the interconnection of the ritual that pertains to 'Ideological State Apparatuses' and of the act of interpellation: when I believe that I knelt down because of my belief, I simultaneously 'recognize' myself in the call of the Other-God who dictated that I kneel down. . . .

Things are even more complex in the case of interpellation – Althusser's 'example' contains more than his own theorization gets out of it. Althusser evokes an individual who, while carelessly walking down the street, is suddenly addressed by a policeman: 'Hey, you there!'. By answering the call – that is, by stopping and turning round towards the policeman – the individual recognizes-constitutes himself as the subject of Power, of the big Other-Subject: ideology

'transforms' the individuals into subjects (it transforms them all) by that very precise operation which I have called *interpellation* or hailing, and which can be imagined along the lines of the most commonplace everyday police (or other) hailing: 'Hey, you there!'

Assuming that the theoretical scene I have imagined takes place in the street, the hailed individual will turn round. By this mere one-hundred-and-eighty-degree physical conversion, he becomes a *subject*. Why? Because he has recognized that the hail was 'really' addressed to him, and that 'it was *really him* who was hailed' (and not someone else). Experience shows that the practical transmission of hailings is such that they hardly ever miss their man: verbal call or whistle, the one hailed always recognizes that it is really him who is being hailed. And yet it is a strange phenomenon, and one which cannot be explained solely by 'guilt feelings', despite the large numbers who 'have something on their consciences'.

Naturally for the convenience and clarity of my little theoretical theatre I have had to present things in the form of a sequence, with a before and an after, and thus in the form of a temporal succession. There are individuals walking along. Somewhere (usually behind them) the hail rings out: 'Hey, you there!' One individual (nine times out of ten it is the right one) turns round, believing/suspecting/knowing that it is for him, i.e. recognizing that 'it really is he' who is meant by the hailing. But in reality these things happen without any succession. The existence of ideology and the hailing or interpellation of individuals as subjects are one and the same thing.[4]

The first thing that strikes the eye in this passage is Althusser's implicit reference to Lacan's thesis on a letter that 'always arrives at its destination': the interpellative letter cannot miss its addressee since, on account of its 'timeless' character, it is only the addressee's recognition-acceptance that constitutes it as a letter.[5] The crucial feature of the quoted passage, however, is the double denial at work in it: the denial of the explanation of interpellative recognition by means of a 'guilt feeling', as well as the denial of the temporality of the process of interpellation (strictly speaking, individuals do not 'become' subjects, they 'always-already' *are* subjects). This double denial is to be read as a Freudian denial: what the 'timeless' character of interpellation renders invisible is a kind of atemporal sequentiality that is far more complex than the 'theoretical theatre' staged by Althusser on behalf of the suspicious alibi of 'convenience and clarity'.

This 'repressed' sequence concerns a 'guilt feeling' of a purely formal, 'non-pathological' (in the Kantian sense) nature, a guilt which, for that very reason, weighs most heavily upon those individuals who 'have nothing on their consciences'. That is to say, in what, precisely, consists the individual's first reaction to the policeman's 'Hey, you there!'?[6] In an inconsistent mixture of two elements: (1) why me, what does the policeman want from me? I'm innocent, I was just minding my own business and strolling around ... ; however, this perplexed protestation of innocence is always accompanied by (2) an indeterminate Kafka-esque feeling of 'abstract' guilt, a feeling that, in the eyes of Power, I am a priori terribly guilty of something, although it is not possible for me to know what precisely I am guilty of, and for that reason – since I don't know what I am guilty of – I am even more guilty; or, more pointedly, it is in this very ignorance of mine that my true guilt consists.

What we have here is thus the entire Lacanian structure of the subject split between innocence and abstract, indeterminate guilt, confronted with a non-transparent call emanating from the Other ('Hey, you there!'), a call where it is not clear to the subject what the Other actually wants from him ('Che vuoi?'). In short, what we encounter here is *interpellation prior to identification*. Prior to the recognition in the call of the Other by means of which the individual constitutes himself as 'always-already'-subject, we are obliged to acknowledge this 'timeless' instant of the impasse in which innocence coincides with indeterminate guilt: the ideological identification by means of which I assume a symbolic mandate and recognize myself as the subject of Power takes place only as an answer to *this* impasse.

So we are again at the tension between the public Law and its obscene superego underside: the ideological recognition in the call of the Other is the act of identification, of identifying oneself as the subject of the public Law, of assuming one's place in the symbolic order; whereas the abstract, indeterminate 'guilt' confronts the subject with an impenetrable call that precisely prevents identification, recognition of one's symbolic mandate. The paradox here is that the obscene superego underside is, in one and the same gesture, the necessary *support* of the public symbolic Law and the traumatic vicious circle, the impasse that the subject endeavours to *avoid* by way of taking refuge in public Law – in order to assert itself, public Law has to resist its own foundation, to render it invisible.

What remains 'unthought' in Althusser's theory of interpellation is thus the fact that prior to ideological recognition we have an intermediate moment of obscene, impenetrable interpellation without identification, a kind of 'vanishing mediator' that has to become invisible if the subject is to achieve symbolic identity – to accomplish the gesture of subjectivization. In short, the 'unthought' of Althusser is that there is already an uncanny subject that *precedes* the gesture of subjectivization. Is not this 'subject prior to subjectivization' a pure theoretical construction and, as such, of no use for a concrete social analysis? Evidence to the contrary is offered by the syntagm that recurs regularly when social workers attempt to render their experience of the 'antisocial' adolescent criminal who lacks what we ideologically call the 'elementary sense of compassion and moral responsibility': when you look into his eyes, it seems as if 'there is nobody at home'.[7]

The key Althusserian text here is 'Trois notes sur la théorie des discours' (1966).[8] In the first Note, Althusser proposes the hypothesis according to which each of the four fundamental types of discourse implies a specific mode of subjectivity – that is, brings about its own 'effect-of-subject [*effet-sujet*]': in ideological discourse, the subject is present *en personne*; in scientific discourse, it is absent *en personne*; in aesthetic discourse, it is present through interposed persons [*par personnes interposées*]; in unconscious discourse, the subject is neither present nor simply absent but a gap represented by a place-holder.[9] In the third Note, however, Althusser suddenly and rather unexpectedly pulls back and constrains the subject to *ideological* discourse, emphasizing that one can speak of the 'subject of science' or the 'subject of the unconscious' only in a metaphorical sense. The moment we accept this position, of course, we are compelled to repudiate the very notion of the 'divided subject': as Althusser puts it, there is no divided subject, there is only the subject plus the abyss [*Spaltung*] that gapes between the subject and the order of discourse: 'le manque du sujet ne peut être dit sujet'.[10] In short, Lacan illegitimately identifies the void, the gap that undermines the self-identity of the subject, with the subject itself.

Our Lacanian standpoint compels us here to persist with Althusser I (that of the four 'effects-of-subject') against Althusser II (that of the ideological status of the subject): Althusser's constraining of the subject to ideology is a clear case of theoretical 'regression'. The four 'effects-of-subject' in Althusser I are clearly not of equal weight: there are two candidates for the role of the subject *par excellence* – either the ideological subject, present *en personne*, or the subject of the unconscious, a gap in the structure (\$) that is merely represented by a signifier. Althusser opted for the first choice (ideological status of the subject), whereas from the Lacanian standpoint the second choice seems far more productive: it allows us to conceive of the remaining three 'effects-of-subject' as the derivations-occultations of \$, as the three modes of coming to terms with the gap in the structure that 'is' the subject.

An additional argument for the Lacanian choice is provided by the symptomal reading of Althusser himself: is not the shift in Althusser's theory announced by his essay on 'Lenin and Philosophy' – the self-critical repudiation of 'theoreticist deviation'; the assertion of class struggle in theory; the theory's self-referentiality, that is, the notion that theory is included in its object – a kind of 'return of the repressed', of the dimension of the subject of the signifier? What is indicative here is Althusser's new definition of philosophy, which encapsulates this shift: no longer 'philosophy is the Theory of theoretical practice' but 'philosophy represents politics (class struggle) in theory' – is this not a clear variant of Lacan's 'a signifier represents the subject for another signifier'? Class struggle as the gap that prevents totalization is the sole true 'subject' of history, whereas philosophy is the Master-Signifier (S_1) that represents the subject – the class struggle – for the theory, within the field of knowledge (S_2).[11]

Kundera, or, How to Enjoy Bureaucracy

Emphasis should be laid on the inherent political dimension of the notion of enjoyment – on the way this kernel of enjoyment functions as a political factor. Let us probe this dimension through one of the enigmas of cultural life in post-Socialist Eastern Europe: why does Milan

Kundera even now, after the victory of democracy, suffer a kind of excommunication in Bohemia? His works are rarely published, the media pass them over in silence, everybody is somehow embarrassed to talk about him.... In order to justify such treatment, one rakes up old stories about his hidden collaboration with the Communist regime, about his taking refuge in private pleasures and avoiding the morally upright conflict *à la Havel*, and so on. However, the roots of this resistance lie deeper – Kundera conveys a message that is unbearable to the 'normalized' democratic consciousness:

- At first glance, the fundamental axis that structures the universe of his works seems to be the opposition between the pretentious pathos of the official Socialist ideology and the islands of everyday private life, with its small joys and pleasures, laughter and tears, beyond the reach of ideology. These islands enable us to assume a distance which renders the ideological ritual visible in all its vain, ridiculous pretentiousness and grotesque meaninglessness: it is not worth the trouble to revolt against an official ideology with pathetic speeches on freedom and democracy – sooner or later, such a revolt leads to a new version of the 'Big March', of ideological obsession.... If Kundera is reduced to such an attitude, it is easy to dismiss him via Václav Havel's fundamental 'Althusserian' insight into how the ultimate conformist attitude is precisely such an 'apolitical' stance which, while publicly obeying the imposed ritual, privately indulges in cynical irony: it is not sufficient to ascertain that the ideological ritual is a mere appearance which nobody takes seriously – this appearance is essential, which is why one has to take a risk and refuse to participate in the public ritual (see Havel's famous example, from his essay 'The Power of the Powerless', of a common man, a greengrocer, who, of course, does not believe in Socialism; yet when the occasion demands it he dutifully decorates the windows of his store with official Party slogans, etc.).

- One must therefore go a step further and take into account that there is no way simply to step aside from ideology: the private indulgence in cynicism, the obsession with private pleasures, and so on – all this is precisely how totalitarian ideology operates in 'non-ideological' every-day life, how this life is determined by ideology, how ideology is 'present in it in the mode of absence', if we may resort to this syntagm from the heroic epoch of structuralism. The depoliticization of the private sphere in late-Socialist societies is 'compulsive', marked by the fundamental prohibition of free political discussion; for that reason, such depoliticiza-tion always functions as the evasion of what is truly at stake. This accounts for the most immediately striking feature of Kundera's novels: the depoliticized private sphere in no way functions as the free domain of innocent pleasures; there is always something damp, claustrophobic, inauthentic, even desperate, in the characters' striving for sexual and other pleasures. In this respect, the lesson of Kundera's novels is the exact opposite of a naive reliance on the innocent private sphere: the totalitarian Socialist ideology vitiates from within the very sphere of privacy in which we take refuge.

• This insight, however, is far from conclusive. Another step is needed here, since Kundera's lesson is even more ambiguous. Notwithstanding the dampness of the private sphere, the fact remains that the totalitarian situation gave rise to a series of phenomena attested by numerous chronicles of everyday life in the Socialist East: in reaction to totalitarian ideological domination, there was not only a cynicized escape into the 'good life' of private pleasures, but also an extraordinary flourishing of authentic friendship, of paying visits, of shared dinners, of passionate intellectual conversations in closed societies – features which usually fascinated visitors from the West. The problem, of course, is that there is no way to draw a clear-cut line of separation between the two sides: they are the heads and tails of the same coin, which is why, with the advent of democracy, they *both* get lost. It is to Kundera's credit that he does not conceal this ambiguity: the spirit of 'Middle Europe', of authentic friendship and intellectual sociability, survived only in Bohemia, Hungary and Poland, as a form of resistance to the totalitarian ideological domination.

• Perhaps yet another step is to be ventured here: the very subordination to the Socialist order brought about a specific enjoyment – not only the enjoyment provided by an awareness that people were living in a universe absolved of uncertainty, since the System possessed (or pretended to possess) an answer to everything, but above all the enjoyment of the very stupidity of the System – a relish in the emptiness of the official ritual, in the worn-out stylistic figures of the predominating ideological discourse. (Suffice it to recall the extent to which some key Stalinist syntagms became part of the ironical figures of speech even among Western intellectuals: 'objective responsibility', etc.).

An exemplary case of this enjoyment that pertains to the 'totalitarian' bureaucratic machinery is provided by a scene from Terry Gilliam's *Brazil*: in the labyrinthine corridors of a large government house, a high-ranking functionary marches swiftly, followed by a bunch of lower clerks who desperately try to keep pace with him; the functionary acts as an overbusy man, inspecting documents and shouting orders to the people around him while walking quickly, in a great hurry, as if he is on his way to some important meeting. When the functionary stumbles upon the film's hero (Jonathan Pryce), he exchanges a couple of words with him and rushes forward, busy as ever.... Half an hour later, however, the hero sees him again in a distant corridor, carrying on his senseless ritualistic march. Enjoyment is provided by the very *senselessness* of the functionary's acting: although his frantic walking-officiating imitates the 'efficient' use of every free minute, it is *stricto sensu* purposeless – a pure ritual repeated *ad infinitum.*

The contemporary Russian composer Alfred Schnittke succeeded in exposing this feature in his opera *Life with an Idiot*: so-called 'Stalinism' confronts us with what Lacan designated as the imbecility inherent to the signifier as such. The opera tells the story of an ordinary married man ('I') who, under a punishment imposed by the Party, is compelled to take home from a lunatic asylum a person who is to live with his family; this idiot, Vava, who appears to be a normal bearded, bespectacled intellectual, constantly spouting meaningless political phrases, soon shows his true colours as an obscene intruder by having sex first with I's wife and then with I himself. In so far as we are living in the universe of language, we are condemned to this imbecility of the superego: we can assume a minimal distance towards it, thus rendering it more bearable, but we can never be rid of it....

'Do not give up your desire!'

How, then, on closer examination, is the superego structured? In his perspicacious reading of Zinoviev, Jon Elster proposes a formal definition of the elementary 'totalitarian' mechanism: a short circuit between internal and external negation – that is, at the level of deontic logic, a short circuit between non-obligation and prohibition.[12] The external negation of our obligation to do D is that we *do not have* to do D; the internal negation is that we *have* to do *non-D*. In a totalitarian society, every non-obligation tends to be interpreted as prohibition. This tendency can be illustrated through numerous examples, from elections and the possibility of criticism to the totalitarian obsession with 'conspiracies'. Elections are formally free, everybody *can* vote either for or against; yet everyone knows how he actually must vote – that is to say, he knows he is *prohibited* from voting against. Officially, criticism is not only allowed but invited, yet everyone knows that only 'constructive' – that is to say, no – criticism is actually tolerated. Thus, the *failure of our intention* changes (in Hegelese: is 'reflected into itself') into an *intended failure*: when some project of the Communist regime fails miserably because its unrealistic goals gave rise to passive resistance among the people, this failure is immediately interpreted as the result of a conspiracy hatched by the regime's enemies.

The underlying structure of such a short circuit involves a kind of psychotic distortion of the 'semiotic square' of necessity, possibility, impossibility and contingency: in a perfect 'totalitarian' universe we deal only with necessity and impossibility. A *contingent* decision of the Leadership passes itself off as an expression of historical *Necessity*, which is why every form of resistance to such a decision – although formally *possible* – is actually *impossible*, that is, prohibited. This distortion thus gives rise to the paradox of the *forced choice*, according to which we are actually allowed to choose only one of two options, the other one remaining an empty set (this paradox is none other than that of *servitude volontaire*). And it is this same short circuit that provides the most elementary definition of the superego: *the superego is a law 'run amok' in so far as it prohibits what it formally permits*.[13]

What is the place of the superego within the matrix of different ethical attitudes? Here, reference to the films of Orson Welles can help. Welles is obsessed with the figure of a 'larger-than-life' individual, from Kurtz in his first (non-realized) cinematic project, *Heart of Darkness*, through *Citizen Kane*, *The Magnificent Ambersons*, *The Touch of Evil* and *Mr. Arkadin*, up to Falstaff in *Chimes at Midnight*. This 'larger-than-life' individual is characterized by his ambiguous relationship to morals: he nonchalantly violates common moral norms and disregards the Good of his fellow-creatures, ruthlessly exploiting them for his own purposes, yet he is also thoroughly dedicated to his goal and generous, the very opposite of a petty calculating utilitarian attitude, so that he cannot be said to be simply unethical – his acts irradiate a deeper 'ethics of Life itself' that does not bother with our narrow-minded considerations. Welles used to designate these individuals 'scorpions', after the story of a scorpion who stings the frog carrying him on her back across the stream: he knows that as a result he himself will be drowned, yet he cannot help it, since such is his nature.[14] In an interview for *Cahiers du Cinéma*, Welles even insisted on a difference between Göring and Himmler: Himmler was the 'banality of Evil' personified, a clerk running the Gestapo killing-machine as a small-town post office; whereas Göring was a Renaissance personality, broad-minded in his very Evil.[15]

The underlying notional matrix becomes manifest if we enlarge the opposition of ethics and morals into a Greimasian semiotic square:

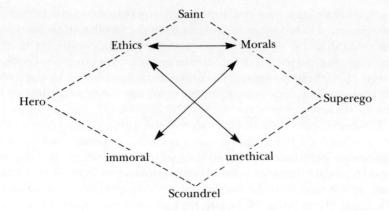

At the top and on the bottom we have two flat positions: the saint is ethical (he does not compromise his desire) and moral (he considers the Good of others), whereas the scoundrel is immoral (he violates moral norms) and unethical (what he is after is not desire but pleasures and profits, so he lacks any firm principles). Far more interesting are the two horizontal positions expressing an inherent antagonism: the hero is immoral, yet ethical – that is to say, he violates (or rather, suspends the validity of) existing explicit moral norms in the name of a higher ethics of life, historical Necessity, and so on, whereas superego designates the very opposite of the hero, an unethical moral Law, a Law in which an obscene enjoyment sticks to obedience to the moral norms (say, a severe teacher who torments his pupils for the sake of their own good, and is not ready to acknowledge his own sadistic investment in this torment).

This, however, in no way entails that, in the ethical domain, there is no way to avoid the tension between Law and superego. Lacan's maxim of the ethics of psychoanalysis ('not to compromise one's desire') is *not* to be confounded with the pressure of the superego. That is to say, in a first approach it may seem that the maxim 'Do not give up your desire!' coincides with the superego command 'Enjoy!' – do we not compromise our desire precisely by renouncing enjoyment? Is it not a fundamental thesis of Freud, a kind of Freudian commonplace, that the superego forms the basic, 'primitive' kernel of the ethical agency? Lacan goes against these commonplaces: between the ethics of desire and the superego, he posits a relationship of radical exclusion. That is to say, Lacan takes seriously and literally the Freudian 'economical paradox' of the superego – that is, the vicious cycle that characterizes the superego: the more we submit ourselves to the superego imperative, the greater its pressure, the more we feel guilty. According to Lacan, this 'feeling of guilt' is not a self-deception to be dispelled in the course of the psychoanalytic cure – we really *are* guilty: superego draws the energy of the pressure it exerts upon the subject from the fact that the subject was not faithful to his desire, that he gave it up. Our sacrificing to the superego, our paying tribute to it, only corroborates our guilt. For that reason our debt to the superego is unredeemable: the more we pay it off, the more we owe. Superego is like the extortioner slowly bleeding us to death – the more he gets, the stronger his hold on us.

The exemplary case of this paradox of the superego is, of course, the literary work of Franz Kafka: the so-called 'irrational guilt' of the Kafkaesque hero bears witness to the fact that, somewhere, he compromised his desire. In order to avoid commonplaces, however, let us rather refer to Choderlos de Laclos's *Les liaisons dangereuses*: when Valmont offers the Marquise de Montreuil his famous 'c'est pas ma faute', 'it's beyond my control', as the excuse for his falling in love with the Présidente de Tourvel, he thereby confirms that he 'compromised his desire' and yielded to a pathological passion – that is, he *is* guilty. In order to redeem himself in the eyes of the Marquise, he then proceeds to sacrifice the Présidente, rebuffing her with the same words ('c'est pas ma faute' if I no longer love you, since it's beyond my control). This sacrifice, however, in no way enables him to get rid of his guilt – quite the contrary, his guilt is redoubled; he betrays the Présidente without reducing his guilt in the slightest in the eyes of the Marquise. Therein consists the vicious cycle into which we are drawn once we 'give up our desire': there is no simple way back, since the more we endeavour to exculpate ourselves by sacrificing the pathological object which induced us to betray our desire, the greater is our guilt.

Lacanian ethics thus involves the radical disjunction between duty and giving consideration to the Good. This is why Lacan refers to Kant, to the Kantian gesture of excluding the Good as the motivation of an ethical act: Lacan insists that the most dangerous form of betrayal is not a direct yielding to our 'pathological' impulses but, rather, a reference to some kind of Good, as when I shirk my duty with the excuse that I might thereby impair the Good (my own or the common) – the moment I invoke 'circumstances' or 'unfavourable consequences' as an excuse, I am on my way to perdition. Reasons on account of which I compromise my desire can be very convincing and well-founded, even honourable; I can invoke anything, up to and including ecological damage. The artifice of looking for excuses is boundless; it may well be 'true' that the well-being of my fellow-men is jeopardized by my act, but the abyss that separates ethics from the consideration of the Good none the less remains insurmountable. Desire and Kantian ethical rigour coincide here in their disregard for the 'demands of reality': neither of them acknowledges the excuse of circumstances or unfavourable consequences, which is why Lacan ultimately identifies them ('the moral law, looked at more closely, is simply desire in its pure state'[16]).

Freud's infamous assertion that women are without superego – or, at least, that a woman's superego is weaker than a man's – appears, therefore, in an entirely new light: women's lack of superego bears witness to their ethics. Women don't need a superego, since they have no guilt on which the superego can parasitize – since, that is, they are far less prone to compromise their desire. It is by no means accidental that Lacan evokes as the exemplary case of a pure ethical attitude Antigone, a woman who 'didn't give up': already, at a pre-theoretical intuitive level, it is clear that she does not do as she does because of superego pressure – superego has no business here. Antigone is not guilty, although she does not trouble herself at all about the Good of the community, about the possible catastrophic consequences of her act. Herein resides the link between the male superego and the fact that in man the sense of the Good of the community is expressed far more than it is in woman: the 'Good of the community' is the standard excuse for compromising our desire. Superego is the revenge that capitalizes upon our guilt – that is to say, the price we pay for the guilt we contract by betraying our desire in the name of the Good. In other words, superego is the necessary inverse, underside, of the Ego-Ideal, of the ethical norms founded upon the Good of the community.[17]

This ethics of persisting in one's desire irrespective of the common Good inevitably gives rise to anxiety: is not such a radical attitude the preserve of a few 'heroes', while we ordinary people also have a right to survive? Consequently, do we not also need an 'ordinary' ethics of 'common Good' and distributive justice that would meet the requirements of the majority, despicable as it may appear in the eyes of the suicidal heroic ethics advocated by Lacan?[18] The fear of this 'excessive' character of the Lacanian ethics of desire, of this *fiat desiderium, pereat mundus*, can be detected even in Kant who, according to Lacan, was the first to formulate an ethics of desire that ignores pathological considerations: is not the restraint imposed by 'What if everyone were to do the same as me?' the elementary form of the way we give up our desire? Renounce your desire, since it is not universalizable!

Does not this taking into account the possibility of universalizing our act silently introduce the pathological consideration of the *consequences* of our act in reality? It is at this level that we can also locate the precise moment of the ethical compromise of Buddhism: when, in Mahayana Buddhism, they accepted the difference between 'big' and 'small' wheel – that is to say, the need to formulate, in addition to a 'pure' teaching for those who are already able to overcome covetousness in this life, a kind of 'minor' ethics, rules of conduct for ordinary people who are unable to renounce sexuality, and so on. In clear contrast to this, Lacan persists in the troubling imperative 'do not give up your desire', although he knows that it is not universalizable.[19]

Ego-Evil, Superego-Evil, Id-Evil

Our contemporary experience compels us to complicate this picture further. That is to say, what strikes the eye in the recent wave of anti-immigrant violence is the 'primitive' level of the underlying libidinal economy – 'primitive' not in the sense of a 'regression' to some archaic stratum, but in the sense of the utmost *elementary* nature of the relationship between pleasure and *jouissance*, between the circle of the pleasure principle that strives for balance, for the reproduction of its closed circuit, and the ex-timate foreign body. The libidinal economy that sustains the infamous battle-cry 'Ausländer raus! [Foreigners out!]' can be exemplified by Lacan's schema of the hoop net where *a* prevents the closure of the circle,[20] or, even better, with the schema of the relationship between the *Ich* and *Lust*[21] where the *Unlust* is defined in the terms of (non)assimilation, as 'what remains *unassimilable*, irreducible to the pleasure principle'.[22] The terms used by Freud and Lacan to describe the relationship between *Ich* and *jouissance* fit the metaphorics of the racist attitude towards foreigners perfectly: assimilation and resistance to assimilation, expulsion of a foreign body, disturbed balance....

In order to locate this type of Evil within the usual types of Evil, one is tempted to use as the classificatory principle the Freudian triad of Ego, Superego and Id:

- the most common kind of Evil is *Ego*-Evil: behaviour motivated by selfish calculation and greed – that is, by disregard for universal ethical principles;
- the Evil attributed to the so-called 'fundamentalist fanatics', on the contrary, is *Superego*-Evil: Evil accomplished in the name of fanatical devotion to some ideological ideal;
- in the skinhead beating up foreigners, however, one can discern neither a clear selfish calculation nor a clear ideological identification. All the talk about foreigners stealing work from us, or the threat they represent to our Western values, should not deceive us: on closer examination, it soon becomes clear that this talk provides a rather superficial secondary rationalization. The answer we ultimately obtain from a skinhead is that it makes him feel good to beat

up foreigners, that their presence disturbs him.... What we encounter here is *Id*-Evil, Evil structured and motivated by the most elementary imbalance in the relationship between the *Ich* and *jouissance,* by the tension between pleasure and the foreign body of *jouissance* at the very heart of it. The Id-Evil thus stages the most elementary 'short circuit' in the subject's relationship to the primordially missing object-cause of his desire: what 'bothers' us in the 'other' (Jew, Japanese, African, Turk ...) is that he appears to entertain a privileged relationship to the object – the other either possesses the object-treasure, having snatched it away from us (which is why we don't have it), or poses a threat to our possession of the object. In short, the skinhead's 'intolerance' of the other cannot be adequately conceived without a reference to the object-cause of desire that is, by definition, missing.

How are we to combat effectively this Id-Evil which, on account of its 'elementary' nature, remains impervious to any rational or even purely rhetorical argumentation? That is to say, racism is always grounded in a particular fantasy (of *cosa nostra,* of our ethnic Thing menaced by 'them', of 'them' who, by means of their excessive enjoyment, pose a threat to our 'way of life') which, by definition, resists universalization. The translation of the racist fantasy into the universal medium of symbolic intersubjectivity (the Habermasian ethics of dialogue) in no way weakens the hold of the racist fantasy upon us.[23] If we are to undermine this power of fantasy, a different political strategy is needed, a strategy that is able to incorporate what Lacan called 'la traversée du fantasme', a strategy of *overidentification,* which takes into account the fact that the obscene superego *qua* basis and support of the public Law is operative only in so far as it remains unacknowledged, hidden from the public eye. What if, instead of critical dissection and irony which reveal their impotence in the face of racism's phantasmic kernel, we proceed *a contrario* and identify publicly with the obscene superego?

In the process of the disintegration of Socialism in Slovenia, the post-punk group Laibach staged an aggressive inconsistent mixture of Stalinism, Nazism and *Blut und Boden* ideology. The first reaction of enlightened Leftist critics was to conceive of Laibach as the ironic imitation of totalitarian rituals; however, their support of Laibach was always accompanied by an uneasy feeling: 'What if they really mean it? What if they truly identify with the totalitarian ritual?' – or (a more cunning version) a transferring of one's own doubt on to the other: 'What if Laibach overestimate their public? What if the public take seriously what Laibach mockingly imitate, so that Laibach actually strengthen what they purport to undermine?' This uneasy feeling is fed on the assumption that ironic distance is automatically a subversive attitude. What if, on the contrary, the dominant attitude of the contemporary 'post-ideological' universe is precisely a cynical distance towards public values? What if this distance, far from posing any threat to the system, designates the supreme form of conformism, since the normal functioning of the system requires cynical distance? In this case, the Laibach strategy appears in a new light: *it 'frustrates' the system (the ruling ideology) precisely in so far as it is not its ironic imitation, but overidentification with it* – by bringing to light the obscene superego underside of the system, overidentification suspends its efficiency.[24]

The ultimate expedient of Laibach is their deft manipulation of transference: their public (especially intellectuals) is obsessed with the 'desire of the Other' – What is Laibach's actual position? Are they truly totalitarians or not? – that is, they ask Laibach a question and expect an answer from them, failing to notice that Laibach themselves *function not as an answer but as a question*. By means of the elusive character of their desire, of the undecidability as to 'where they actually stand', Laibach compel us to take up our position and decide upon *our* desire.

Here Laibach actually accomplish the reversal that defines the end of psychoanalytic cure. At the outset of the cure is transference: the transferential relationship is in force as soon as the analyst appears in the guise of the subject supposed to know – to know the truth about the analysand's desire. When, in the course of the psychoanalysis, the analysand complains that he doesn't know what he wants, all his moaning and groaning is addressed to the analyst, with the implicit supposition that the analyst *does* know. In other words – in so far as the analyst stands for the big Other – the analysand's illusion lies in reducing his ignorance about his desire to an 'epistemological' *incapacity*: the truth about his desire already exists, it is registered somewhere in the big Other, one has only to bring it to light and his desiring will run smoothly.... The end of the psychoanalysis, the dissolution of trans-ference, occurs when this 'epistemological' incapacity shifts into 'onto-logical' *impossibility*: the analysand has to experience how the big Other does not possess the truth about his desire either, how his desire is without guarantee, groundless, authorized only in itself. In this precise sense, the dissolution of transference designates the moment when the arrow of the question that the analysand pointed at the analyst turns back towards the analysand himself: first the analysand's (hysterical) question is addressed to the analyst who is supposed to possess the answer; then the analysand is forced to acknowledge that the analyst himself is nothing but a big question mark addressed to the analysand. Here one can specify Lacan's thesis that an analyst is authorized only by himself: an analysand becomes an analyst upon assuming that his desire has no support in the Other, that the authorization of his desire can come only from himself. And in so far as this same reversal of the direction of the arrow defines drive, we could say (as Lacan says) that what takes place at the end of psychoanalysis is the shift from desire to drive.[25]

The Impotent Gaze and Its Guilt

The fundamental fantasy of contemporary technological warfare, the fantasy that structured our perception of the Gulf War, involves the suspension of 'raw' physical violence. The first 'materialization' of this fantasy was the construction of the 'Maginot line' in the 1930s. First, we have an absolute barrier separating us from the other side, the 'enemy'; by preventing any direct contact with the enemy, this barrier thoroughly depersonalizes warfare and thus renders possible the organization of warfare as an ordinary profession. A soldier fights eight hours a day (at his post behind the gun, etc.); he then moves to residential quarters, has a rest, reads, goes to the cinema, then does another eight-hour shift.... In this way, 'nothing real happens': the raw reality of blood and death is 'sublated' into abstract data – location of the target, our bombing score....

The fundamental fantasy of contemporary technological warfare, therefore, is simply *fantasy itself,* since in fantasy the subject is reduced to a pure impassive gaze witnessing the phantasmic scene whose reality is suspended. How, then, are we to conceive of the link between this position of impassive witness – of pure gaze – and the outburst of 'real' violence? One of the commonplaces of deconstructionist feminism concerns the link between gaze and power: the one who 'sees', whose point of view organizes and dominates the field of vision, is also the bearer of power; already in Bentham's fantasy of Panopticon, the place of power is located in the central gaze. On that account, the power relation in cinema is determined by the fact that the male gaze controls the field of vision, whereas the status of woman is that of the privileged object of the male gaze. The lesson of Hitchcock's great masterpieces from *Notorious* to *Rear Window,* however, is that the dialectic of gaze and power is far more refined: the gaze does connote power, yet simultaneously, and at a more fundamental level, it connotes the very opposite of power – *impotence* – in so far as it involves the position of an immobilized witness who cannot but observe what goes on.

The recent war in Bosnia raises very acutely the question of the *guilt of the gaze*: why does the impotent gazer forced to witness some unspeakable horror inevitably seem to be infected with guilt, even though 'it isn't his fault'? What we have in mind here is rape as 'weapon', used especially by Serbs against Muslims. The form it takes – the raping of a girl (or a boy, for that matter) *in the presence of her father*, forced to witness the affair – is bound to set in motion the vicious cycle of guilt: the father – the representative of authority, of the big Other – is exposed in his utter impotence, which makes him guilty in his own eyes as well as in those of his daughter; the daughter is guilty for causing her father's humiliation; and so on. The rape thus entails, besides the girl's physical and psychic suffering, the disintegration of the entire familial socio-symbolic network.

Impotent gaze is at work already in the 'primordial scene' of Poe's 'The Purloined Letter', the Minister's pilfering of the letter in the presence of the Queen and the King: here the impotent gaze is the gaze of the Queen herself, who can only observe the act, unable as she is to do anything to prevent it, since any action on her part would reveal her complicity to the King. The impotent gaze is thus an element in the triangle comprising also the ignorant gaze of the big Other and the act of the criminal-torturer. Strictly speaking, who is impotent here? In the first place, of course, the subject of the impotent gaze. At a deeper level, however, a more radical impotence pertains to the ignorant third, the big Other, the agent of social authority (the King in 'The Purloined Letter'): the criminal's act lays bare the big Other's impotence, without the latter being aware of it at all.[26] The subject of the impotent gaze can only passively observe the affair, since his hands are bound on account of *his hidden complicity, solidarity, with the criminal*: unbeknownst to the big Other, he himself has trespassed against him.

This position of 'powerless witness' is also a crucial component of the experience of the Sublime: this experience takes place when we find ourselves in the face of some horrifying event whose comprehension exceeds our capacity of representation; it is so overwhelming that we can do nothing but stare at it in horror; yet at the same time this event poses no immediate threat to our physical well-being, so that we can maintain the safe distance of an observer. Kant confines the experience of the Sublime to examples from nature (rough sea, mountain precipices ...), bypassing the fact that a *human* act can also trigger such an experience: the act of torture and *murder* – here also, we can only stare at it in horror. Thomas de Quincey articulated his theory of the 'sublime art of murder' through a reference to Kant; in his literary practice, he rendered this sublime dimension by presenting the murder from the standpoint of an observer (the housemaid who knows that the murderer who has just killed her master is lurking beyond the doors; the hotel guest who observes from a dark corner at the top of the stairs how the murderer slaughters the hotel owner's entire family).[27] And the lesson of psychoanalysis is that one has to add to torture and murder as the sources of possible experience of the Sublime *intense (sexual) enjoyment.*

The position of impotent observer is also the matrix of one of the standard scenes in *film noir.* In Howard Hawks's *The Big Sleep*, for example, Marlowe, concealed behind a wooden fence, witnesses how a paid killer finishes off a small crook who prefers losing his life to betraying the girl he loves. Perhaps the clearest example occurs at the beginning of Fritz Lang's *Scarlet Street*, when Edward Robinson witnesses Dan Duryea's violent outburst against Joan Bennett: blinded by his fantasy frame, Robinson misperceives a simple 'lovers' tiff', which Joan Bennett is clearly *enjoying*, as the suffering she is to be *rescued* from. This scene provides the key to the constellation of the impotent gaze: the unbearable, traumatic element witnessed by this gaze is ultimately the *feminine enjoyment* whose presence suspends the authority of the big Other, of the Name-of-the-Father, and fantasy (the fantasy of the 'threat' woman is to be 'rescued' from) is a scenario we construct in order to elude feminine enjoyment. Freud's 'A child is being beaten' is to be supplemented by what is perhaps an even more elementary example of fantasy scene: 'A woman is being tortured-coited'.

Why, then, is the observer passive and impotent? Because his desire is split, divided between fascination with enjoyment and repulsion at it; or – to put it another way – because his yearning to rescue the woman from her torturer is hindered by the implicit knowledge that the victim is *enjoying* her suffering.[28] The observer's ability to act – to rescue the victim-woman from the torturer or from herself – bears witness to the fact that he became 'dupe of his own fantasy' (as Lacan put it apropos of Sade): *the blow aims at the unbearable surplus-enjoyment.*[29]

The War of Fantasies

The doxa about violence in the postmodern 'society of spectacle' goes like this: today, our perception of reality is mediated by aestheticized media manipulations to such an extent that it is no longer possible for us to distinguish reality from its media image – reality itself is experienced as an aesthetic spectacle. Outbursts of 'irrational' violence are to be apprehended against this background: as desperate attempts to draw a distinction between fiction and reality by way of a *passage à l'acte* – that is, to dispel the cobweb of the aestheticized pseudo-reality and to arrive at the hard, true reality. Far from being simply wrong, this doxa, rather, is *right for the wrong reasons*: what is missing from it is the crucial distinction between imaginary order and symbolic fiction.

75

The problem of contemporary media resides not in their enticing us to confound fiction with reality but, rather, in their 'hyperrealist' character by means of which they *saturate the void that keeps open the space for symbolic fiction*. The symbolic order can function only by maintaining a minimal distance towards reality, on account of which it ultimately has the status of a fiction. Suffice it to recall the anxiety that arises when our words realize themselves 'to the letter'. In Hitchcock's *Rope*, Professor Cadell is unpleasantly surprised when two of his pupils 'take literally' his theories about supermen's right to murder, and realize them: this surprise bears witness to Cadell's 'normality'. Thus if it is to function normally, symbolic order is not to be taken 'literally'. When, for example, a waiter greets me with a complimentary 'How are you today?', the best way to cause surprise is to take this question seriously and answer it ('I really had a bad day. First, a terrible headache in the morning. Then ...'). In the 'society of spectacle', the overgrowth of imaginary 'realistic presentations' leaves less and less space open for this symbolic fiction. What gets lost with media realism, from toys to videos, is the experience of 'less is more': when you listen to an opera on CD, the very fact that 'you don't see anything' enables you to fill out this void with creative fiction. In contrast, there is always something vulgar about an opera on video, due to the very fact that 'you can see everything'.

What, then, takes place when this imaginary overgrowth saturates the space for symbolic fiction? The void filled out by creative symbolic fiction is the *objet petit a*, the object-cause of desire, the empty frame that provides the space for the articulation of desire. When this void is saturated, the distance separating *a* from reality gets lost: *a* falls into reality. However, reality itself is constituted by means of the withdrawal of *objet a*: we can relate to 'normal' reality only in so far as *jouissance* is evacuated from it, in so far as the object-cause of desire is missing from it. The necessary consequence of *a*'s overproximity to reality, which suffocates the activity of symbolic fiction, is therefore a 'de-realization' of reality itself: reality is no longer structured by symbolic fictions; fantasies which regulate the imaginary overgrowth get a direct hold on it. And it is here that violence comes on to the stage, in the guise of the psychotic *passage à l'acte*.

When Hamlet the hysteric, hidden behind the arras, observes the praying Claudius, he cannot decide if he should strike him with the sword or not: will his killing of Claudius *qua* flesh-and-blood also deal a blow at the sublime substance in Claudius, at what is 'in him more than himself', *objet petit a*? Hamlet's doubt enables us to apprehend *per negationem* the psychotic *passage à l'acte*. In psychosis *a* is not excluded from reality; it does not function as the void of its formal frame. Consequently the psychotic, in contrast to the hysteric, does not doubt, he *knows* that *a* is contained in reality; this is why he can act and actually kill the other, thereby dealing a blow at *a*. The psychotic *passage à l'acte* is to be conceived of as a desperate attempt of the subject to evict *objet a* from reality by force, and thus gain access to reality. (The psychotic 'loss of reality' does not arise when something is missing in reality, but, on the contrary, when there is *too much* of a Thing in reality.) This eviction of *a* also produces the matrix of 'irrational' war violence. Here, Richard Rorty's reading of Orwell's *Nineteen Eighty-four* can perhaps be of some help: apropos of Winston's breakdown in the hands of O'Brien, his torturer, Rorty points out that people can experience

> the ultimate humiliation of saying to themselves, in retrospect, 'Now that I have believed or desired *this*, I can never be what I hoped to be, what I thought I was. The story I have been telling myself about myself . . . no longer makes sense. I no longer have a self to make sense of. There is no world in which I can picture myself as living, because there is no vocabulary in which I can tell a coherent story about myself.' For Winston, the sentence he could not utter sincerely and still be able to put himself back together was 'Do it to Julia!' and the worst thing in the world happened to be rats. But presumably each of us stands in the same relations to some sentence, and to some thing.[30]

One of the fundamental propositions of Lacanian psychoanalysis is that this sentence or thing which encapsulates the kernel of the subject's being beyond imaginary identifications is irreducibly decentred with regard to the symbolic texture which defines the subject's identity: the subject can confront this ex-timate kernel only at the price of his temporary *aphanisis*. This is what Lacan's formula of fantasy – $\$ \lozenge a$ – designates: the subject's self-erasure in the face of this strange, 'ex-timate' body (belief, desire, proposition) which forms the core of his or her being.[31] Suffice it to recall how we blush red as a rose when our most intimate mode of enjoyment is publicly revealed: we would like to sink into the ground. In other words, *aphanisis* bears witness to the irreducible discord between the phantasmic hard core and the texture of symbolic narrative: when I risk confrontation with this hard core, 'the story I have been telling myself about myself no longer makes sense', 'I no longer have a self to make sense of' – or, in Lacanian terms, the big Other (the symbolic order) collapses into the small other, *objet petit a*, the fantasy-object. The extraction of *objet a* from the field of reality gives this field its consistency: in *aphanisis*, the *objet a* is no longer extracted, it acquires full presence – in consequence, not only does the symbolic texture which constituted my reality disintegrate, but the very phantasmic kernel of my enjoyment is laid open, and thus comes under attack.

Perhaps, in a sense, there is no greater violence than that suffered by the subject who is forced, against his or her will, to expose to public view the *objet a* in himself or herself. And, incidentally, therein resides the ultimate argument against rape: even if, in a sense, male chauvinism is right – even if some women somehow and sometimes *do* want to be taken roughly – for that very reason there is nothing more humiliating than to force a woman, against her will, to comply with her desire. This is what Shakespeare's Coriolanus had in mind when he refused to 'hear my nothings monster'd': he preferred to become a traitor rather than resort to public self-praise and lay open that 'nothing' which was the kernel of his being.

The present war in Bosnia, therefore, is a paradigmatic case of a 'postmodern' war: it materializes in an exemplary way the triad of Ego-Evil, Superego-Evil, and Id-Evil. Here we are dealing with extreme physical violence, conquering of territory, plunder; with symbolic violence, the destruction of the enemy's symbolic universe, 'culturocide', as a consequence of which 'the story the community has been telling itself about itself no longer makes sense'; and, at the most radical level, with an endeavour to strike a blow at the unbearable surplus-enjoyment, *a*, contained in the Other. Since hatred is not limited to the 'actual properties' of its object but targets its real kernel, *objet a*, what is 'in the object more than itself', the object of hatred is, *stricto sensu, indestructible*: the more we destroy the object in reality, the more powerfully its sublime kernel rises before us.

This paradox, which has already emerged apropos of the Jews in Nazi Germany (the more they were ruthlessly exterminated, the more horrifying were the dimensions acquired by those who remained), can be perceived today apropos of Muslims in Bosnia: the more they are slaughtered and starved out, the more powerful is the danger of 'Muslim fundamentalism' in Serbian eyes. Our relationship to this traumatic-real kernel of surplus-enjoyment that 'bothers us' in the Other is structured in fantasies (about the Other's omnipotence, about 'their' strange sexual practices, etc.). In this precise sense, war is always also a *war of fantasies*.

As for the social background of this 'postmodern' warfare, Étienne Balibar[32] articulated acutely the double displacement of contemporary racism with regard to 'classical' racism. Classical racism functions as a supplement to nationalism: it is a secondary formation that emerges against the background of the assertion of national identity and designates its 'pathological' intensification, its negative, its inversion, its change of direction towards the 'internal' otherness, towards the foreign body that threatens our Nation-Body from within. Today, the relationship seems to be reversed – or, in Hegelese, reflected-into-itself:

nationalism itself functions as a species or a supplement to racism, as a delimitation from the 'internal' foreign body. On that account, 'non-racist nationalism' is formally impossible today, since nationalism itself, in its very notion, is posited as a species of racism (the 'other' against whom we assert our national identity always threatens us 'from within'). Leftist misgivings about 'non-aggressive', 'good' nationalism – about the possibility of drawing a clear line of demarcation between the 'good' nationalism of small, menaced nations and 'bad' aggressive nationalism – are thus fully justified.

Within the field of racism itself, the counterpart to this displacement is the structural change in the role of anti-Semitism. In classical racism, anti-Semitism functions as an *exception*: in Nazi discourse, for example, the attitude towards Jews (who are the *unheimlich* double of the Germans themselves and, as such, have to be annihilated) differs radically from the attitude towards other 'inferior' nations, in whose case the aim is not their annihilation but only their subordination – they have to assume their 'proper place' in the hierarchy of nations. Jews are the disturbing element that incites other inferior nations to insubordination, so that it is only through the annihilation of Jews that other nations will accept their proper subordinate place. Here also, however, a specific inversion is taking place today: we are dealing with *universalized anti-Semitism* – that is, every ethnic 'otherness' is conceived of as an *unheimliches* double that threatens our enjoyment; in short, 'normal', non-exceptional, non-anti-Semitic racism is no longer possible. The universalization of the Holocaust metaphor (apropos of every ethnic cleansing it is asserted that it is comparable to the Nazi Holocaust), excessive as it may appear, is therefore founded in the inherent logic of the thing itself, in the universalization of anti-Semitism.

This reversal, this changing of places between genus and its species, hinges on the gradual disintegration of the Nation-State *qua* predominant frame of the identification with the ethnic Thing. Today, this frame is under attack from both sides, through transnational processes of integration as well as through the emergence of new local, intra-national, ethnic and proto-ethnic forms of identification, up to and including the 'Gay Nation'. Within this global field, every ethnic difference is *eo ipso* perceived as 'internal' – which is why every nationalism is already a species of racism, and every racism already possesses the structure of anti-Semitism.

Traversing the Fantasy

Aldous Huxley's *The Grey Eminence*, a biography of Père Joseph, political adviser to Cardinal Richelieu, should be on the reading list of anyone who wants to shed some light on the obscure relationship between ethics and fantasy. If, in a fictional reconstruction of modern European history, one wanted to isolate the episode that disrupted the 'normal' course of events and introduced the imbalance whose final consequence was the two world wars in our century, the main candidate for this role is undoubtedly the parcelling out of the German *Reich* in the Thirty Years War in the first half of the seventeenth century – as a result of this parcelling out, Germany's assertion of nation-statehood was delayed. And if there is one person who, within this fictitious reconstruction, can be considered responsible for the catastrophic results, the main candidate for this role is Père Joseph who, through his phenomenal capacity for intrigue, succeeded in introducing a rupture into the Protestant camp, concluding a pact between Catholic France and Protestant Sweden, and thus shifting the centre of war to German territory.

Père Joseph is the ultimate embodiment of the plotting, Machiavellian politician ready to sacrifice thousands of lives and to resort to spying, lies, murder and extortion for the *raison d'État*. But – and this was the feature that fascinated Huxley – there was another side to this same Père Joseph: he was not only a priest but a mystic of the most authentic kind. Every evening, after a day full of painful and tortuous diplomatic intrigues, he plunged into deep meditation; his mystical visions bear witness to an authenticity worthy of Saint Teresa or John of the Cross; he corresponded regularily with the Sisters of a small French convent, and always found time to advise them on their spiritual distress.... How are we to think of these two sides together? At this crucial point, Huxley himself avoids the true paradox and opts for an easy way out by putting the blame on the alleged weak point of Père Joseph's mystical experience itself: its excessive Christocentrism, its obsession with Christ's suffering on the Way of the Cross, is made responsible for rendering possible the reckless manipulation of other people's suffering. (For that reason, Huxley turned away from Christianity and sought spiritual salvation in Eastern wisdom.) What we must do, however, is precisely to persist in this seemingly impossible conjunction: a person can be a monstrous plotter, yet his 'self-understanding', his existential-religious experience, can be impeccably 'authentic'. No 'non-ideological' self-experience, 'authentic' as it may be, can guarantee that horrifying politics will not be carried out in its name. Is not a supreme literary example of this paradox Dostoevsky's *The Brothers Karamazov*? As we now know from the post-humously published sketches, it is Alyosha, the model of innocent and humble spirituality, who, in the unwritten continuation of the novel, was to become a revolutionary terrorist.

It is becoming fashionable today to interview skinheads 'at home', demonstrating how in their home environment they are 'normal people like us', caring members of the family, tender husbands or sons – here, also, we have to endure a contradiction: a person can brutally beat up immigrants, yet in his family circle he can be the loving husband taking care of his old and infirm mother-in-law.... The case of the skinhead-at-home is even clearer than that of Père Joseph, since we are dealing here with an exemplary case of the Hegelian 'coincidence of the opposites': a brutal skinhead is not the external opposition to – the other of – the sentimental family man, but *this very sentimental family man in his otherness*; that is, he presents the brutal reaction of this same man when his safe family haven is threatened. In other words, the skinhead who gets into a fury and starts to beat 'them' up without any 'deeper' rational or ideological foundation, simply because 'it makes him feel good', is none other than the narcissistic individual of the so-called 'society of consumption' in a different modality: the line that separates them is extremely thin; it consists of a purely formal conversion, since we are dealing with one and the same fundamental attitude inscribed either inside or outside the ideological framework of what is 'socially permissible'.

It is not difficult to discern how this example of the skinhead differs from other previously mentioned examples of the constitutive splitting of ideology into the public Law and its obscene underside, hidden from public view ('Code Red', Ku Klux Klan lynchings). The example of the skinhead almost symmetrically inverts the previous ones: in it, the surface itself gets 'besmirched' – the skinhead performs in full public view what the two soldiers in *A Few Good Men* or members of Ku Klux Klan do under the cover of darkness – whereas the 'honest', 'human' side recedes into the sphere of privacy. Notwithstanding the cruelty of his public deeds, the skinhead is privately a warm person like ourselves who loves his mother, and so on – instead of the public law-and-order face with an obscene backside, we have a horrifying face concealing a tender, honest, 'human' backside. Something similar was at work in the Stalinist hagiography of Lenin: the Stalinist texts admit openly that Lenin, in his effort to fulfil historical Necessity, was forced to resort to resolute measures – that is, to violate many a gentle bourgeois moral norm and to order the summary execution of a great number of people – yet notwithstanding, he was deeply stirred by Beethoven's piano sonatas, he liked children and cats.... This difference is thus the very difference between traditional and 'totalitarian' power: in traditional power, the superego is active clandestinely, whereas in the 'totalitarian' order, it takes over the public space, and so-called 'warm humanity' appears as the private feature of people to whom the necessity of History imposes the accomplishment of obscene horrors. . . .

Recent events in ex-Yugoslavia prove that one of the most stupid proverbs at our disposal is the infamous 'To understand means to forgive'. What does this amount to in terms of the ethnic slaughter in Bosnia? To 'understand' the Serbs means to transpose oneself into their self-understanding and to 're-experience' the way they perceive and justify their acts – to plunge oneself into the bric-à-brac of Serbian myths by means of which the Serbs narrativize their historical self-experience. The paradox one has to endure here is that the monstrosity of Serbian crimes in no way diminishes the authenticity, and a kind of tragic beauty, that pertain to these myths.

Herein resides the ethical attitude of psychoanalysis, the reversal baptized by Lacan 'la traversée du fantasme', going-through the fantasy: in the distance we are obliged to assume towards our most 'authentic' dreams, towards the myths that guarantee the very consistency of our symbolic universe.

Notes

1. This also sheds a new light on the resistance of the US Army against legalizing the status of homosexuals in its ranks: the very libidinal structure of army life is latently homosexual – that is to say, the 'spirit of (military) community' turns on a disavowed homosexuality, a homosexuality thwarted, hindered from attaining its goal [zielgehemmte]. For that reason, the open, public acknowledgement of homosexuality would undermine the perverted 'sublimation' which forms the very basis of the 'spirit of (military) community'.

2. From what we have just said it should be clear why the Marquis de Sade himself was not a sadist: he subverted, rendered inoperative, the logic of sadism by publicly exhibiting it in his writings – this, precisely, is the gesture that is unbearable for sadism proper. Sadism proper is the 'nightly', obscene underside of institutional power; it cannot survive its own public disclosure. (In this precise sense Lacan points out that Sade was not a victim of his own sadistic fantasy: it was the distance maintained towards this fantasy that enabled him to reveal its functioning.) The entire content of Sade's work is 'sadistic' – the non-sadistic element in it is only its position of enunciation, that is, the fact that there is a subject ready to articulate it. This act of putting-into-words the sadistic fantasy locates Sade himself on the side of the victim.

3. See Jean-Claude Milner, Les noms indistincts, Paris: Seuil 1981.

4. Louis Althusser, 'Ideology and Ideological State Apparatuses', in Essays in Ideology, London: Verso 1984, p. 163.

5. For a more detailed account of how 'the letter always arrives at its destination', see Chapter 1 of Slavoj Žižek, Enjoy Your Symptom!, New York: Routledge 1992.

6. Here I follow the perspicacious observations of Henry Krips; see his excellent unpublished manuscript 'The Subject of Althusser and Lacan' (Department of Communication, University of Pittsburgh).

7. A similar case of pure theoretical construction seems to be the notion of freedom as the state 'between the two deaths' when my symbolic identity is suspended – is it an accident that all examples, from Antigone to Poe's Valdemar, are from the domain of literature? The state 'between the two deaths' can none the less be exemplified by an everyday experience. When I answer the phone and an unknown voice says 'Mary, are you there?' – an obvious case of wrong number – I am always tempted (I do not actually do it, yet it was Plato who said that there are two kinds of people, those who actually do nasty things and those who only dream about doing them) – I am instantaneously tempted to give an answer that would cause panic at the other end – to say: 'Don't you know?! She's had an accident, she's just been taken away in an ambulance, it's not certain whether she'll survive!', or 'She's just left in the arms of Robert!' ... In cases like this I am, for a brief moment, allowed to speak as it were from a symbolic void (since – in Europe, at least – the list of numbers you have called is not attached to the phone bill): nobody will be able to identify me, so I am disengaged, freed of any responsibility for my words.

What is here a mere example of morbid imagination assumes tragic ethical colours in the case of the gay community. That is to say, the latest trend in San Francisco is to take a risk and omit the precautions of 'safe sex' – the certainty that AIDS lies ahead is considered preferable to the procrastinating uncertainty of defensive compromises. Or – as one of the Castro Street gays recently put it – 'When you learn that you are HIV-positive, you are finally free.' Here freedom designates precisely the state between-the-two-deaths when the subject is 'alive, although already branded by death' – the shadow of death frees him from symbolic links.

Kieslowski's *Blue*, the first part of the *Three Colours* trilogy, deploys the deadlocks of such radical freedom: the theme of the film is 'abstract freedom', (the impossibility of) a break with the entire symbolic tradition in which the subject has been embedded. After the tragic death of her husband and child, the wife (Juliette Binoche) endeavours to get rid of the ghosts of her past by restarting her life from scratch (breaking with her friends, changing residence, ignoring her husband's artistic inheritance, etc.). The *Blue* in the film's title thus effectively stands for 'freedom', the first term of the 'three colours' of the French Revolution, *liberté–égalité–fraternité* – Kieslowski wisely chose to unfold the consequences of the politico-ideological notion of freedom in the most 'intimate', apparently 'apolitical' domain.

8. Printed for the first time in Louis Althusser, *Écrits sur la psychanalyse*, Paris: Stock/ IMEC 1993.

9. See ibid., p. 131.

10. Ibid., pp. 164–6.

11. This unacknowledged problematic of the subject also marks Althusser's reflection on psychoanalysis. Althusser's passionate assertion of the primacy of countertransference over transference aims precisely at *undermining* the epistemological barrier that separates the analysand caught in the imaginary trappings of transference from the analyst who is already freed from its constraints. Consequently, the point is that the analyst himself is involved in his object, caught in transference, since – as Althusser puts it in his ironic *pasticcio* of Freud – one should not forget that the analyst's countertransference is also a species of transference. (See 'Sur le transfert et le contre-transfert', ibid., pp. 175–86.) One is even tempted to go a step further and claim that what 'returns' here is the problematic of *self-consciousness*, this ultimate *bête noire* of Althusserianism: is not the assertion that transference always-already is countertransference (in his work with the analysand, the analyst continues with his self-analysis) a variation on the fundamental motif of Kant and Hegel according to which consciousness (of an object) always-already is self-consciousness?

12. See Chapter 2 of Jon Elster, *Political Psychology*, Cambridge: Cambridge University Press 1993.

13. In democracy and constitutional monarchy, however, there is also a point at which the imposed necessity assumes the form of a free act: when the President or (in constitutional monarchy) the King expresses the decision of the parliament as his free act. This was the problem that bothered all advocates of constitutional monarchy: Necker, for example, argued that the King's right to two consecutive vetos was essential, as it allowed

him to yield to the assembly's wishes in the second legislature *without appearing to be forced to do so* – that is, without losing his dignity and majesty. See Elster, *Political Psychology*, p. 28.

14. See Bazin's description of this type apropos of Quinlan in *Touch of Evil*:

> Quinlan is physically monstrous, but is he morally monstrous as well? The answer is yes and no. Yes, because he is guilty of committing a crime to defend himself; no, because from a higher moral standpoint, he is, at least in certain respects, above the honest, just, intelligent Vargas, who will always lack that sense of life which I shall call Shakespearean. These exceptional beings should not be judged by ordinary laws. They are both weaker and stronger than others ... so much stronger because directly in touch with the true nature of things, or perhaps one should say, with God.
>
> (André Bazin, *Orson Welles: A Critical View*, New York: Harper & Row 1979, p. 74)

15. The underlying libidinal economy of the Wellesian hero can be detected apropos of what is perhaps, in its very exceptional character, its exemplary case: George in *The Magnificent Ambersons*. Interpreters were quite justified in conceiving of *The Ambersons* as a permutation of *Hamlet*: here, as in *Hamlet*, the key scene is the hero's confrontation with his mother. The hero reproaches her that by her intended new marriage to the car-maker Eugene, she will betray his father's memory and the honour of her class. In *Hamlet*, however, the mother persists in her sexual need and betrays the father's noble memory, whereas in *The Ambersons* the son succeeds in breaking her down: although she loves Eugene, the mother renounces him for the sake of her love for her son; as a consequence she survives as an empty shell of her former self. In other words, what confers the 'larger-than-life' dimension upon the subject is the victory over the foreign intruder in the oedipal duel for the mother's love, the victory which enables him to continue to occupy the structural place of the mother's phallus.

16. Jacques Lacan, *The Four Fundamental Concepts of Psycho-Analysis*, Harmondsworth: Penguin 1979, p. 275.

17. The reference to this problem of not compromising one's desire opens up a way to approach Kieslowski's *The Double Life of Véronique* without falling prey to the obscurantist New Age lumber that pervades the film (the 'deep' mystical connection of the two Véroniques, the presentiment of each of them that 'she is not alone', that she has a double). The first half of the film depicts the short life of the Polish Véronique who knows she has a heart weakness, yet prefers the strain of art (singing) to a quiet private life, paying for this choice with a heart attack and death on stage. The other Véronique 'learns' from the sad fate of her double via a mysterious intuition, and refrains from following her fate to the end: she avoids the Polish Véronique's mistake, and chooses instead a quiet life in a small town.... Yet was the choice of the Polish Véronique really a mistake? Are not the two Véroniques, the Polish and the French, related to each other in the same way as Antigone and Ismene in Sophocles, or Juliette and Justine in de Sade? Does not their difference hinge on the fact that the Polish Véronique persists in her desire, whereas the French one compromises her desire and sticks to everyday 'human, all too human' considerations? In other words, do not the two Véroniques confront us with the two alternative histories of *one and the same person* who makes two fundamentally opposed ethical choices? Does not the French Véronique 'pull back' because she is frightened of the consequences of her own true desire, rendered visible to her in her premonition about the fate of her double?

18. I myself yielded to this temptation in the last chapter of *Looking Awry* (Cambridge, MA: MIT Press 1991), where I propose the maxim 'do not violate the other's fantasy-space' as a complement to Lacan's ethics of persisting in one's desire.

19. For a strict Lacanian reading of the Kantian ethics, see Alenka Zupančič, *Die Ethik des Realen. Kant–Lacan*, Vienna: Turia & Kant 1994.

20. Lacan, *The Four Fundamental Concepts of Psycho-Analysis*, p. 144.

21. Ibid., p. 240.

22. Ibid., p. 241.

23. See Chapter 6 of Slavoj Žižek, *Tarrying with the Negative*, Durham, NC: Duke University Press 1993. This insensitivity of the racist fantasy to rational-symbolic argumentation means that fantasy can only be shown, not spoken out. What we have in mind here,

of course, is the Wittgensteinian opposition, from his *Tractatus*, of what we can speak about and what can only be shown: we can speak about symptoms, dreams, slips of the tongue, and so on, we can interpret them, whereas fantasy – the phantasmic frame – is a 'form of (psychic) life' that can be shown only via a kind of purely demonstrative gesture.

24. In order to clarify the way this baring, this public staging of the obscene phantasmic kernel of an ideological edifice, suspends its normal functioning, let us recall a somewhat homologous phenomenon in the sphere of individual experience: each of us has some private ritual, phrase (nicknames, etc.) or gesture, used only within the most intimate circle of our closest friends or relatives; when these rituals are rendered public, the effect is necessarily one of extreme embarrassment and shame – we want to sink into the ground....

25. The inherent logic of the triad of hysteria–perversion–psychosis can be formulated precisely by a reference to the status of the *question* in each of the three cases. In hysteria the subject himself has the status of a question addressed to the big Other, a question that articulates his anxiety about his status in the eyes of the Other: 'What am I for the Other?' In perversion the question is displaced on to the Other – that is, a pervert has the answer (say, a Stalinist Communist who knows what people really want, in opposition to actual people who are confused and disorientated by enemy propaganda), whereas the question is foisted on the Other in whom the pervert endeavours to arouse anxiety. In psychosis the dimension of the question disappears: psychotic symptom (hallucination, for example) is an 'answer of the real' in the precise sense of an answer without question, an answer that cannot be placed in its symbolic context. The psychotic breaks the circle of communication in which the speaker receives from the addressee his own message in its true, inverted form – that is to say, in which the speaker, by means of his address, sets props, as it were, to the space of the possible answer. In psychosis, an answer emerges without its symbolic context.

26. It is possible to draw the conclusion that 'The Purloined Letter' deals quite literally with the consequences of the King's impotence: Poe gives us to understand that the secret of the 'purloined letter' is the Queen's illicit love affair – and why would the Queen look for a lover if it were not for the King's incapacity to satisfy her ... ?

27. See Chapter 1 of Joel Black, *The Aesthetics of Murder*, Baltimore, MD: Johns Hopkins University Press 1991.

28. This mysterious figure of the torturer who has a hold on woman and prevents the subject's access to her, the ultimate target of the subject's outburst of violence, is what Lacan calls Father-Enjoyment [*Père-Jouissance*], the fantasy-image of the Master of feminine enjoyment – the very opposite of the symbolic-dead father whose death means precisely that he is thoroughly ignorant of enjoyment. As to this figure of Father-Enjoyment, see Chapter 4 of Žižek, *Enjoy Your Symptom!*.

29. This constellation is at work in a whole series of American films, from John Ford's *Searchers* to Martin Scorsese's *Taxi Driver*, in which Travis (Robert de Niro) resorts to a violent *passage à l'acte* to resolve the impasse of his relationship with the young prostitute who refuses to be rescued (Jodie Foster). See Chapter 4 of Black, *The Aesthetics of Murder*.

30. Richard Rorty, *Contingency, Irony, and Solidarity*, Cambridge: Cambridge University Press 1989, p. 179.

31. For a link between *aphanisis* and the motif of amnesia (loss of memory and the sense of personal identity) in the *film noir*, see Chapter 5 of Žižek, *Enjoy Your Symptom!*.

32. Unpublished manuscript, 'Violence et politique', pp. 24–5.

PART II

Woman

4

Courtly Love, or,
Woman as Thing

Why talk about courtly love [*l'amour courtois*] today, in an age of permissiveness when the sexual encounter is often nothing more than a 'quickie' in some dark corner of an office? The impression that courtly love is out of date, long superseded by modern manners, is a lure blinding us to how the logic of courtly love still defines the parameters within which the two sexes relate to each other. This claim, however, in no way implies an evolutionary model through which courtly love would provide the elementary matrix out of which we generate its later, more complex variations. Our thesis is, instead, that history has to be read retroactively: the anatomy of man offers the key to the anatomy of the ape, as Marx put it. It is only with the emergence of masochism, of the masochist couple, towards the end of the last century that we can now grasp the libidinal economy of courtly love.

The Masochistic Theatre of Courtly Love

The first trap to be avoided apropos of courtly love is the erroneous notion of the Lady as the sublime object: as a rule, one evokes here the process of spiritualization, the shift from raw sensual coveting to elevated spiritual longing. The Lady is thus perceived as a kind of spiritual guide into the higher sphere of religious ecstasy, in the sense of Dante's Beatrice. In contrast to this notion, Lacan emphasizes a series of features which belie such a spiritualization: true, the Lady in courtly love loses concrete features and is addressed as an abstract Ideal, so that 'writers have noted that all the poets seem to be addressing the same person. . . . In this poetic field the feminine object is emptied of all real substance.'[1] However, this abstract character of the Lady has nothing to do with spiritual purification; rather, it points towards the abstraction that pertains to a cold, distanced, inhuman partner – the Lady is by no means a warm, compassionate, understanding fellow-creature:

89

By means of a form of sublimation specific to art, poetic creation consists in positing an object I can only describe as terrifying, an inhuman partner.

The Lady is never characterized for any of her real, concrete virtues, for her wisdom, her prudence, or even her competence. If she is described as wise, it is only because she embodies an immaterial wisdom or because she represents its functions more than she exercises them. On the contrary, she is as arbitrary as possible in the tests she imposes on her servant.[2]

The knight's relationship to the Lady is thus the relationship of the subject-bondsman, vassal, to his feudal Master-Sovereign who subjects him to senseless, outrageous, impossible, arbitrary, capricious ordeals. It is precisely in order to emphasize the non-spiritual nature of these ordeals that Lacan quotes a poem about a Lady who demanded that her servant literally lick her arse: the poem consists of the poet's complaints about the bad smells that await him down there (one knows the sad state of personal hygiene in the Middle Ages), about the imminent danger that, as he is fulfilling his duty, the Lady will urinate on his head. . . . The Lady is thus as far as possible from any kind of purified spirituality: she functions as an inhuman partner in the sense of a radical Otherness which is wholly incommensurable with our needs and desires; as such, she is simultaneously a kind of automaton, a machine which utters meaningless demands at random.

This coincidence of absolute, inscrutable Otherness and pure machine is what confers on the Lady her uncanny, monstrous character – the Lady is the Other which is not our 'fellow-creature'; that is to say, she is someone with whom no relationship of empathy is possible. This traumatic Otherness is what Lacan designates by means of the Freudian term *das Ding*, the Thing – the Real that 'always returns to its place',[3] the hard kernel that resists symbolization. The idealization of the Lady, her elevation to a spiritual, ethereal Ideal, is therefore to be conceived of as a strictly secondary phenomenon: it is a narcissistic projection whose function is to render her traumatic dimension invisible. In this precise and limited sense, Lacan concedes that 'the element of idealizing exaltation that is expressly sought out in the ideology of courtly love has certainly been demonstrated; it is fundamentally narcissistic in character'.[4] Deprived of every real substance, the Lady functions as a mirror on to which the subject projects his narcissistic ideal. In other words – those of Christina Rossetti, whose sonnet 'In an Artist's Studio' speaks of Dante Gabriel Rossetti's relationship to Elizabeth Siddal, his Lady – the Lady appears 'not as she is, but as she fills his dream'.[5] For Lacan, however, the crucial accent lies elsewhere:

The mirror may on occasion imply the mechanisms of narcissism, and especially the dimension of destruction or aggression that we will encounter subsequently. But it also fulfills another role, a role as limit. It is that which cannot be crossed. And the only organization in which it participates is that of the inaccessibility of the object.[6]

Thus, before we embrace the commonplaces about how the Lady in courtly love has nothing to do with actual women, how she stands for the man's narcissistic projection which involves the mortification of the flesh-and-blood woman, we have to answer this question: where does that empty surface come from, that cold, neutral screen which opens up the space for possible projections? That is to say, if men are to project on to the mirror their narcissistic ideal, the mute mirror-surface must already be there. This surface functions as a kind of 'black hole' in reality, as a limit whose Beyond is inaccessible.

The next crucial feature of courtly love is that it is thoroughly a matter of courtesy and etiquette; it has nothing to do with some elementary passion overflowing all barriers, immune to all social rules. We are dealing with a strict fictional formula, with a social game of 'as if', where a man pretends that his sweetheart is the inaccessible Lady. And it is precisely this feature which enables us to establish a link between courtly love and a phenomenon which, at first, seems to have nothing whatso-ever to do with it: namely, masochism, as a specific form of perversion articulated for the first time in the middle of the last century in the literary works and life-practice of Sacher-Masoch. In his celebrated study of masochism,[7] Gilles Deleuze demonstrates that masochism is not to be conceived of as a simple symmetrical inversion of sadism. The sadist and his victim never form a complementary 'sado–masochist' couple. Among those features evoked by Deleuze to prove the asymmetry between sadism and masochism, the crucial one is the opposition of the modalities of negation. In sadism we encounter direct negation, violent destruction and tormenting, whereas in masochism negation assumes the form of disavowal – that is, of feigning, of an 'as if' which suspends reality.

Closely depending on this first opposition is the opposition of institution and contract. Sadism follows the logic of institution, of institutional power tormenting its victim and taking pleasure in the victim's helpless resistance. More precisely, sadism is at work in the obscene, superego underside that necessarily redoubles and accom-panies, as its shadow, the 'public' Law. Masochism, on the contrary, is made to the measure of the victim: it is the victim (the servant in the masochistic relationship) who initiates a contract with the Master (woman), authorizing her to humiliate him in any way she considers appropriate (within the terms defined by the contract) and binding himself to act 'according to the whims of the sovereign lady', as Sacher-Masoch put it. It is the servant, therefore, who writes the screenplay – that is, who actually pulls the strings and dictates the activity of the woman [*dominatrix*]: he stages his own servitude.[8] One further differential feature is that masochism, in contrast to sadism, is inherently theatrical: violence is for the most part feigned, and even when it is 'real', it functions as a component of a scene, as part of a theatrical performance. Furthermore, violence is never carried out, brought to its conclusion; it always remains suspended, as the endless repeating of an interrupted gesture.

It is precisely this logic of disavowal which enables us to grasp the fundamental paradox of the masochistic attitude. That is to say, how does the typical masochistic scene look? The man-servant establishes in a cold, businesslike way the terms of the contract with the woman-master: what she is to do to him, what scene is to be rehearsed endlessly, what dress she is to wear, how far she is to go in the direction of real, physical torture (how severely she is to whip him, in what precise way she is to enchain him, where she is to stamp him with the tips of her high heels, etc.). When they finally pass over to the masochistic game proper, the masochist constantly maintains a kind of reflective distance; he never really gives way to his feelings or fully abandons himself to the game; in the midst of the game, he can suddenly assume the stance of a stage director, giving precise instructions (put more pressure on that point, repeat that movement ...), *without thereby in the least 'destroying the illusion'*. Once the game is over, the masochist again adopts the attitude of a respectful bourgeois and starts to talk with the Sovereign Lady in a matter-of-fact, businesslike way: 'Thank you for your favour. Same time next week?' and so on. What is of crucial importance here is the total self-externalization of the masochist's most intimate passion: the most intimate desires become objects of contract and composed negotiation. The nature of the masochistic theatre is therefore thoroughly 'non-psychological': the surrealistic passionate masochistic game, which suspends social reality, none the less fits easily into that everyday reality.[9]

For this reason, the phenomenon of masochism exemplifies in its purest form what Lacan had in mind when he insisted again and again that psychoanalysis is not psychology. Masochism confronts us with the paradox of the symbolic order *qua* the order of 'fictions': there is more truth in the mask we wear, in the game we play, in the 'fiction' we obey and follow, than in what is concealed beneath the mask. The very kernel of the masochist's being is externalized in the staged game towards which he maintains his constant distance. And the Real of violence breaks out precisely when the masochist is hystericized – when the subject refuses the role of an object-instrument of the enjoyment of his

Other, when he is horrified at the prospect of being reduced in the eyes of the Other to *objet a*; in order to escape this deadlock, he resorts to *passage à l'acte*, to the 'irrational' violence aimed at the other. Towards the end of P.D. James's *A Taste for Death*, the murderer describes the circumstances of the crime, and lets it be known that the factor which resolved his indecision and pushed him towards the act (the murder) was the attitude of the victim (Sir Paul Berowne):

> 'He wanted to die, God rot him, he wanted it! He practically asked for it. He could have tried to stop me, pleaded, argued, put up a fight. He could have begged for mercy, "No, please don't do it. Please!" That's all I wanted from him. Just that one word. . . . He looked at me with such contempt. . . . He knew then. Of course he knew. And I wouldn't have done it, not if he'd spoken to me as if I were even half-human.'[10]

> 'He didn't even look surprised. He was supposed to be terrified. He was supposed to prevent it from happening. . . . He just looked at me as if he were saying "So it's you. How strange that it has to be you." As if I had no choice. Just an instrument. Mindless. But I did have a choice. And so did he. Christ, he could have stopped me. Why didn't he stop me?'[11]

Several days before his death, Sir Paul Berowne experienced an 'inner breakdown' resembling symbolic death: he stepped down as a government Minister and cut all his principal 'human ties', assuming thereby the 'excremental' position of a saint, of *objet petit a*, which precludes any intersubjective relationship of empathy. This attitude was what the murderer found unbearable: he approached his victim as $, a split subject – that is to say, he wanted to kill him, yet he was simultaneously waiting for a sign of fear, of resistance, from the victim, a sign which would prevent the murderer from accomplishing the act. The victim, however, did not give any such sign, which would have subjectivized the murderer, acknowledging him as a (divided) subject. Sir Paul's attitude of non-resistance, of indifferent provocation, objectivized the murderer, reducing him to an instrument of the Other's will, and so left him with no choice. In short, what compelled the murderer to act was the experience of having his desire to kill the victim coincide with the victim's death drive.

This coincidence recalls the way a male hysterical 'sadist' justifies his beating of a woman: 'Why does she make me do it? She really wants me to do it hurt her, she compels me to beat her so that she can enjoy it – *so I'll beat her black and blue and teach her what it really means to provoke me!*' What we encounter here is a kind of loop in which the (mis)perceived effect of the brutal act upon the victim retroactively legitimizes the act: I set out to beat a woman and when, at the very point where I think that

I thoroughly dominate her, I notice that I am actually her slave – since she wants the beating and provoked me to deliver it – I get really mad and beat her. . . .[12]

The Courtly 'Imp of the Perverse'

How, on closer examination, are we to conceptualize the inaccessibility of the Lady-Object in courtly love? The principal mistake to avoid is reducing this inaccessibility to the simple dialectic of desire and prohibition according to which we covet the forbidden fruit precisely in so far as it is forbidden – or, to quote Freud's classic formulation:

> . . . the psychical value of erotic needs is reduced as soon as their satisfaction becomes easy. An obstacle is required in order to heighten libido; and where natural resistances to satisfaction have not been sufficient men have at all times erected conventional ones so as to be able to enjoy love.[13]

Within this perspective, courtly love appears as simply the most radical strategy for elevating the value of the object by putting up conventional obstacles to its attainability. When, in his seminar *Encore*, Lacan provides the most succinct formulation of the paradox of courtly love, he says something that is apparently similar, yet fundamentally different: 'A very refined manner to supplant the absence of the sexual relationship is by feigning that it is us who put the obstacle in its way.'[14] The point, therefore, is not simply that we set up additional conventional hindrances in order to heighten the value of the object: *external hindrances that thwart our access to the object are there precisely to create the illusion that without them, the object would be directly accessible* – what such hindrances thereby conceal is the inherent impossibility of attaining the object. The place of the Lady-Thing is originally empty: she functions as a kind of 'black hole' around which the subject's desire is structured. The space of desire is bent like space in the theory of relativity; the only way to reach the Object-Lady is indirectly, in a devious, meandering way – proceeding straight on ensures that we miss the target. This is what Lacan has in mind when, apropos of courtly love, he evokes 'the meaning we must attribute to the negotiation of the detour in the psychic economy':

> The detour in the psyche isn't always designed to regulate the commerce between whatever is organized in the domain of the pleasure principle and whatever presents itself as the structure of reality. There are also detours and obstacles which are organized so as to make the domain of the vacuole stand

out as such. .... The techniques involved in courtly love – and they are precise enough to allow us to perceive what might on occasion become fact, what is properly speaking of the sexual order in the inspiration of this eroticism – are techniques of holding back, of suspension, of *amor interruptus*. The stages courtly love lays down previous to what is mysteriously referred to as *le don de merci*, 'the gift of mercy' – although we don't know exactly what it meant – are expressed more or less in terms that Freud uses in his *Three Essays* as belonging to the sphere of foreplay.[15]

For that reason, Lacan accentuates the motif of anamorphosis (in his Seminar on the Ethics of Psychoanalysis, the title of the chapter on courtly love is 'Courtly Love as Anamorphosis'): the Object can be perceived only when it is viewed from the side, in a partial, distorted form, as its own shadow – if we cast a direct glance at it we see nothing, a mere void. In a homologous way, we could speak of temporal anamorphosis: the Object is attainable only by way of an incessant postponement, as its absent point of reference. The Object, therefore, is literally something that is created – whose place is encircled – through a network of detours, approximations and near-misses. It is here that *sublimation* sets in – sublimation in the Lacanian sense of the elevation of an object into the dignity of the Thing: 'sublimation' occurs when an object, part of everyday reality, finds itself at the place of the impossible Thing. Herein resides the function of those artificial obstacles that suddenly hinder our access to some ordinary object: they elevate the object into a stand-in for the Thing. This is how the impossible changes into the prohibited: by way of the short circuit between the Thing and some positive object rendered inaccessible through artificial obstacles.

The tradition of Lady as the inaccessible object is alive and well in our century – in surrealism, for example. Suffice it to recall Luis Buñuel's *That Obscure Object of Desire*, in which a woman, through a series of absurd tricks, postpones again and again the final moment of sexual re-union with her aged lover (when, for example, the man finally gets her into bed, he discovers beneath her nightgown an old-fashioned corset with numerous buckles which are impossible to undo ...). The charm of the film lies in this very nonsensical short circuit between the fundamental, metaphysical Limit and some trivial empirical impediment. Here we find the logic of courtly love and of sublimation at its purest: some common, everyday object or act becomes innaccessible or impossible to accomplish once it finds itself in the position of the Thing – although the thing should be easily within reach, the entire universe has somehow been adjusted to produce, again and again, an unfathomable contingency blocking access to the object. Buñuel himself was quite aware of this paradoxical logic: in his autobiography he speaks of 'the non-explainable impossibility of the fulfilment of a simple desire', and a whole series of films offers variations on this motif: in *The Criminal Life of Archibaldo de la Cruz* the hero wants to accomplish a simple murder, but all his attempts fail; in *The Exterminating Angel*, after a party, a group of rich people cannot cross the threshold and leave the house; in *The Discreet Charm of the Bourgeoisie* two couples want to dine together, but unexpected complications always prevent the fulfilment of this simple wish....

It should be clear, now, what determines the difference with regard to the usual dialectic of desire and prohibition: the aim of the prohibition is not to 'raise the price' of an object by rendering access to it more difficult, but to raise this object itself to the level of the Thing, of the 'black hole', around which desire is organized. For that reason, Lacan is quite justified in inverting the usual formula of sublimation, which involves shifting the libido from an object that satisfies some concrete, material need to an object that has no apparent connection to this need: for example, destructive literary criticism becomes sublimated aggressivity, scientific research into the human body becomes sublimated voyeurism, and so on. What Lacan means by sublimation, on the contrary, is shifting the libido from the void of the 'unserviceable' Thing to some concrete, material object of need that assumes a sublime quality the moment it occupies the place of the Thing.[16]

What the paradox of the Lady in courtly love ultimately amounts to is thus the paradox of *detour*: our 'official' desire is that we want to sleep with the Lady; whereas in truth, there is nothing we fear more than a Lady who might generously yield to this wish of ours – what we truly expect and want from the Lady is simply yet another new ordeal, yet one more postponement. In his *Critique of Practical Reason*, Kant offers a parable about a libertine who claims that he cannot resist the temptation to gratify his illicit sexual desire, yet when he is informed that the gallows now await him as the price to be paid for his adultery, he suddenly discovers that he can resist the temptation after all (proof, for Kant, of the pathological nature of sexual desire – Lacan opposes Kant by claiming that a man of true amorous passion would be even more aroused by the prospect of the gallows ...). But for the faithful servant of a Lady the choice is structured in a totally different way: perhaps he would even prefer the gallows to an immediate gratification of his desire for the Lady. The Lady therefore functions as a unique short circuit in which *the Object of desire itself coincides with the force that prevents its attainment* – in a way, the object 'is' its own withdrawal, its own retraction.

It is against this background that one must conceive of the often mentioned, yet no less often misunderstood, 'phallic' value of the woman in Lacan – his equation Woman = Phallus. That is to say, precisely the same paradox characterizes the phallic signifier *qua* signifier of castration. 'Castration means that *jouissance* must be refused, so that it can be reached on the inverted ladder of the Law of desire.'[17] How is this 'economic paradox' feasible, how can the machinery of desire be 'set in motion' – that is to say, how can the subject be made to renounce enjoyment not for another, higher Cause but simply in order to gain access to it? Or – to quote Hegel's formulation of the same paradox – how is it that we can attain identity only by losing it? There is only one solution to this problem: the phallus, the signifier of enjoyment, had simultaneously to be the signifier of 'castration', that is to say, *one and the same signifier had to signify enjoyment as well as its loss.* In this way, it becomes possible that the very agency which entices us to search for enjoyment induces us to renounce it.[18]

Back to the Lady: are we, therefore, justified in conceiving of the Lady as the personification of the Western metaphysical passion, as an exorbitant, almost parodical example of metaphysical *hubris*, of the elevation of a particular entity or feature into the Ground of all being? On closer examination, what constitutes this metaphysical or simply philosophical *hubris*? Let us take what might appear to be a surprising example. In Marx, the specifically *philosophical* dimension is at work when he points out that production, one of the four moments of the totality of production, distribution, exchange and consumption, is simultaneously the encompassing totality of the four moments, conferring its specific colour on that totality. (Hegel made the same point in asserting that every genus has two species, itself and its species – that is to say, the genus is always one of its own species.) The 'philosophical' or 'metaphysical' is this very 'absolutization', this elevation of a particular moment of the totality into its Ground, this *hubris* which 'disrupts' the harmony of a balanced Whole.

Let us mention two approaches to language: that of John L. Austin and that of Oswald Ducrot. Why is it legitimate to treat their work as 'philosophy'? Austin's division of all verbs into performatives and constatives is not yet philosophy proper: we enter the domain of philosophy with his 'unbalanced', 'excessive' hypothesis that every proposition, including a constative, *already is a performative* – that the performative, as one of the two moments of the Whole, simultaneously *is* the Whole. The same goes for Oswald Ducrot's thesis that every predicate possesses, over and above its informative value, an argumentative value. We remain within the domain of positive science as long as we simply endeavour to discern in each predicate the level of information and the level of argumentation – that is, the specific modality of how certain information 'fits' some argumentative attitude. We enter philosophy with the 'excessive' hypothesis that *the predicate as such, including its informative content, is nothing but a condensed argumentative attitude,* so that we can never 'distil' from it its 'pure' informative content, untainted by some argumentative attitude. Here, of course, we encounter the paradox of 'non-all': the fact that 'no aspect of a predicate's content remains unaffected by some argumentative attitude' does not authorize us to draw the seemingly obvious universal conclusion that 'the entire content of a predicate is argumentative' – the elusive surplus that persists, although it cannot be pinned down anywhere, is the Lacanian Real.

This, perhaps, offers another way of considering Heidegger's 'onto-logical difference': as the distance that always yawns between the (specific feature, elevated into the) Ground of the totality and the Real which eludes this Ground, which itself cannot be 'Grounded' in it. That is to say, 'non-metaphysical' is not a 'balanced' totality devoid of any *hubris*, a totality (or, in more Heideggerian terms: the Whole of entities) in which no particular aspect or entity is elevated into its Ground. The domain of entities gains its consistency from its sup-posited Ground, so that 'non-metaphysics' can only be an insight into the difference between Ground and the elusive Real which – although its positive content ('reality') is grounded in the Ground – none the less eludes and undermines the reign of the Ground.

And now, back to the Lady again: this is why the Lady is *not* another name for the metaphysical Ground but, on the contrary, one of the names for the self-retracting Real which, in a way, grounds the Ground itself. And in so far as one of the names for the metaphysical Ground of all entities is 'supreme Good', the Lady *qua* Thing can also be designated as the embodiment of radical Evil, of the Evil that Edgar Allan Poe, in two of his stories, 'The Black Cat' and 'The Imp of the Perverse', called the 'spirit of perverseness':

> Of this spirit philosophy takes no account. Yet I am not more sure that my soul lives, than I am that perverseness is one of the primitive impulses of the human heart. ... Who has not, a hundred times, found himself committing a vile or a stupid action, for no other reason than because he knows he should *not*? Have we not a perpetual inclination, in the teeth of our best judgment, to violate that which is *Law,* merely because we understand it to be such?
>
> ('The Black Cat')

> ... it is, in fact, a *mobile* without motive, a motive not *motiviert*. Through its promptings we act without comprehensible object; or, if this shall be understood as a contradiction in terms, we may so far modify the proposition as to say, that through its promptings we act, for the reason that we should *not*. In theory, no reason can be more unreasonable; but, in fact, there is none more strong. ... I am not more certain that I breathe, than that the assurance of the wrong or error of any action is often the one unconquerable *force* which

impels us, and alone impels us to its prosecution. Nor will this overwhelming tendency to do wrong for the wrong's sake, admit of analysis, or resolution into ulterior elements. It is a radical, a primitive impulse – elementary.

('The Imp of the Perverse')

The affinity of crime as an unmotivated *acte gratuit* to art is a standard topic of Romantic theory (the Romantic cult of the artist comprises the notion of the artist *qua* criminal): it is deeply significant that Poe's formulas ('a *mobile* without motive, a motive not *motiviert*') immediately recall Kant's determinations of the aesthetic experience ('purposeful-ness without purpose', etc.). What we must not overlook here is the crucial fact that this command – 'You must because you are not allowed to!', that is to say, a purely negative grounding of an act accomplished only because it is prohibited – is possible only within the differential symbolic order in which negative determination as such has a positive reach – in which the very *absence* of a feature functions as a *positive feature*. Poe's 'imp of the perverse' therefore marks the point at which the motivation of an act, as it were, cuts off its external link to empirical objects and grounds itself solely in the immanent circle of self-reference – in short, Poe's 'imp' corresponds to the point of freedom in the strict Kantian sense.

This reference to Kant is far from accidental. According to Kant, the faculty of desiring does not possess a transcendental status, since it is wholly dependent upon pathological objects and motivations. Lacan, on the contrary, aims to demonstrate the transcendental status of this faculty – that is, the possibility of formulating a motivation for our desire that is totally independent of pathology (such a non-pathological object-cause of desire is the Lacanian *objet petit a*). Poe's 'imp of the perverse' offers us an immediate example of such a pure motivation: when I accomplish an act 'only because it is prohibited', I remain within the universal-symbolic domain, without reference to any empirical-contingent object – that is to say, I accomplish what is *stricto sensu* a non-pathological act. Here, then, Kant miscalculated his wager: by cleansing the domain of ethics of pathological motivations, he wanted to extirpate the very possibility of doing Evil in the guise of Good; what he actually did was to open up a new domain of Evil far more uncanny than the usual 'pathological' Evil.

Exemplifications

From the thirteenth century to modern times, we encounter numerous variations on this matrix of courtly love. In *Les liaisons dangereuses*, for example, the relationship between the Marquise de Montreuil and Valmont is clearly the relationship between a capricious Lady and her servant. The paradox here turns on the nature of the task the servant must perform in order to earn the promised gesture of Mercy: he must seduce other ladies. His Ordeal requires that, even at the height of passion, he maintain a cold distance towards his victims: in the very moment of triumph, he must humiliate them by abandoning them without reason, thereby proving his fidelity to the Lady. Things get complicated when Valmont falls in love with one of his victims (Présidente de Tourvel) and thereby 'betrays his Duty': the Marquise is quite justified in dismissing his excuse (the famous 'c'est pas ma faute': it's beyond my control, it's the way things are ...) as beneath Valmont's dignity, as a miserable recourse to a 'pathological' state of things (in the Kantian sense of the term).

The Marquise's reaction to Valmont's 'betrayal' is thus strictly ethical: Valmont's excuse is exactly the same as the excuse invoked by moral weaklings when they fail to perform their duty – 'I just couldn't help it, such is my nature, I'm simply not strong enough ...'. Her message to Valmont recalls Kant's motto 'Du kannst, denn du sollst! [You can, because you must!]'. For that reason, the punishment imposed by the Marquise on Valmont is quite appropriate: in renouncing the Présidente de Tourvel, he must have recourse to exactly the same words – that is, he must compose a letter to her, explaining to her that 'it's not his fault' if his passion for her has expired, it's simply the way things are....

Another variation on the matrix of courtly love emerges in the story of Cyrano de Bergerac and Roxane. Ashamed of his obscene natural deformity (his too-long nose), Cyrano has not dared to confess his love to the beautiful Roxane; so he interposes between himself and her a good-looking young soldier, conferring on him the role of proxy through whom he expresses his desire. As befits a capricious Lady, Roxane demands that her lover articulate his love in elegant poetic terms; the unfortunate simple-minded young soldier is not up to the task, so Cyrano hastens to his assistance, writing passionate love letters for the soldier from the battlefield. The dénouement takes place in two stages, tragic and melodramatic. Roxane tells the soldier that she does not love his beautiful body alone; she loves his refined soul even more: she is so deeply moved by his letters that she would continue to love him even if his body were to become mutilated and ugly. The soldier shudders at these words: he realizes that Roxane does not love him as he really is but as the author of his letters – in other words, she unknowingly loves Cyrano. Unable to endure this humiliation, he rushes suicidally into an attack and dies. Roxane enters a cloister, where she has regular visits from Cyrano, who keeps her informed about the social life of Paris.

COURTLY LOVE, OR, WOMAN AS THING

During one of these visits Roxane asks him to read aloud the last letter of her dead lover. The melodramatic moment now sets in: Roxane suddenly notices that Cyrano does not read the letter, he recites it – thereby proving that he is its true author. Deeply shaken, she recognizes in this crippled merrymaker her true love. But it is already too late: Cyrano has come to this meeting mortally wounded....

One of the most painful and troubling scenes from David Lynch's *Wild at Heart* is also comprehensible only against the matrix of the logic of suspension that characterizes courtly love. In a lonely motel room, Willem Dafoe exerts a rude pressure on Laura Dern: he touches and squeezes her, invading the space of her intimacy and repeating in a threatening way 'Say fuck me!', that is, extorting from her a word that would signal her consent to a sexual act. The ugly, unpleasant scene drags itself on, and when, finally, the exhausted Laura Dern utters a barely audible 'Fuck me!', Dafoe abruptly steps away, assumes a nice, friendly smile and cheerfully retorts: 'No thanks, I don't have time today; but on another occasion I would do it gladly ...'. He has attained what he really wanted: not the act itself, just her consent to it, her symbolic humiliation. What intervenes here is the function of the big Other, the trans-subjective symbolic order: by means of his intrusive pressure, Dafoe wants to extort the inscription, the 'registration', of her consent in the field of the big Other.

The reverse variation on the same motif is at work in a short love scene from Truffaut's *La nuit américaine* (*Day for Night*). When, on the drive from the hotel to the studio, a car tyre blows, the assistant cameraman and the script-girl find themselves alone on a lake shore. The assistant, who has pursued the girl for a long time, seizes the opportunity and bursts into a pathetic speech about how much he desires her and how much it would mean to him if, now that they are alone, she were to consent to a quick sexual encounter; the girl simply says 'Yes, why not?' and starts to unbutton her trousers.... This non-sublime gesture, of course, totally bewilders the seducer, who conceived of her as the unattainable Lady: he can only stammer 'How do you mean? Just like that?' What this scene has in common with the scene from *Wild at Heart* (and what sets it within the matrix of courtly love) is the unexpected gesture of refusal: the man's response to the woman's 'Yes!', obtained by long, arduous effort, is to refuse the act.

We encounter a more refined variation on the matrix of courtly love in Eric Rohmer's *Ma nuit chez Maud*: courtly love provides the only logic that can account for the hero's lie at the end. The central part of the film depicts the night that the hero and his friend Maud spend together; they talk long into the small hours and even sleep in the same bed, but the sexual act does not take place, owing to the hero's indecision – he is unable to seize the opportunity, obsessed as he is by the mysterious blonde woman whom he saw the evening before in a church. Although he does not yet know who she is, he has already decided to marry her (i.e. the blonde is his Lady). The final scene takes place several years later. The hero, now happily married to the blonde, encounters Maud on a beach; when his wife asks him who this unknown woman is, the hero tells a lie – apparently to his detriment; he informs his wife that Maud was his last love adventure before marriage. Why this lie? Because the truth could have aroused the suspicion that Maud also occupied the place of the Lady, with whom a brief, noncommittal sexual encounter is not possible – precisely by telling a lie to his wife, by claiming that he did have sex with Maud, he assures her that Maud was not his Lady, but just a passing friend.

The definitive version of courtly love in recent decades, of course, arrives in the figure of the *femme fatale* in *film noir*: the traumatic Woman-Thing who, through her greedy and capricious demands, brings ruin to the *hard-boiled* hero. The key role is played here by the third person (as a rule the gangster boss) to whom the *femme fatale* 'legally' belongs: his presence renders her inaccessible and thus confers on the hero's relationship with her the mark of transgression. By means of his involvement with her, the hero betrays the paternal figure who is also his boss (in *The Glass Key, Killers, Criss-cross, Out of the Past*, etc.).

This link between the courtly Lady and the *femme fatale* from the *noir* universe may appear surprising: is not the *femme fatale* in *film noir* the very opposite of the noble sovereign Lady to whom the knight vows service? Is not the hard-boiled hero ashamed of the attraction he feels for her; doesn't he hate her (and himself) for loving her; doesn't he experience his love for her as a betrayal of his true self? However, if we bear in mind the original traumatic impact of the Lady, not its secondary idealization, the connection is clear: like the Lady, the *femme fatale* is an 'inhuman partner', a traumatic Object with whom no relationship is possible, an apathetic void imposing senseless, arbitrary ordeals.[19]

From the Courtly Game to *The Crying Game*

The key to the extraordinary and unexpected success of Neil Jordan's *The Crying Game* is perhaps the ultimate variation that it delivers on the motif of courtly love. Let us recall the outlines of the story: Fergus, a member of the IRA guarding a captured black British soldier, develops friendly links with him; the soldier asks him, in the event of his liquidation, to pay a visit to his girlfriend, Dil, a hairdresser in a London suburb, and to give her his last regards. After the death of the soldier,

Fergus withdraws from the IRA, moves to London, finds a job as a bricklayer and pays a visit to the soldier's love, a beautiful black woman. He falls in love with her, but Dil maintains an ambiguous ironic, sovereign distance towards him. Finally, she gives way to his advances; but before they go to bed together she leaves for a brief moment, returning in a transparent nightgown; while casting a covetous glance at her body, Fergus suddenly perceives her penis – 'she' is a transvestite. Sickened, he crudely pushes her away. Shaken and wet with tears, Dil tells him that she thought he knew all the time how things stood (in his obsession with her, the hero – as well as the public – did not notice a host of telltale details, including the fact that the bar where they usually met was a meeting-place for transvestites). This scene of the failed sexual encounter is structured as the exact inversion of the scene referred to by Freud as the primordial trauma of fetishism: the child's gaze, sliding down the naked female body towards the sexual organ, is shocked to find nothing where one expects to see something (a penis) – in the case of *The Crying Game*, the shock is caused when the eye finds *something* where it expected *nothing*.

After this painful revelation, the relationship between the two is reversed: now it turns out that Dil is passionately in love with Fergus, although she knows her love is impossible. From a capricious and ironic sovereign Lady she changes into the pathetic figure of a delicate, sensitive boy who is desperately in love. It is only at this point that true love emerges, love as a metaphor in the precise Lacanian sense:[20] we witness the sublime moment when *eromenos* (the loved one) changes into *erastes* (the loving one) by stretching out her hand and 'returning love'. This moment designates the 'miracle' of love, the moment of the 'answer of the Real'; as such, it perhaps enables us to grasp what Lacan has in mind when he insists that the subject itself has the status of an 'answer of the Real'. That is to say, up to this reversal the loved one has the status of an object: he is loved on account of something that is 'in him more than himself' and that he is unaware of – I can never answer the question 'What am I as an object for the other? What does the other see in me that causes his love?'. We thus confront an asymmetry – not only the asymmetry between subject and object, but asymmetry in a far more radical sense of a discord between what the lover sees in the loved one and what the loved one knows himself to be.

Here we find the inescapable deadlock that defines the position of the loved one: the other sees something in me and wants something from me, but I cannot give him what I do not possess – or, as Lacan puts it, there is no relationship between what the loved one possesses and what the loving one lacks. The only way for the loved one to escape this deadlock is to stretch out his hand towards the loving one and to 'return love' – that is, to exchange, in a metaphorical gesture, his status as the loved one for the status of the loving one. This reversal designates the point of subjectivization: the object of love changes into the subject the moment it answers the call of love. And it is only by way of this reversal that a genuine love emerges: I am truly in love not when I am simply fascinated by the *agalma* in the other, but when I experience the other, the object of love, as frail and lost, as lacking 'it', and my love none the less survives this loss.

We must be especially attentive here so that we do not miss the point of this reversal: although we now have two loving subjects instead of the initial duality of the loving one and the loved one, the asymmetry persists, since it was the object itself that, as it were, confessed to its lack by means of its subjectivization. Something deeply embarrassing and truly scandalous abides in this reversal by means of which the mysterious, fascinating, elusive object of love discloses its deadlock, and thus acquires the status of another subject.

We encounter the same reversal in horror stories: is not the most sublime moment in Mary Shelley's *Frankenstein* the moment of the monster's subjectivization – the moment when the monster-object (who has been continually described as a ruthless killing machine) starts talking in the first person, revealing his miserable, pitiful existence? It is deeply symptomatic that all the films based on Shelley's *Frankenstein* have avoided this gesture of subjectivization. And perhaps, in courtly love itself, the long-awaited moment of highest fulfilment, when the Lady renders *Gnade*, mercy, to her servant, is not the Lady's surrender, her consent to the sexual act, nor some mysterious rite of initiation, but simply a sign of love on the part of the Lady, the 'miracle' that the Object answered, stretching its hand out towards the supplicant.[21]

So, back to *The Crying Game*: Dil is now ready to do anything for Fergus, and he is more and more moved and fascinated by the absolute, unconditional character of her love for him, so that he overcomes his aversion and continues to console her. At the end, when the IRA again tries to involve him in a terrorist act, he even sacrifices himself for Dil and assumes responsibility for a killing she committed. The last scene of the film takes place in the prison where she visits him, again dressed up as a provocatively seductive woman, so that every man in the visiting room is aroused by her looks. Although Fergus has to endure more than four thousand days of prison – they count them up together – she cheerfully pledges to wait for him and visit him regularly.... The external impediment – the glass-partition in the prison preventing any physical contact – is here the exact equivalent to the obstacle in courtly love that renders the object inaccessible; it thereby accounts for the absolute, unconditional character of this love in spite of its inherent impossibility – that is, in spite of the fact that their love will never be consummated, since he is a 'straight' heterosexual and she is a homosexual transvestite. In his Introduction to the published screen-play, Jordan points out that

> the story ended with a kind of happiness. I say a kind of happiness, because it involved the separation of a prison cell and other more profound separations, of racial, national, and sexual identity. But for the lovers, it was the irony of what divided them that allowed them to smile. So perhaps there is hope for our divisions yet.[22]

Is not the division – the unsurmountable barrier – that allows for a smile the most concise mechanism of courtly love? What we have here is an 'impossible' love which will never be consummated, which can be realized only as a feigned spectacle intended to fascinate the gaze of the spectators present, or as an endlessly postponed expectation; this love is absolute precisely in so far as it transgresses not only the barriers of class, religion and race, but also the ultimate barrier of sexual orientation, of sexual identification. Herein resides the film's paradox and, at the same time, its irresistible charm: far from denouncing heterosexual love as a product of male repression, it renders the precise circumstances in which this love can today retain its absolute, unconditional character.

The Crying Game Goes East

This reading of *The Crying Game* immediately brings to mind one of the standard reproaches to Lacanian theory: in all his talk about feminine inconsistency, and so on, Lacan speaks about woman only as she appears or is mirrored in male discourse, about her distorted reflection in a medium that is foreign to her, never about woman as she is in herself: to Lacan, as earlier to Freud, feminine sexuality remains a 'dark continent'. In answer to this reproach, we must emphatically assert that if the fundamental Hegelian paradox of reflexivity remains in force anywhere, it is here: the remove, the step back, from woman-in-herself to how woman *qua* absent Cause distorts male discourse brings us much closer to the 'feminine essence' than a direct approach. That is to say, is not 'woman' ultimately just the name for a distortion or inflection of the male discourse? Is not the spectre of 'woman-in-herself', far from being the active cause of this distortion, rather its reified-fetishized effect?

All these questions are implicitly addressed by *M. Butterfly* (directed by David Cronenberg, script by David Henry Hwang from his own play), a film whose subtitle could well have been *'The Crying Game' Goes to China*.

The first feature of this film that strikes the eye is the utter 'improbability' of its narrative: without the information (given in the credits) that the story is based on true events, nobody would take it seriously. During the Great Cultural Revolution, a minor French diplomat in Beijing (Jeremy Irons) falls in love with a Chinese opera singer who sings some Puccini arias at a reception for foreigners (John Lone). His courting leads to a lasting love relationship; the singer, who is to him the fatal love object (with reference to Puccini's opera, he affectionately calls her 'my butterfly'), apparently becomes pregnant, and produces a child. While their affair is going on she induces him to spy for China, claiming that this is the only way the Chinese authorities will tolerate their association. After a professional failure the diplomat is transferred to Paris, where he is assigned to the minor post of diplomatic courier. Soon afterwards, his love joins him there and tells him that if he will carry on spying for China, the Chinese authorities will allow 'their' child to join them. When, finally, French security discovers his spying activities and they are both arrested, it turns out that 'she' is not a woman at all, but a man – in his Eurocentric ignorance, the hero did not know that in Chinese opera, female roles are sung by men.

It is here that the story stretches the limits of our credulity: how was it that the hero, in their long years of consummated love, did not see that he was dealing with a man? The singer incessantly evoked the Chinese sense of shame, s/he never undressed, they had (unbeknownst to him, anal) sex discreetly, s/he sitting on his lap ... in short, what he mistook for the shyness of the Oriental woman was, on 'her' side, a deft manipulation destined to conceal the fact that 'she' was not a woman at all. The choice of the music that obsesses the hero is crucial here: the famous aria 'Un bel di, vedremo' from *Madama Butterfly*, perhaps the most expressive example of Puccini's gesture that is the very opposite of bashful self-concealment – the obscenely candid self-exposure of the (feminine) subject that always borders upon *kitsch*. The subject pathetically professes what she is and what she wants, she lays bare her most intimate and frail dreams – a confession which, of course, reaches its apogee in the desire to die (in 'Un bel di, vedremo', Madama Butterfly imagines the scene of Pinkerton's return: at first, she will not answer his call, 'in part for fun and in part not to die at the first encounter [*per non morir al primo incontro*]').

From what we have just said, it may seem that the hero's tragic blunder consists in projecting his fantasy-image on to an inadequate object – that is to say, in mistaking a real person for his fantasy-image of the love object, the Oriental woman of the Madama Butterfly type. However, things are definitely more complex. The key scene of the film occurs after the trial, when the hero and his Chinese partner, now in an ordinary man's suit, find themselves alone in the closed compartment of a police car on their way to prison. The Chinese takes off his clothes and offers himself naked to the hero, desperately proclaiming his availability: 'Here I am, your butterfly!' He proposes himself as what he is outside the hero's fantasy-frame of a mysterious Oriental woman. At this crucial moment, the hero retracts: he avoids his lover's eyes and rejects the offer. It is here that he gives up his desire and is thereby marked by an indelible guilt: he betrays the true love that aims at the real kernel of the object beneath the phantasmic layers. That is to say, the paradox resides in the fact that although he loved the Chinese without any underhand thoughts, while the Chinese manipulated his love on behalf of the Chinese secret service, it now becomes obvious that the Chinese's love was in some sense purer and far more authentic. Or, as John le Carré put it in *A Perfect Spy*: 'Love is whatever you can still betray'.

As every reader of 'true' spy adventures knows very well, a large number of cases in which a woman has seduced a man out of duty, in order to extract from him some vital piece of information (or vice versa) end with a happy marriage – far from dispelling the mirage of love, the disclosure of the deceitful manipulation that brought the lovers together only strengthened their bond. To put it in Deleuzian terms: we are dealing here with a split between the 'depth' of reality, the intermixture of bodies in which the other is the instrument I mercilessly exploit, in which love itself and sexuality are reduced to means manipulated for politico-military purposes, and the level of love *qua* pure surface event. Manipulation at the level of bodily reality renders all the more manifest love *qua* surface event, *qua* effect irreducible to its bodily support.[23]

The painful final scene of the film conveys the hero's full recognition of his guilt.[24] In prison, the hero stages a performance for his vulgar and noisy fellow-prisoners: dressed as Madama Butterfly (a Japanese kimono, heavily made-up face) and accompanied by excerpts from Puccini's opera, he retells his story; at the very climax of 'Un bel di, vedremo', he cuts his throat with a razor and collapses dead. This scene of a man performing public suicide dressed as a woman has a long and respectable history: suffice it to mention Hitchcock's *Murder* (1930), in which the murderer Handel Fane, dressed as a female trapeze artist, hangs himself in front of a packed house after finishing his number. In *M. Butterfly*, as in *Murder*, this act is of a strictly ethical nature: in both cases the hero stages a psychotic identification with his love object, with his *sinthome* (synthetic formation of the nonexistent woman, 'Butterfly') – that is, he 'regresses' from the object-choice to an immediate identification with the object; the only way out of the insoluble deadlock of this identification is suicide *qua* the ultimate *passage à l'acte*. By his suicidal act the hero makes up for his guilt, for his rejection of the object when the object was offered to him outside the fantasy-frame.

Here, of course, the old objection again awaits us: ultimately, does not *M. Butterfly* offer, a tragicomic confused bundle of male fantasies about women, not a true relationship with a woman? The entire action of the film takes place among men. Does not the grotesque incredibility of the plot simultaneously mask and point towards the fact that what we are dealing with is a case of homosexual love for the transvestite? The film is simply dishonest, and refuses to acknowledge this obvious fact. This 'elucidation', however, fails to address the true enigma of *M. Butterfly* (and of *The Crying Game*): how can a hopeless love between the hero and his partner, a man dressed up as a woman, realize the notion of heterosexual love far more 'authentically' than a 'normal' relationship with a woman?

How, then, are we to interpret this perseverance of the matrix of courtly love? It bears witness to a certain deadlock in contemporary feminism. True, the courtly image of man serving his Lady is a semblance that conceals the actuality of male domination; true, the masochist's theatre is a private *mise en scène* designed to recompense the guilt contracted by man's social domination; true, the elevation of woman to the sublime object of love equals her debasement into the passive stuff or screen for the narcissistic projection of the male ego-ideal, and so on. Lacan himself points out how, in the very epoch of courtly love, the actual social standing of women as objects of exchange in male power-plays was probably at its lowest. However, this very semblance of man serving his Lady provides women with the fantasy-substance of their identity whose effects are real: it provides them with all the features that constitute so-called 'femininity' and define woman not as she is in her *jouissance féminine*, but as she refers to herself with regard to her (potential) relationship to man, as an object of his desire. From this fantasy-structure springs the near-panic reaction – not only of men, but also of many a woman – to a feminism that wants to deprive woman of her very 'femininity'. By opposing 'patriarchal domination', women simultaneously undermine the fantasy-support of their own 'feminine' identity.

The problem is that once the relationship between the two sexes is conceived of as a symmetrical, reciprocal, voluntary partnership or contract, the fantasy matrix which first emerged in courtly love remains in power. Why? In so far as sexual difference is a Real that resists symbolization, the sexual relationship is condemned to remain an asymmetrical non-relationship in which the Other, our partner, prior to being a subject, is a Thing, an 'inhuman partner'; as such, the sexual relationship cannot be transposed into a symmetrical relationship between pure subjects. The bourgeois principle of contract between equal subjects can be applied to sexuality only in the form of the *perverse* – masochistic – contract in which, paradoxically, the very form of balanced contract serves to establish a relationship of domination. It is no accident that in the so-called alternative sexual practices ('sadomaso-chistic' lesbian and gay couples) the Master-and-Slave relationship re-emerges with a vengeance, including all the ingredients of the masochistic theatre. In other words, we are far from inventing a new 'formula' capable of replacing the matrix of courtly love.

For that reason, it is misleading to read *The Crying Game* as an anti-political tale of escape into privacy – that is to say, as a variation on the theme of a revolutionary who, disillusioned by the cruelty of the political power-play, discovers sexual love as the sole field of personal realization, of authentic existential fulfilment. Politically, the film remains faithful to the Irish cause, which functions as its inherent background. The paradox is that in the very sphere of privacy where the hero hoped to find a safe haven, he is compelled to accomplish an even more vertiginous revolution in his most intimate personal attitudes. Thus *The Crying Game* eludes the usual ideological dilemma of 'privacy as the island of authenticity, exempt from political power-play' versus 'sexuality as yet another domain of political activity': it renders visible the *antagonistic* complicity between public political activity and personal sexual subver-sion, the antagonism that is already at work in Sade, who demanded a sexual revolution as the ultimate accomplishment of the political revolution. In short, the subtitle of *The Crying Game* could have been 'Irishmen, yet another effort, if you want to become republicans!'.

Notes

1. Jacques Lacan, *The Ethics of Psychoanalysis*, London: Routledge 1992, p. 149.
2. Ibid., p. 150; translation modified.
3. Is not Lacan's definition of the Real as that which always returns to its place 'pre-Einsteinian' and, as such, de-valorized by the relativization of space with regard to the observer's point of view – that is, by the cancellation of the notion of absolute space and time? However, the theory of relativity involves its own absolute constant: the space–time interval between two events is an absolute that never varies. Space–time interval is defined as the hypotenuse of a right-angled triangle whose legs are the time and space distance between the two events. One observer may be in a state of motion such that for him there is a time and a distance involved between the two events; another may be in a state of motion such that his measuring devices indicate a different distance and a different time between the events, but the space–time interval between them does not vary. *This* constant is the Lacanian Real that 'remains the same in all possible universes'.
4. Lacan, *The Ethics of Psychoanalysis*, p. 151.
5. It is clear, therefore, that it would be a fateful mistake to identify the Lady in courtly love, this unconditional Ideal of the Woman, with woman in so far as she is not submitted to phallic enjoyment: the opposition of everyday, 'tamed' woman, with whom sexual

relationship may appear possible, and the Lady *qua* 'inhuman partner', has nothing whatsoever to do with the opposition of woman submitted to phallic signifier and woman *qua* bearer of the Other enjoyment. The Lady is the projection of man's narcissistic Ideal, her figure emerges as the result of the masochistic pact by way of which woman accepts the role of *dominatrix* in the theatre staged by man. For that reason, Rossetti's *Beata Beatrix*, for example, is not to be perceived as the figuration of the Other enjoyment: as with Isolde's love death in Wagner's *Tristan*, we are dealing with *man's* fantasy.

6. Lacan, *The Ethics of Psychoanalysis*, p. 151.

7. Gilles Deleuze, 'Coldness and Cruelty', in *Masochism*, New York: Zone Press 1991.

8. For that reason lesbian sadomasochism is far more subversive than the usual 'soft' lesbianism, which elevates tender relationships between women in contrast to aggressive-phallic male penetration: although the content of lesbian sadomasochism imitates 'aggressive' phallic heterosexuality, this content is subverted by the very contractual form.

9. Here the logic is the same as in the 'non-psychological' universe of *Twin Peaks*, in which we encounter two main types of people: 'normal', everyday people (based on soap-opera clichés) and 'crazy' eccentrics (the lady with a log, etc.); the uncanny quality of the *Twin Peaks* universe hinges on the fact that the relationship between these two groups follows the rules of 'normal' communication: 'normal' people are not at all amazed or outraged by the strange behaviour of the eccentrics; they accept them as part of their daily routine.

10. P.D. James, *A Taste for Death*, London and Boston, MA: Faber & Faber 1986, p. 439.

11. Ibid., p. 440.

12. An exemplary case of the inverse constellation – of the gaze *qua objet a* hystericizing the other – is provided by Robert Montgomery's *Lady in the Lake*, a film whose interest consists in its very failure. The point of view of the hard-boiled detective to which we are confined via a continuous subjective camera in no way arouses in us, the spectators, the impression that we are actually watching the events through the eyes of the person shown by the camera in the prologue or the epilogue (the only 'objective shots' in the film) or when it confronts a mirror. Even when Marlowe 'sees himself in the mirror', the spectator does not accept that the face he sees, the eyes on it, is the point of view of the camera. When the camera drags on in its clumsy, slow way it seems, rather, that the point of view is that of a living dead from Romero's *Night of the Living Dead* (the same association is further encouraged by the Christmas choral music, very unusual for a *film noir*). More precisely, it is as if the camera is positioned next to or closely behind Marlowe and somehow looks over his back, imitating the virtual gaze of his shadow, of his 'undead' sublime double. There is no double to be seen next to Marlowe, since this double, what is in Marlowe 'more than himself', is the gaze itself as the Lacanian *objet petit a* that does not have a specular image. (The voice that runs a commentary on the story belongs to this gaze, not to Marlowe *qua* diegetic person.) This object-gaze is the cause of the desire of women who, all the time, turn towards it (i.e. look into the camera): it lays them bare in an obscene way – or, in other words, it hystericizes them by simultaneously attracting and repelling them. It is on account of this objectivization of the gaze that *The Lady in the Lake* is not a *film noir*: the essential feature of a *film noir* proper is that the point of view of the narration is that of a *subject*.

13. Sigmund Freud, 'On the Universal Tendency to Debasement in the Sphere of Love' (1912), in James Strachey, ed., *The Standard Edition of the Complete Psychological Works of Sigmund Freud*, vol. 11, London: Hogarth Press 1986, p. 187.

14. Jacques Lacan, *Le séminaire, livre XX: Encore*, Paris: Éditions du Seuil 1975, p. 65.

15. Lacan, *The Ethics of Psychoanalysis*, p. 152.

16. '... par une inversion de l'usage du terme de sublimation, j'ai le droit de dire que nous voyons ici la déviation quant au but se faire en sens inverse de l'objet d'un besoin' (Jacques Lacan, *Le séminaire, livre VIII: Le transfert*, Paris: Éditions du Seuil 1991, p. 250). The same goes for every object which functions as a sign of love: its use is suspended, it changes into a means of the articulation of the demand for love.

17. Jacques Lacan, *Écrits: A Selection*, New York: Norton 1977, p. 324. The first to formulate this 'economic paradox of castration' in the domain of philosophy was Kant. One of the standard reproaches to Kant is that he was a contradictory thinker who got stuck

halfway: on the one hand *already* within the new universe of democratic rights (*égaliberté*, to use Étienne Balibar's term), on the other hand *still* caught in the paradigm of man's subordination to some superior Law (imperative). However, Lacan's formula of fetishism (a fraction with *a* above minus phi of castration) enables us to grasp the co-dependence of these two allegedly opposed aspects. The crucial feature that distinguishes the democratic field of *égaliberté* from the pre-bourgeois field of traditional authority is the potential *infinity* of rights: rights are never fully realized or even explicitly formulated, since we are dealing with an unending process of continually articulating new rights. On that account, the status of rights in the modern democratic universe is that of *objet petit a*, of an evasive object-cause of desire. Where does this feature come from? Only one consistent answer is possible: *rights are (potentially) infinite because the renunciation upon which they are based is also infinite*. The notion of a radical, 'infinite' renunciation as the price the individual must pay for his entry into the social-symbolic universe – that is to say, the notion of a 'discontent in civilization', of an irreducible antagonism between man's 'true nature' and the social order – emerged only with the modern democratic universe. Previously, within the field of traditional authority, 'sociability', a propensity for subordination to authority and for aligning oneself with some community, was conceived of as an integral part of the very 'nature' of man *qua zōon politikon*. (This, of course, does not mean that this renunciation – 'symbolic castration', in psychoanalytic terms – was not, implicitly, at work from the very beginning: we are dealing here with the logic of retroactivity where things 'become what they always-already were': the modern bourgeois universe of Rights made visible a renunciation that was *always-already* there.) And the infinite domain of rights arises precisely as a kind of 'compensation': it is what we *get in exchange* for the infinite renunciation as the price we had to pay for our entry into society.

18. This paradox of castration also offers the key to the function of perversion, to its constitutive loop: the pervert is a subject who directly assumes the paradox of desire and inflicts pain in order to enable enjoyment, who introduces schism in order to enable reunion, and so on. And, incidentally, theology resorts to obscure talk about the 'inscrutable divine mystery' precisely at the point where it would otherwise be compelled to acknowledge the perverse nature of God: 'the ways of the Lord are mysterious', which usually means that when misfortune pursues us everywhere, we must presuppose that He plunged us into misery in order to force us to take the opportunity to achieve spiritual salvation. . . .

19. Films that transpose the *noir* matrix into another genre (science fiction, musical comedy, etc.) often exhibit some crucial ingredient of the *noir* universe more patently than the *noir* proper. When, for example, in *Who Framed Roger Rabbit?*, Jessica Rabbit, a cartoon character, answers the reproach of her corruption with 'I'm not bad, I was just drawn that way!', she thereby displays the truth about *femme fatale* as a male fantasy – that is, as a creature whose contours are drawn by man.

20. See Chapters 3 and 4 of Lacan, *Le séminaire, livre VIII: Le transfert* (1960–61).

21. This moment when the object of fascination subjectivizes itself and stretches out its hand is the magical moment of crossing the frontier that separates the fantasy-space from 'ordinary' reality: it is as if, at this moment, the object that otherwise belongs to another, sublime space intervenes in 'ordinary' reality. Suffice it to recall a scene from *Possessed*, Clarence Brown's early Hollywood melodrama with Joan Crawford. Crawford, a poor small-town girl, stares amazed at the luxurious private train that slowly passes in front of her at the local railway station; through the windows of the carriages she sees the rich life going on in the illuminated inside – dancing couples, cooks preparing dinner, and so on. The crucial feature of the scene is that we, the spectators, together with Crawford, perceive the train as a magic, immaterial apparition from another world. When the last carriage passes by, the train comes to a halt and we see on the observation desk a good-natured drunkard with a glass of champagne in his hand, which stretches over the railing towards Crawford – as if, for a brief moment, the fantasy-space intervened in reality. . . .

22. *A Neil Jordan Reader*, New York: Vintage Books 1993, pp. xii–xiii. The question to be raised here is also that of inserting *The Crying Game* into the series of Jordan's other films: are not the earlier *Mona Lisa* and *Miracle* variations on the same motif? In all three cases, the relationship between the hero and the enigmatic woman he is obsessed with is doomed

111

to fail – because she is a lesbian, because she is the hero's mother, because she is not a 'she' at all but a transvestite. Jordan thus provides a veritable matrix of the impossibilities of sexual relationship.

23. As for this Deleuzian opposition of surface event and bodily depth, see Chapter 5 below.

24. At this point the film differs from 'reality': the 'true' hero is still alive and rotting in a French prison.

5

David Lynch, or,
the Feminine Depression

Lynch as a Pre-Raphaelite

In art history, the Pre-Raphaelites offer a paradoxical borderline case of the avant-garde overlapping with *kitsch*: they were first perceived as bearers of an anti-traditionalist revolution in painting, breaking with the entire tradition from the Renaissance onwards; but only a short time later – with the rise of Impressionism in France – they were devalued as the epitome of damp Victorian pseudo-Romantic *kitsch*. This scornful evaluation persisted until the 1960s – that is to say, until the emergence of postmodernism, when the Pre-Raphaelites suddenly staged a critical comeback. How was it that the Pre-Raphaelites became 'readable' only retroactively, through the postmodernist paradigm?

In this respect, the crucial artist is William Holman Hunt, usually dismissed as the first of the Pre-Raphaelites to sell out to the establishment by changing into a well-paid producer of 'sugared' religious paintings (*The Triumph of the Innocents*, etc.). A closer look, however, confronts us with an uncanny, deeply disturbing dimension of his work – his paintings cannot fail to produce a certain uneasiness, an indeterminate feeling that, in spite of their idyllic and elevated 'official' content, something is still amiss. Let us take *The Hireling Shepherd*, ostensibly a simple pastoral idyll depicting a shepherd engaged in seducing a country girl and, for that reason, neglecting his sheep (an obvious allegory of the Church neglecting its flock). The longer we observe the painting, the more we become aware of how many details testify to Hunt's intense relationship with enjoyment, with *jouissance* as life-substance – that is to say, his disgust at sexuality. The shepherd is muscular, dull, crude and rudely voluptuous; the girl's cunning gaze indicates a sly, vulgarly manipulative exploitation of her own sexual attraction; the all too vivacious red and green palette stains the entire painting with a repulsive tone, as if we were dealing with a putrid overripe nature. The same goes for *Isabella and the Pot of Basil*, where

113

numerous details – such as the snaky hairs and the skulls on the brim of the vase – belie the 'official' tragic-religious content.

The sexuality radiated by the painting is damp, 'unwholesome', permeated with the rot of death ... we are thereby already in the midst of David Lynch's universe. That is to say, Lynch's entire 'ontology' is based upon the discordance between reality, observed from a safe distance, and the absolute proximity of the Real. His elementary procedure involves moving forward from the establishing shot of reality to a disturbing proximity that renders visible the disgusting substance of enjoyment, the crawling and glistening of indestructible life.[1] Suffice it to recall the opening sequence of Blue Velvet. After the vignettes of the idyllic American small town and the heart attack of the hero's father as he waters the lawn (when he collapses, the jet of hose water uncannily recalls surrealistic, heavy urination), the camera noses into the lawn, disclosing the bursting life there: the crawling insects and beetles, their rattling and devouring of the grass.... At the very beginning of Twin Peaks: Fire Walk with Me, we encounter the opposite procedure, which amounts to the same effect: first we see abstract white protoplasmic shapes floating in a blue background, a kind of elementary form of life in its primordial twinkling; then, as the camera moves slowly away, we gradually become aware that what we saw was the extreme close-up of a TV screen.[2] Here we come to recognize the fundamental feature of postmodernist 'hyperrealism': the overproximity to reality brings about the 'loss of reality'; uncanny details stick out and perturb the pacifying effect of the overall picture.[3]

The second feature, closely linked to the first, resides in the very designation 'Pre-Raphaelitism': the reaffirmation of rendering things as they 'really are', not yet distorted by the rules of academic painting first established by Raphael. However, the Pre-Raphaelites' own practice belies this naive ideology of returning to the 'natural' way of painting. The first thing about their paintings that strikes the eye is their flatness. This feature necessarily appears to us, accustomed as we are to modern perspective-realism, as a sign of clumsiness: Pre-Raphaelite paintings somehow lack the 'depth' that pertains to space organized along perspective lines which meet at a distant point – it is as if the very 'reality' these paintings depict is not a 'true' reality but, rather, a reality structured as in bas-relief. (Another aspect of this same feature is the 'dollish', mechanically composite, artificial quality that clings to the depicted individuals: they somehow lack the abyssal depth of personality that we usually associate with the notion of 'subject'.) The designation 'Pre-Raphaelitism' is thus to be taken literally: as indicating the shift from Renaissance perspectivism to the 'closed' medieval universe.

In Lynch's films, this 'flatness' of depicted reality, which effectively cancels the perspective of infinite openness, finds its precise counterpart at the level of sound. Let us return to the opening sequence of *Blue Velvet*: its crucial feature is the uncanny noise that emerges when we approach the Real. This noise is difficult to locate in reality; in order to determine its status one is tempted to invoke contemporary cosmology, which speaks of the noises at the borders of the universe. Such noises are not simply internal to the universe; they are the remainders, the last echoes, of the Big Bang that created the universe itself. The ontological status of this noise is more interesting than it may seem, since it subverts the fundamental notion of the 'open', infinite universe that defines the space of Newtonian physics.

This modern notion of the 'open' universe is based on the hypothesis that every positive entity (noise, matter) occupies some (empty) space: it hinges on the difference between space *qua* void and positive entities occupying space, 'filling it out'. Here space is phenomenologically viewed as something existing prior to the entities that 'fill it out': if we destroy or remove the matter occupying a given space, the space *qua* void still remains. But the primordial noise, the last remainder of the Big Bang, is *constitutive of space itself*: it is not a noise 'in' space, but a noise that keeps space open as such. If, therefore, we were to erase this noise, we would not get the 'empty space' that the noise filled out: space itself, the receptacle for every 'inner-worldly' entity, would vanish. This noise is therefore, in a sense, the very 'sound of silence'. Along the same lines, the fundamental noise in Lynch's films is not simply caused by objects that are part of reality; instead, this noise forms the ontological horizon, the frame of reality itself, the very texture that holds reality together – if this noise were to be eradicated, reality itself would collapse. From the 'open' infinite universe of Cartesian–Newtonian physics, we thus revert to the pre-modern 'closed' universe, bounded by a fundamental 'noise'.

We encounter this same noise in the nightmare sequence of *The Elephant Man*, as it crosses the borderline that separates interior from exterior; that is to say, in this noise, the extreme externality of a machine coincides uncannily with the utmost intimacy of the bodily interior, with the rhythm of the palpitating heart. Another point not to be missed is that this noise appears after the camera enters the hole in the elephant man's hood which stands for the gaze: the reversal of reality into the Real corresponds to the reversal of the look (of the subject peering at reality) into the gaze – that is, this reversal occurs when we enter the 'black hole', the tear in the fabric of reality.

A Voice That Skins the Body

What we encounter in this 'black hole' is simply the body stripped of its skin. That is to say, Lynch perturbs our most elementary phenomenological relationship to the living body, which is based on the radical separation between the surface of the skin and what lies beneath it. Let us recall the uncanniness, even disgust, we experience when we endeavour to imagine what goes on just under the surface of a beautiful naked body – muscles, organs, veins.... In short, relating to the body implies suspending what goes on beneath the surface. This suspension is an effect of the symbolic order; it can occur only in so far as our bodily reality is structured by language. In the symbolic order, even when we are undressed, we are not really naked, since skin itself functions as the 'dress of the flesh'.[4] This suspension excludes the Real of the life-substance, its palpitation: one of the definitions of the Lacanian Real is that it is the flayed body, the palpitation of the raw, skinless red flesh.

How, then, does Lynch perturb our most elementary phenomenological relationship to the bodily surface? By means of *voice*, of a word that 'kills', breaking through the skin surface to cut directly into raw flesh – in short, by means of a word whose status is that of the *Real*. This feature is most expressive in Lynch's version of Herbert's *Dune*. Suffice it to recall the members of the space-guild who, because they have overindulged in 'spice', the mysterious drug around which the story revolves, have became distorted beings with gigantic heads; as worm-like creatures made of skinless, raw flesh, they represent the indestructible life-substance, the pure embodiment of enjoyment.

A similar distortion arises in the corrupted kingdom of the evil baron Harkonnen, where many faces are disfigured in an uncanny way, with sewn-up eyes and ears, and so on. The face of the baron himself is full of disgusting protuberances, 'sprouts of enjoyment' in which the inside of the body breaks through the surface. The bizarre scene of the baron assaulting a young boy in an oral-homoerotic way also plays on this ambiguous relationship between the inside and the surface – the baron attacks the youth by pulling out his heart-cork, so that blood starts squirting out. (What we have here is the typical Lynch child-fantasy notion of the human body as a balloon, a form made of inflated skin, with no solid substance inside....) The skulls of the space-guild servants also start to crack when they run out of the spice – again a case of distorted, fractured surfaces.

What is crucial here is the correlation between these cracks in the skull and the distorted *voice*: the guild-servant utters unintelligible whispers, which are transformed into articulated speech only by passing through the microphone – or, in Lacanian terms, by passing through the medium

of the big Other. In *Twin Peaks* also, the dwarf in the Red Lodge spo
an incomprehensible, distorted English, rendered intelligible onl
the help of subtitles, which assume here the role of the microphone –
that is, the role of the medium of the big Other. This delay – the process
by which the inarticulate sounds we utter become speech only through
the intervention of the external, mechanical, symbolic order – is usually
concealed. It is rendered visible only when the relationship between
surface and its beyond is perturbed. What we have here, therefore, is the
hidden reverse of the Derridean critique of logocentrism, in which the
voice functions as the medium of illusory self-transparency and self-
presence: instead, we have the obscene, cruel, superegotistical, incomprehensible, impenetrable, traumatic dimension of the Voice, which
functions as a kind of foreign body perturbing the balance of our lives.[5]

In *Dune*, our – the spectators' – experience of the bodily surface is also
perturbed in the hero, Paul Atreid's, mystical experience of drinking the
'water of life' (mysticism, of course, stands for the encounter with the
Real). Here again the inside endeavours to erupt through the surface –
blood drips not only from Paul's eyes but also from the mouths of his
mother and sister, who are aware of his ordeal by direct, non-symbolic
empathy. (The ruler's counsellors, the 'living computers' who are able
to read other people's thoughts and see into the future, also have strange
blood-like stains around their lips.)

Finally, the voice of Paul himself has a direct, physical impact: by
raising his voice, he can not only derange his adversary, he can even blow
up the hardest rock. At the end of the film, Paul raises his voice and
shouts back at the old priestess who tried to penetrate his mind, causing
her to jump away as if she has been dealt a physical blow. As Paul himself
says, his words can kill – that is, his speech does not only function as a
symbolic act, it cuts directly into the Real. The disintegration of the
'normal' relationship between bodily surface and its beneath or beyond
is strictly correlative to this change in the status of speech, to this
emergence of a word that operates directly at the level of the Real.

A Crack in the Causal Chain

Another crucial feature marks this last scene: the old priestess reacts to
Paul's words in an exaggerated, almost theatrical way, so that it is not
clear if she is reacting to his actual words or to the distorted, overblown
way she perceived them. In short, the 'normal' relationship between
cause (Paul's words) and effect (woman's reaction to them) is here
perturbed, as if a gap separates them, as if the effect never corresponds
to its alleged cause. The usual way to read this gap would be to figure it

as an index of woman's hysteria: women cannot perceive external causes clearly, they always project into them their own distorted vision.... Michel Chion, however, in a true stroke of genius, proposes quite a different reading of this disturbance.[6] One is tempted to 'set in order' his rather non-systematic progression, scattered throughout his book on Lynch, by arranging it into three consecutive steps.

• Chion's starting point is the gap, the discrepancy, *décalage*, between action and reaction that is always at work in Lynch: when a subject – a man as a rule – addresses a woman or 'electrocutes' her in some other way, the woman's reaction is always somehow incommensurable with the signal or 'impulse' she received. At stake in this incommensurability is a kind of short circuit between cause and effect: their relationship is never 'pure' or linear, we can never be quite certain about the extent to which the effect itself retroactively 'coloured' its own cause. Here we encounter the logic of *anamorphosis* presented in an exemplary way in Act II scene ii of Shakespeare's *Richard II* by the words of the Queen's faithful servant Bushy:

> Like perspectives, which rightly gaz'd upon
> Show nothing but confusion; ey'd awry
> Distinguish form: so your sweet majesty
> Looking awry upon your lord's departure,
> Finds shapes of grief more than himself to wail;
> Which, look'd on as it is, is nought but shadows
> Of what is not.

In her answer to Bushy, the Queen herself locates her fears in the context of causes and effects:

> ... conceit is still deriv'd
> From some forefather grief; mine is not so,
> For nothing hath begot my something grief;
> Or something hath the nothing that I grieve:
> 'Tis in reversion that I do possess;
> But what it is, that is not yet known; what
> I cannot name; 'tis nameless woe, I wot.[7]

The incommensurability between cause and effect thus results from the anamorphic perspective of the subject who distorts the 'real' preceding cause, so that his act (his reaction to this cause) is never a direct effect of the cause but, rather, a consequence of his distorted perception of the cause.

• Chion's next step consists of a 'crazy' gesture worthy of the most daring Freudian interpretation: he hypothesizes that the fundamental matrix, the paradigmatic case, of this discrepancy between action and reaction is the sexual (non-)relationship between man and woman. In sexual activity, men 'do certain things to women', and the question is: *is woman's enjoyment reducible to an effect, is it a simple consequence of what a man does to her?* From the good old times of Marxist hegemony, one perhaps remembers the vulgar-materialist 'reductionist' efforts to locate the genesis of the notion of causality in human practice, in man's active relating to his environment: we arrive at the notion of causality by generalizing from the experience of witnessing how, every time we make a certain gesture, the same effect occurs in reality.... Chion proposes an even more radical 'reductionism': the elementary matrix of the relationship between cause and effect is offered by the sexual relationship. In the last analysis, the irreducible gap that separates an effect from its cause amounts to the fact that '*not all* of the feminine enjoyment is an effect of the masculine cause'. This 'not-all' has to be conceived precisely in the sense of the Lacanian logic of 'not-all [*pas-tout*]': it does not in any way entail that a part of a woman's enjoyment is *not* the effect of what a man does to her. In other words, 'not-all' designates inconsistency, not incompleteness: in a woman's reaction there is always something unforeseen, the woman never reacts in the expected way – one day she does not react to something that hitherto has never failed to arouse her; another day she is aroused by something the man does in passing, and inadvertently.... Woman is not fully submitted to the causal link; with her, the linear order of causality breaks down – or, to quote Nicolas Cage when, in Lynch's *Wild at Heart*, he is struck by an unexpected reaction from Laura Dern: 'The way your mind works is God's own private mystery.'[8]

• Chion's last step is in itself double: a further specification, followed by a generalization. *Why* is it precisely woman who, by way of her incommensurate reaction to man's signal, breaks the causal chain asunder? The specific feature of woman, which seems to be reducible to a link in the causal chain yet actually suspends and inverts the causal connection, is *feminine depression*, her suicidal propensity to slide into permanent lethargy: man 'bombards' woman with 'shocks' in order to rouse her out of this depression.

The Birth of Subjectivity out of the Feminine Depression

At the centre of *Blue Velvet* (and of Lynch's entire *oeuvre*) lies the enigma of woman's depression. That the fatal Dorothy (Isabella Rossellini) is depressed goes without saying, since the reasons for her anguish seem obvious: her child and husband have been kidnapped by the cruel Frank (Dennis Hopper), who even cut off one of her husband's ears, and he blackmails Dorothy by exacting sexual favours from her as the price for keeping her husband and child alive. So the causal link seems clear and unambiguous: Frank has caused all her troubles by breaking into the happy family and provoking the trauma. Whatever masochist enjoyment Dorothy experiences is a simple after-effect of this initial shock – the victim is so bewildered and derailed by the sadistic violence she is submitted to that she 'identifies with the aggressor' and sets out to imitate his game.... However, detailed analysis of the most famous scene from *Blue Velvet* – the sadomasochistic sexual play between Dorothy and Frank, observed by Jeffrey (Kyle MacLachlan), hidden in the closet – compels us to invert our entire perspective. That is to say, the crucial question to be asked here is: *for whom* is this scene staged?

• The first answer seems obvious: for Jeffrey. Is not this scene an exemplary case of the child witnessing parental coitus? Is not Jeffrey reduced to a pure gaze present at the act of his own conception (the elementary matrix of fantasy)? Such an interpretation gains support from two peculiar features of what Jeffrey observes: Dorothy stuffing some blue velvet material into Frank's mouth; Frank breathing heavily into an oxygen mask held to his mouth. Are not both these features visual hallucinations based on what the child hears? When the child eavesdrops on his parents' lovemaking, he hears hollow speaking and heavy, gasping breathing, so he imagines that something must be in his father's mouth (perhaps a piece of sheet, since he is in bed), or that he is breathing under a mask....[9]

• But what this reading ignores is the crucial fact that the sadomasochistic game between Dorothy and Frank is thoroughly staged, deliberately theatrical: both of them act, not just Dorothy, who knows that Jeffrey is watching, since she put him in the closet. In fact, both of them overact – as if they both know they are being observed. Jeffrey is not an unacknowledged, accidental witness to a secret ritual: the ritual is staged for his gaze from the outset. From this perspective, the true organizer of the game seems to be Frank. His noisy, theatrical mannerisms, bordering on the comical and recalling the classic image of the arch-villain, reveal how desperately he is trying to fascinate and impress the third gaze. In order to prove what? The key, perhaps, is offered by Frank's obsessive repeating to Dorothy: 'Don't you look at me!' – why not? There can be only one possible answer: *because there is nothing to see* – that is to say, there is no erection, since Frank is impotent. Read this way, the scene takes on quite a different meaning: Frank and Dorothy feign a wild sexual act in order to conceal the father's impotence from the child; all Frank's shouting and swearing, his comical-spectacular imitation of coital gestures, serve to mask the absence of coitus. In traditional terms, the accent shifts from voyeurism to exhibitionism: Jeffrey's gaze is nothing but an element in the exhibitionist's scenario – that is, instead of a son witnessing parental coitus, we have the father's desperate attempt to convince the son of his potency.

• Yet a third possible reading centres on Dorothy herself. What we have in mind here, of course, are not the anti-feminist commonplaces about female masochism, about how women secretly enjoy being brutally mistreated, and so forth. Our point, rather, is the following hypothesis: given that with woman the linear causal link is suspended, even reversed, what if *depression is the original fact*, what if it comes first, and all subsequent activity – Frank's terrorizing of Dorothy – far from being the cause of her malaise, is, rather, a desperate 'therapeutic' attempt to prevent the woman from sliding into the abyss of absolute depression, a kind of 'electroshock' therapy that endeavours to focus her attention?[10] The crudeness of his 'treatment' (kidnapping her husband and son; cutting off the husband's ear; requiring her participation in the sadistic sexual game) simply corresponds to the depth of her depression: only such raw shocks can keep her active.

In this sense Lynch can be said to be truly anti-Weininger: if, in Otto Weininger's *Sex and Character*, the paradigm of modern anti-feminism, woman presents herself to man, endeavouring to fascinate his gaze and thus to drag him down from the spiritual heights into the pit of sexual debauchery – if, then, for Weininger, the 'original fact' is man's spirituality, whereas his fascination with a woman results from his Fall – with Lynch, the 'original fact' is the woman's depression, her sliding into the abyss of self-annihilation, of absolute lethargy; whereas, on the contrary, it is man who presents himself to woman as the object of her gaze. Man 'bombards' her with shocks in order to arouse her attention and thereby pull her out of her numbness – in short, in order to reinstate her in the 'proper' order of causality.[11]

The tradition of a deadened, lethargic woman aroused from her numbness by a man's call was well under way in the nineteenth century: suffice it to recall Kundry from Wagner's *Parsifal* who, at the beginning of Act II and Act III, is awakened from a catatonic sleep (first through Klingsor's rude summons, then through Gurnemanz's kind care), or – from 'real' life – the unique figure of Jane Morris, wife of William Morris and mistress of Dante Gabriel Rossetti. The famous photo of Jane from 1865 presents a depressive woman, deeply absorbed in her thoughts, who seems to await man's stimulation to pull her out of her lethargy: this photo offers, perhaps, the closest approximation to what Wagner had in mind when he created the figure of Kundry.[12]

What is of crucial importance is the universal, formal structure at work here: the 'normal' relationship between cause and effect is inverted; the 'effect' is the original fact, it comes first, and what appears as its cause – the shocks that allegedly set the depression in motion – is actually a reaction to this effect, a struggle against the depression. Here again the logic is that of 'not-all': 'not-all' of depression results from the causes that trigger it; yet, at the same time, there is no element of depression that is not triggered by some external active cause. In other words, everything in depression is an effect – everything except depression as such, except the *form* of depression. The status of depression is thus strictly 'transcendental': depression provides the a priori frame within which causes can act as they do.[13]

It may seem that we have simply trotted out the most common prejudices about female depression – the notion of woman who can be aroused only by man's stimuli. There is, however, another way to consider the issue: the elementary structure of subjectivity turns on how *not-all of the subject is determined by the causal chain.* The subject 'is' this very gap that separates the cause from its effect; it emerges precisely in so far as the relationship between cause and effect becomes 'unaccountable'.[14] In other words, what is this feminine depression that suspends the causal link, the causal connection between our acts and external stimuli, if not the founding gesture of subjectivity, the primordial act of freedom, of refusing our insertion into the nexus of causes and effects?[15] The philosophical name for this 'depression' is absolute negativity – what Hegel called 'the night of the world', the subject's withdrawal into itself. In short, woman, not man, is the subject *par excellence.*[16] And the link between this depression and the indestructible life-substance is also clear: depression, withdrawal-into-self, is the primordial act of retreat, of maintaining a distance towards the indestructible life-substance, making it appear as a repulsive scintillation.

The Pure Surface of the Sense-Event

The fundamental axis of Lynch's universe consists of the tension between the abyss of 'feminine' depth and the pure skin surface of the symbolic order: bodily depth constantly invades the surface and threatens to swallow it. Which philosophical dyad provides the co-ordinates of this axis? In his *Logic of Sense,* Deleuze aims to displace the opposition that defines the Platonic space, that of suprasensible Ideas and their sensible-material copies, into the opposition of substantial-opaque depth of the Body and the pure surface of the Sense-Event. This surface depends on the emergence of language: it is the non-substantial void that separates Things from Words. As such, it has two faces: one face is turned towards Things – that is, it is the pure, non-substantial surface of Becoming, of Events heterogeneous with regard to substantial Things to which these Events happen; the other face is turned towards Language – that is, it is the pure flux of Sense in contrast to representational Signification, to the referring of a sign to bodily objects. Deleuze, of course, remains a materialist: the surface of Sense is an effect of the interplay of bodily causes – it is, however, a heterogeneous effect, an effect of a radically different order from that of (corporeal) Being. We thus have, on the one hand, the generative bodily mixture of causes and effects and, on the other, the incorporeal surface of pure effects-events that are 'sterile', 'asexual', neither active nor passive.

This other, anti-Platonic line emerged for the first time in Stoicism, with the Stoic perversion (rather than subversion) of Platonism through the theory of Sense *qua* incorporeal Event (our principal, albeit scarce, source here is Chrysippos' fragments on logic); it reappeared triumphantly in the 'anti-ontological' turn of philosophy at the beginning of the century. The Deleuzian opposition of bodies and sense-effect thus opens up a new approach not only to Husserl's phenomenology but also to its less well known double, Alexis Meinong's 'theory of objects [*Gegenstandstheorie*]': both aim *to set phenomena free from the constraints of substantial being*. Husserl's 'phenomenological reduction' brackets the substantial bodily depth – what remain are 'phenomena' *qua* the pure surface of Sense. Meinong's philosophy similarly deals with 'objects in general': according to Meinong, an object is everything that is possible to conceive intellectually, irrespective of its existence or non-existence. Thus Meinong admits not only Bertrand Russell's notorious 'present French king who is bald' but also objects like 'wooden iron' or 'round square'. Apropos of every object, Meinong distinguishes between its *Sosein* (being-thus) and its *Sein* (being): a round square has its *Sosein*, since it is defined by the two properties of being round and square, yet it does not have *Sein*, since, due to its self-contradictory nature, such an object cannot exist.

Meinong's name for such objects is 'homeless' objects: there is no place for them, either in reality or in the domain of the possible. More precisely, Meinong classifies objects into those that have being, that exist in reality; those that are formally possible (since they are not self-contradictory) although they do not exist in reality, like the 'golden mountain' – in this case, it is their non-being that exists; and finally 'homeless' objects that do not exist *tout court*. Furthermore, Meinong claims that every subject's attitude, not only the assertoric attitude of knowledge, possesses its objective correlative: the correlative of representation is object [*Gegenstand*]; the correlative of thought is objective [*Objektiv*]; the correlative of feeling dignity, and the correlative of drive desiderative. So a new field of objects opens up that is not only 'wider' than reality but constitutes a separate level of its own: objects are determined only by their quality, *Sosein*, irrespective of their real existence or even of their mere possibility – in a sense they 'take off' from reality.

Does not Wittgenstein's *Tractatus* also belong to the same 'Stoicist' line? In its very first proposition, Wittgenstein establishes a distinction between things [*Dinge*] and the world [*die Welt*] as the entirety of facts [*Tatsachen*], of everything that is a case [*der Fall*], that can occur: 'Die Welt ist die Gesamtheit der Tatsachen, nicht der Dinge.' In his Preface, which is usually reprinted with *Tractatus*, Bertrand Russell endeavours precisely to domesticate this 'homelessness' of the event by means of reinscribing the event back into the order of things.

The first association to which this tension between pre-symbolic depth and the surface of events gives rise in the domain of popular culture is, of course, the 'alien' from the film of the same name. Our first response is to conceive of it as a creature of the chaotic depth of the maternal body, as the primordial Thing. However, does not the 'alien''s incessant changing of its form, the utter 'plasticity' of its being, also point in exactly the opposite direction: are we not dealing with a being whose entire consistency resides in the phantasmic surface, with a series of pure events-effects devoid of any substantial support?

Perhaps this difference of the two levels also offers the key to Mozart's *Così fan tutte*. One of the commonplaces about this opera is that it constantly subverts the line that separates sincere from feigned emotions: not only is pathetic heroism (that of Fiordiligi, who wants to join her fiancé on the battlefield, for example) denounced again and again as empty posturing, the subversion also goes in the opposite direction – the philosopher Alfonso, that supreme cynic, becomes dupe of his own manipulation from time to time and is carried away by his feigned emotions, which unexpectedly prove sincere (in the trio 'Soave il vento', for example).

This pseudo-dialectics of sincere and feigned emotions, although it is not entirely out of place, none the less fails to take into account the gap that separates the bodily machine from the surface of its effects-events. Alfonso's point of view is that of mechanical materialism: man or woman is a machine, a puppet; his or her emotions – love, in this case – do not express some spontaneous authentic freedom but can be brought about automatically, by way of submitting him or her to proper causes. Mozart's answer to this philosopher's cynicism is the autonomy of the 'effect' *qua* pure event: emotions are effects of the bodily machine, but they are also effects in the sense of an effect-of-emotion (as when we speak about an 'effect-of-beauty'), and this surface of the effect *qua* event possesses its own authenticity and autonomy. Or, to put it in contemporary terms: even if biochemistry succeeds in isolating the hormones that regulate the rise, intensity and duration of sexual love, the actual experience of love *qua* event will maintain its autonomy, its radical heterogeneity with regard to its bodily cause.

This opposition of bodily machine and surface event is personified in the couple of Alfonso and Despina. Alfonso is a mechanicist-materialist cynic who believes only in the bodily machine, while Despina stands for love *qua* pure surface event. The lesson of the philosopher Alfonso is – as usual – 'Renounce your desire, acknowledge its vanity!': if it were possible, by way of a carefully conducted experiment, to induce the two sisters to forget their fiancés and fall in love anew with unequalled passion in the span of a single day, then it is useless to ask which love is true and which is false – one love equals the other; all of them result from the bodily mechanism to which man is enslaved.

Despina, on the contrary, maintains that in spite of all this it is still worthy to remain faithful to one's desire – hers is the ethics displayed by Sam Spade who, in a well-known passage from Hammett's *Maltese Falcon*, reports how he was hired to find a man who had suddenly left his settled job and family and vanished. Spade is unable to track him down, but a few years later he stumbles into him in a bar in another city, where the man lives under an assumed name and leads a life remarkably similar to the one from which he had fled. The man is none the less convinced that the change was not in vain....[17] One of the key arias of the entire opera is Despina's 'Una donna a quindici anni' from the beginning of Act II. If one pays proper attention to it, as Peter Sellars did in his deservedly famous production, it attests to an unexpected ambiguity in Despina's character: what lurks beneath the mask of a jovial intriguer is the melancholic ethic of persisting in one's desire notwithstanding its fragility and fickleness.

Deleuze as a Dialectical Materialist

Perhaps the most acute experience of the gap that separates the surface from the bodily depth concerns our relationship to our partner's naked body: we can take this body as a pure object of knowledge (and concentrate on flesh, bones, and glands beneath the skin), as an object of disinterested aesthetic pleasure, as an object of sexual desire.... To put it in a somewhat simplified way: the 'wager' of phenomenology is that each of these attitudes and/or its objective correlative possesses an autonomy of its own: it is not possible to 'translate' our experience of our partner's body as the object of sexual desire into terms of a biochemical process. The surface, of course, is an effect of bodily causes – but an effect that is irreducible to its cause, since it belongs to a radically heterogeneous order.

The fundamental problem for Deleuze in *The Logic of Sense* (but also for Lacan) is how we are to conceive theoretically the passage from bodily depth to the surface event, the rupture that has to occur at the level of bodily depth if the effect-of-sense is to emerge – in short: *how are we to articulate the 'materialist' genesis of Sense?* To ask this question is to enter the problematic of *dialectical materialism* – here we use the term 'dialectical materialism' in its fullest sense, as the name which designates the dimension that is irreducible to the problematic of 'historical materialism'.[18] Historical materialism *qua* the theory of socio-symbolic processes presupposes the horizon of symbolic *praxis* as always-already there, and does not raise the question of its 'genesis'. Thus conceived, dialectical materialism is strictly opposed to mechanical materialism, which is reductionist by definition: it does not acknowledge the radical heteronomy of the effect with regard to the cause – that is, it conceives of the sense-effect-surface as a simple appearance, the appearance of an underlying deeper material Essence. Idealism, on the contrary, denies that the sense-effect is an effect of bodily depth; it fetishizes the sense-effect into a self-generated entity; the price it pays for this denial is the *substantialization* of the sense-effect: idealism covertly qualifies the sense-effect as a new Body (the immaterial body of Platonic Forms, for example). Paradoxical as it may sound, only dialectical materialism can think the effect of Sense, sense *qua* event, in its specific autonomy, without a substantialist reduction (which is why vulgar mechanical materialism forms the necessary complement to idealism).

The universe of Sense *qua* 'autonomous' forms a vicious circle: we are always-already part of it, since the moment we assume the attitude of external distance towards it and turn our gaze from the effect to its cause, we lose the effect.[19] The fundamental problem of dialectical materialism, therefore, is: how does this circle of Sense, which allows of no externality, emerge? How can the immixture of bodies give rise to 'neutral' thought – to the symbolic field that is 'free' in the precise sense of not being bound by the economy of bodily drives, of not functioning as a prolongation of the drive's striving for satisfaction? The Freudian hypothesis is: through the inherent impasse of sexuality. It is not possible to derive the emergence of 'disinterested' thought from other bodily drives (hunger, self-preservation...) – why not?

Sexuality is the only drive that is in itself hindered, perverted:

simultaneously insufficient and excessive, with the excess as the form of appearance of the lack. On the one hand, sexuality is characterized by the universal capacity to provide the metaphorical meaning or innuendo of any activity or object – any element, including the most abstract reflection, can be experienced as 'alluding to *that*' (suffice it to recall the proverbial example of the adolescent who, in order to forget his sexual obsessions, takes refuge in pure mathematics and physics – whatever he does here again reminds him of 'that': how much volume is needed to fill out an empty cylinder? How much energy is discharged when two bodies collide? . . .).

This universal surplus – this capacity of sexuality to overflow the entire field of human experience so that everything, from eating to excretion, from beating up our fellow-man (or getting beaten up by him) to the exercise of power, can acquire a sexual connotation – is not the sign of its preponderance. Rather, it is the sign of a certain structural faultiness: sexuality strives outwards and overflows the adjoining domains precisely because it cannot find satisfaction in itself, because it never attains its goal. How, precisely, does an activity that is in itself definitely asexual acquire sexual connotations? It is 'sexualized' when it fails to achieve its asexual goal and gets caught in the vicious circle of futile repetition. We enter sexuality when a gesture that 'officially' serves some instrumental goal becomes an end in itself, when we start to enjoy the very 'dysfunctional' repetition of this gesture, and thereby suspend its purposefulness.

Sexuality can function as a co-sense that supplements the 'desexualized' neutral-literal meaning precisely in so far as this neutral meaning *is already here*. As Deleuze has demonstrated, perversion enters the stage as an inherent reversal of this 'normal' relationship between the asexual literal sense and the sexual co-sense: in perversion, sexuality is made into a direct object of our speech, but the price we pay for it is the desexualization of our attitude towards sexuality – sexuality becomes one desexualized object among others. The exemplary case of such an attitude is the 'scientific' disinterested approach to sexuality or the Sadeian approach that treats sexuality as the object of an instrumental activity. Suffice it to recall Jennifer Jason Leigh's role in Robert Altman's *Short Cuts*: a housewife who earns supplementary money by paid phone sex, entertaining customers with pep talk. She is so well accustomed to her job that she can improvise into the receiver on how she is all wet between her thighs, and so on, while changing her baby or preparing lunch – she maintains a wholly external, instrumental attitude towards sexual fantasies; they simply do not concern her.[20]

What Lacan aims at with the notion of 'symbolic castration' is precisely this *vel*, this choice: *either* we accept the desexualization of the literal sense that entails the displacement of sexuality to a 'co-sense', to the supplementary dimension of sexual connotation-innuendo; *or* we approach sexuality 'directly', we make sexuality the subject of literal speech, for which we pay with the 'desexualization' of our subjective attitude to it. What we lose in every case is a direct approach, a literal talk about sexuality, which would remain 'sexualized'.

In this precise sense, phallus is the signifier of castration: far from acting as the potent organ-symbol of sexuality *qua* universal creative power, it is the *signifier and/or organ of the very desexualization*, of the 'impossible' passage of 'body' into symbolic 'thought', the signifier that sustains the neutral surface of 'asexual' sense. Deleuze conceptualizes this passage as the inversion of the 'phallus of co-ordination' into the 'phallus of castration': 'phallus of co-ordination' is an *imago*, a figure the subject refers to in order to co-ordinate the dispersed erogenous zones into the totality of a unified body; whereas 'phallus of castration' is a signifier. Those who conceive of the phallic signifier after the model of the mirror stage, as a privileged image or bodily part that provides the central point of reference enabling the subject to totalize the dispersed multitude of erogenous zones into a unique, hierarchically ordered totality, remain at the level of the 'phallus of co-ordination' and reproach Lacan with what is actually his fundamental insight: this co-ordination through the central phallic image necessarily fails. The outcome of this failure, however, is not a return to the uncoordinated plurality of erogenous zones, but precisely 'symbolic castration': sexuality retains its universal dimension and continues to function as the (potential) connotation of every act, object, and so on, only if it 'sacrifices' literal meaning – only if literal meaning is 'desexualized': the step from the 'phallus of co-ordination' to the 'phallus of castration' is the step from the impossible-failed total sexualization, from the state in which 'everything has sexual meaning', to the state in which this sexual meaning becomes secondary, changes into the 'universal innuendo', into the co-sense that potentially supplements every literal, neutral-asexual sense.[21]

How, then, do we pass from the state in which 'the meaning of everything is sexual', in which sexuality functions as the universal *signified*, to the surface of the neutral-desexualized literal sense? The desexualization of the *signified* occurs when the very element that (failed to) co-ordinate(d) the universal sexual meaning (i.e. the phallus) is reduced to a *signifier*. The phallus is the 'organ of desexualization' precisely in its capacity of a signifier without signified: it is the operator of the evacuation of sexual meaning – that is, of the reduction of sexuality *qua* signified content to an empty signifier. In short, the phallus designates the following paradox: sexuality can universalize itself only by way of desexualization, only by undergoing a kind of transubstantiation and changing into a supplement-connotation of the neutral, asexual literal sense.

The Problems of 'Real Genesis'

The difference between Lacan and someone who, like Habermas, accepts the universal medium of intersubjective communication as the ultimate horizon of subjectivity, is therefore not where it is usually sought: it does not reside in the fact that Lacan, in a postmodern fashion, emphasizes the remainder of some particularity that forever prevents our full access to universality and condemns us to the multiple texture of particular language-games. Lacan's basic reproach to someone like Habermas is, on the contrary, that he fails to acknowledge and to thematize *the price the subject has to pay for his access to universality*, to the 'neutral' medium of language: this price, of course, is none other than the traumatism of 'castration', the sacrifice of the object that 'is' the subject, the passage from S (the full 'pathological' subject) to $ (the 'barred' subject). This is also the difference between Heidegger and Gadamer: Gadamer remains an 'idealist' in so far as for him the horizon of language is 'always-already here', whereas Heidegger's problematic of the dif-ference [*Unter-Schied*] as pain [*Schmerz*] that inheres in the very essence of our dwelling in language, 'obscurantist' as it may sound, points towards the materialist problematic of the traumatic cut, 'castration', which marks our entry into language.

The first to formulate this materialist problematic of 'real genesis' as the obverse of the transcendental genesis was Schelling: in his *Weltalter*-fragments (1811–15) he deploys the programme of deriving the emergence of the Word, *Logos*, out of the abyss of the 'real in God', of the vortex of drives [*Triebe*] that is God prior to the creation of the world. Schelling distinguishes between God's existence and the obscure, impenetrable Ground of Existence, the horrendous pre-symbolic Thing as 'that in God which is not yet God'. This Ground consists of the antagonistic tension between 'contraction [*Zusammenziehung, contractio*]' – withdrawal-into-self, egotistic rage, all-destructive madness – and 'extension' – God's giving away, pouring out, of his Love. (How can we fail to recognize in this antagonism Freud's duality of the ego drives and the love drives that precedes his duality of libido and death drive?) This unbearable antagonism is timelessly past, a past that was never 'present', since the present already implies *Logos*, the clearing of the spoken Word that transposes the antagonistic pulsation of the drives into the symbolic difference.

God is thus first the abyss of 'absolute indifference', the volition that does not want anything, the reign of peace and beatitude; in Lacanian terms: pure feminine *jouissance*, the pure expansion into the void that lacks any consistency, the 'giving away' held together by nothing. God's 'pre-history' proper begins with an act of primordial contraction by means of which God procures himself a firm Ground, constitutes himself as One, a subject, a positive entity. Upon 'contracting' being as an illness, God gets caught up in the mad, 'psychotic' alternation of contraction and expansion; he then creates the world, speaks out the Word, gives birth to the Son, in order to escape this madness. Before the emergence of the Word, God is a 'depressive maniac', and this provides the most perspicuous answer to the enigma of why God created the universe – as a kind of creative therapy that allowed him to pull himself out of madness....[22] The late Schelling of the 'philosophy of revelation' recoiled from his previous radicality by conceding that God possesses his existence in advance: contraction now no longer concerns God himself; it designates solely the act by means of which God creates the matter that is later formed into the universe of creatures. This way, God himself is no longer involved in the process of 'genesis': genesis concerns only creation, whereas God supervises the historical process from a safe place outside history, and guarantees its happy outcome. In this withdrawal, in this shift from *Weltalter* to the 'philosophy of revelation', the problematic of *Weltalter* is translated into traditional Aristotelian ontological terms: the opposition of Existence and its Ground now becomes the opposition of Essence and Existence – that is, *Logos* is conceived as the divine Essence that needs a positive Existence if it is to achieve its effectuation, and so on.[23]

Therein resides the materialist 'wager' of Deleuze and Lacan: the 'desexualization', the miracle of the advent of the neutral-desexualized surface of Sense-Event, does not rely on the intervention of some transcendent, extra-bodily force; it can be derived from the inherent impasse of the sexualized body itself. In this precise sense – shocking as it may sound to vulgar materialists and obscurantists in their unacknowl-edged solidarity – *the phallus, the phallic element as the signifier of 'castration', is the fundamental category of dialectical materialism.* The phallus *qua* signifier of 'castration' mediates the emergence of the pure surface of Sense-Event; as such, it is the 'transcendental signifier' – non-sense within the field of Sense, which distributes and regulates the series of Sense. Its 'transcendental' status means that there is nothing 'sub-stantial' about it: the phallus is the semblance *par excellence*. What the phallus 'causes' is the gap that separates the surface event from bodily density: it is the 'pseudo-cause' that sustains the autonomy of the field of Sense with regard to its true, effective, bodily cause. Here one should recall Adorno's observation on how the notion of transcendental constitution results from a kind of perspective inversion: what the subject (mis)perceives as his constitutive power is actually his impotence, his incapacity to reach beyond the imposed limitations of his horizon – the transcendental constitutive power is a pseudo-power that is the obverse of the subject's blindness as to true bodily causes. Phallus *qua* cause is the pure semblance of a cause.[24]

There is no structure without the 'phallic' moment as the crossing point of the two series (of signifier and signified), as the point of the short circuit at which – as Lacan puts it very precisely – 'the signifier falls into the signified'. The point of non-sense within the field of Sense is the point at which the signifier's cause is inscribed into the the field of Sense – without this short circuit, the signifier's structure would act as an external bodily cause, and would be unable to produce the effect of Sense. On that account, the two series (of the signifier and the signified) always contain a paradoxical entity that is 'doubly inscribed' – that is simultaneously surplus and lack – surplus of the signifier over the signified (the empty signifier without a signified) *and* the lack of the signified (the point of non-sense within the field of Sense). That is to say, as soon as the symbolic order emerges, we are dealing with the minimal difference between a structural place and the element that occupies, fills out, this place: an element is always logically preceded by the place in the structure it fills out. The two series can therefore also be described as the 'empty' formal structure (signifier) and the series of elements filling out the empty places in the structure (signified).

From this perspective, the paradox consists in the fact that the two series never overlap: we always encounter an entity that is simultaneously – with regard to the structure – an *empty, unoccupied, place,* and – with regard to the elements – a rapidly moving, elusive object, an *occupant without a place.*[25] We have thereby produced Lacan's formula of fantasy $ \lozenge a $, since the mathem for the subject is $, an empty place in the structure, an elided signifier, while *objet a* is, by definition, an excessive object, an object that lacks its place in the structure. Consequently, the point is not that there is simply the surplus of an element over the places available in the structure or the surplus of a place that has no element to fill it out – an empty place in the structure would still sustain the fantasy of an element that will emerge and fill out this place; an excessive element lacking its place would still sustain the fantasy of an as yet unknown place waiting for it. The point is, rather, that the empty place in the structure is strictly correlative to the errant element lacking its place: they are not two different entities but the obverse and reverse of one and the same entity – one and the same entity inscribed into the two surfaces of a Moebius band. In short, the subject *qua* $ does not belong to the depth: it emerges from a topological twist of the surface itself.

Are we not now, however, at the exact opposite of our starting point? We began by conceiving of the subject as the 'night of the world', as the abyss of the impenetrable depth, whereas now the subject appears as the topological twist of the surface itself. Why does this ambiguity occur? The problem with Deleuze is that he does not distinguish bodily depth from the symbolic pseudo-depth. That is to say, there are two depths: the opaque impenetrability of the body, and the pseudo-depth generated by the 'ply' of the symbolic order itself (the abyss of the 'soul', what one experiences when one looks into another person's eyes . . .). The subject is such a pseudo-depth that results from the ply of the surface. Let us recall the very last shot of Ivory's *The Remains of the Day*: the slow fade-out of the window of Lord Darlington's castle, passing into the helicopter shot of the entire castle moving away. This fade-out lasts a little bit too long, so that for a brief moment the spectator cannot avoid the impression that a third reality emerged, over and above the common reality of the window and the castle: it is as if, instead of the window being simply a small part of the castle, the castle itself, in its entirety, is reduced to a reflection in the window glass, to a fragile entity that is a pure semblance, neither a being nor a non-being. The subject is such a paradoxical entity that emerges when the Whole itself (the entire castle) appears comprised in its own part (a window).

Deleuze is obliged to ignore this symbolic pseudo-depth: there is no place for it in his dichotomy of body and Sense. What opens up here, of course, is the possibility of a Lacanian critique of Deleuze: is not the signifier *qua* differential structure an entity which, precisely, belongs neither to the bodily depth nor to the surface of the Sense-Event? In concrete terms, with regard to Mozart's *Così fan tutte*: is not the 'machine', the automatism on which the philosopher Alfonso relies, the *symbolic* machine, the 'automatism' of the symbolic 'custom', this big motif of Pascal's *Pensées*? Deleuze distinguishes between bodily causality 'proper' and the paradoxical 'phallic' moment, the crossroads of the series of the signifier and the series of the signified, the nonsense *qua* pseudo-cause – that is, the decentred cause of sense inherent to the surface flux of Sense itself. What he fails to take into account here is the radically heterogeneous nature of the series of the signifier with regard to the series of the signified, of the synchrony of a differential structure with regard to the diachrony of the flux of the Sense-Event. What becomes visible here, perhaps, is the limitation of Deleuze who, in the end, remains a *phenomenologist* – it was this limitation that ultimately brought about his theoretical 'regression' into the 'anti-Oedipus', the rebellion against the Symbolic. In this precise sense, one could say that stoics, Husserl, and so forth, are psychotics rather than perverts: it is the psychotic foreclosure of the proper symbolic level that gives rise to the paradoxical short circuits between sense and reality ('when you say "carriage", a carriage runs through your mouth', etc.).[26]

If we are to clarify this crucial distinction between bodily depth and the symbolic pseudo-depth that determines the status of the subject, we have to descend to what is perhaps the most abominable point of modern European ideology, to the author who brought the logic of anti-feminism to its unsurpassed acme: Otto Weininger.

Notes

1. What we encounter here is the Lacanian motif of the 'lamella', the indestructible life-substance. In Freud, this motif is announced in Chapter 4 of *Beyond the Pleasure Principle*, where he talks about the 'little fragment of living substance ... suspended in the middle of an external world charged with the most powerful energies':

> it would be killed by the stimulation emanating from these if it were not provided with a protective shield against stimuli. It acquires the shield in this way: its outermost surface ceases to have the structure proper to living matter, becomes to some degree inorganic and thenceforward functions as a special envelope or membrane resistant to stimuli.

> (Sigmund Freud, *Beyond the Pleasure Principle*, New York and London: Norton 1989, p. 30)

The whole point of Freud's argument, of course, is that this sensitive cortex also receives excitations from *within*.

2. The same procedure was employed by Tim Burton in the outstanding credits sequence of *Batman*: the camera wanders along nondescript winding, ridgy metal funnels; after it gradually removes itself and acquires a 'normal' distance towards its object, it becomes clear what this object actually is: Batman's tiny badge....

3. The counterpart to this Lynchean attitude, perhaps, is the philosophy of Leibniz: Leibniz was fascinated by microscopes because they confirmed for him that what appears from the 'normal', everyday point of view to be a lifeless object is actually full of life – one has only to take a closer look at it, to observe it from absolute proximity: under the lens of a microscope, one can perceive the wild crawling of innumerable tiny living beings.... See Chapter 2 of Miran Božovič, *Der grosse Andere: Gotteskonzepte in der Philosophie der Neuzeit*, Vienna and Berlin: Turia & Kant 1993.

4. An exception to this notion is provided by the naked body of Isabella Rossellini towards the end of *Blue Velvet*: when, having endured the nightmare, she leaves the house and approaches Jeffrey, it is as if a body belonging to another, dark, infernal realm suddenly found itself in our 'normal' daily universe, having stepped out of its own element, like a stranded octopus or some other deep-sea creature – a wounded, exposed body whose material presence exerts an almost unbearable pressure on us.

5. Chaplin's *Great Dictator* bore witness to a homologous disturbance in the relationship between the voice and the written word: the spoken word (in the speeches of the dictator Hynkel) is obscene, incomprehensible, absolutely incommensurable with the written word.

6. See Michel Chion, *David Lynch*, Paris: Cahiers du Cinéma 1992, especially pp. 108–17, 227–8.

7. For a more detailed reading of these lines from *Richard II*, see Chapter 1 of Slavoj Žižek, *Looking Awry*, Cambridge, MA: MIT Press 1991.

8. Since this gap that separates effect from its cause is not a positive feature of a woman, it not only surprises the man, it also confounds woman herself *qua* psychological 'person', as illustrated by a scene from *Blue Velvet* just before the infamous sadomasochistic

encounter: Isabella Rossellini first threatens Kyle MacLachlan with a large kitchen knife, ordering him to undress, and then wonders at his reaction. Here the effect is reflected back into its cause, so that in a way *the cause itself is bewildered at its own effect*. This, of course, means that this cause (woman) must in itself be decentred – the true cause is 'something in the cause more than the cause itself'. And does not this reversal demonstrate that, at a more fundamental level, the true Cause *qua* the Real is the woman who, at the level of the symbolic chain of causes and effects, appears to be the passive object of man's activity? Perhaps this bewilderment of the Cause at its own effect provides a key to the Hegelian category of 'reciprocal action [*Wechselwirkung*]': far from involving a kind of symmetrical interplay of cause and effect, the retroaction of the effect upon the cause points towards an inner decentrement of the Cause itself.

9. In analysing films, therefore, it is crucial to expose homogeneous, continuous, diegetic reality as a product of 'secondary elaboration' – to discern in it the role of (symbolic) reality and the role of fantasy hallucination. Suffice it to recall *Home Alone*: the entire film hinges on the fact that the boy's family – his proper intersubjective environment, his 'big Other' – and the two burglars who threaten him when the family is away *never cross each other's paths*. The burglars enter the scene when the boy finds himself alone, and when, at the end of the film, the family return to their home, all traces of the burglars' presence almost magically evaporate, although as a result of the burglars' confrontation with the boy, practically the entire house lies in ruins. The fact that the burglars' existence *is not acknowledged on the part of the big Other* undoubtedly bears witness to the fact that we are dealing with the boy's fantasy: the moment the two burglars come on the scene, we change terrain and jump from social reality into the fantasy universe in which there is neither death nor guilt; into the universe of silent slapstick pictures and cartoons in which a heap of ironware falls on your head, yet all you feel is a slight bump; in which a gallon of petrol explodes on your head, yet the only damage you suffer is that some of your hair is burned.... Perhaps this is how one has to conceive of Macaulay Culkin's notorious scream: not as an expression of his fear of the burglars but, rather, as an expression of his horror at the prospect of being thrown (again) into his own fantasy universe.

10. A holomogous inversion of the order of causality is one of the features of psychoanalytic practice: its standard device is to interpret as a cause what presents itself as an effect. If, say, a patient-analysand claims that he cannot open himself up and 'tell everything' to the analyst, because he finds the analyst personally repulsive, or because the analyst does not arouse the patient's necessary confidence in him, we can be sure that the relation between the two terms is to be reversed: the analyst is experienced as 'repulsive' so that the patient can avoid 'telling him everything' – that is, the true kernel of his traumas. What comes first is the analysand's resistance to 'telling everything', and the analyst's 'repulsive character' only gives body to this resistance, it is the 'reified' form in which the analysand (mis)perceives his resistance. The analysand's excuse thus merely confirms that transference is already at work: in the guise of the analyst's 'repulsive character' the analysand takes note, in an inverted form, of the repulsion he feels towards the truth about his own desire, and of his unreadiness to confront his own desire. Finding the analyst 'repulsive' implies that the analyst already functions as the 'subject supposed to know' the truth about the analysand's desire.

11. One also encounters this motif of a woman pulled out of her lethargic numbness where one would not normally look for it – in Henry James's *Aspern Papers*, for example. The narrator forces his way into a decaying Venetian *palazzo*, the home of two ladies: an old American who was ages ago, in her youth, a mistress of the great American poet Aspern, and her somewhat younger niece. He makes use of all possible ruses in order to obtain the object of his desire: a bundle of Aspern's love letters, carefully kept secret by the old lady. What he fails to take into account, obsessed as he is by the object of his desire, is simply his own impact on the life in the decaying *palazzo*: through his activity he introduces a spirit of vivacity which awakens the two ladies from their lethargic vegetation and even stirs up, in the younger one, a sexual interest....

12. How are these three readings related to each other? They are mutually exclusive; it is not possible to think them together within the same homogeneous space; in spite of this,

however, their plurality is irreducible and necessary – that is, none of the three readings can be privileged as the 'proper' one and conceived as the 'truth' of the remaining two. Therein resides an important aspect of Lynch's revolution: in the entire history of cinema, it is only one subjective perspective that organizes the narrative space (in the *film noir*, for example, this perspective is the perspective of the hero himself, whose voice-over comments on the action); whereas in Lynch, the domination of sound over imagery (i.e. in his films, the structuring principle which guarantees the unity of the diegetic space is the soundtrack) renders possible the multiplication of points of view. See, among others, a peculiarity of *Dune*, which was wrongly dismissed by a number of critics as a recourse to non-filmic naivety: the *multiple* voice-over commentary on the action.

13. This logic is exactly homologous to that articulated by Deleuze apropos of the Freudian duality of the pleasure (and reality) principle and its 'beyond', the death drive (what is the depression of Lynch's heroines if not a manifestation of the death drive?). Freud's point is not that there are phenomena which cannot be accounted for by the pleasure (and reality) principle (it is easy for him to demonstrate, apropos of every example of 'pleasure in pain' apparently running counter to the pleasure principle, the hidden narcissistic gain conveyed by the renunciation of pleasure) but rather that, *in order to account for the very functioning of the pleasure and reality principles*, we are obliged to posit the more fundamental dimension of the 'death drive' and the compulsion-to-repeat, which hold open the space where the pleasure principle can exercise its rule. See Chapter 10 of Gilles Deleuze, 'Coldness and Cruelty', in *Masochism*, New York: Zone Books 1991.

14. This 'unaccountability' is what Freud was aiming at with his concept of *over-determination*: a contingent external cause can trigger unforeseen catastrophic consequences by stirring up the trauma that always-already glows under the ashes – that 'insists' in the unconscious.

15. This suspension of linear causality is, at the same time, the constitutive feature of the symbolic order. In this respect, the case of Jon Elster is very instructive. Within the framework of an 'objective' socio-psychological approach, Elster endeavours to isolate the specific level of *mechanism*, located between a merely descriptive or narrative ideographic method and the construction of general theories: 'A mechanism is a specific causal pattern that can be recognized after the event but rarely foreseen. ... It is less than a theory, but a great deal more than a description' (Jon Elster, *Political Psychology*, Cambridge: Cambridge University Press 1993, pp. 3, 5). The crucial point missed by Elster is that 'mechanisms' are not simply in between – that is to say, they do not occupy the middle position on the common scale at whose extremes we find the true universal theory with predictive power and a mere description; rather, 'mechanisms' constitute a separate domain of symbolic causality whose efficiency obeys radically different laws. That is to say, the specificity of 'mechanisms' turns on how the same cause can trigger opposite effects: if men cannot have what they would like to have, they sometimes simply prefer what they have, or, on the contrary, they prefer what they cannot have for the very reason that they cannot have it; if men follow a certain habit in one sphere, they sometimes tend to follow it also in other spheres (the 'spillover effect'), or, on the contrary, they act in other spheres in an opposite way (the 'crowding-out effect'); and so on. This fact that we can never ascertain in advance how the causes that determine us exert their causal power over us has nothing whatsoever to do with insufficient generality and unpredictability due to overcomplexity: what we are dealing with is the specific symbolic causality in which the subject himself, in a self-reflective way, determines which causes will determine him, or determines the causes of *what* will be the causes that determine him.

16. The infamous view according to which woman is 'illogical', 'does not react rationally', and so on, therefore designates how this feminine suspension of the causal chain is perceived within the dominating ideological space.

17. For a more detailed reading of this story, see Žižek, *Looking Awry*, p. 8.

18. However, is not 'dialectical materialism' the supreme example of philosophical idiocy, the quintessential naive 'world-view', the universal ontology that comprises historical materialism as *metaphysica specialis*, the regional ontology of society? Our choice was determined by this very fact: 'dialectical materialism' is to be read like 'bone' in Hegel's infinite judgement 'The spirit is a bone' – that is to say, its truth is produced by

135

the very nonsense this term evokes. 'Dialectical materialism' stands for its own impossibility; it is no longer the universal ontology: its 'object' is the very gap that forever, constitutively, renders impossible the placement of the symbolic universe within the wider horizon of reality, as its special region – our access to 'reality as such' is always-already mediated by the symbolic universe. Why, then, have recourse to this term at all? It is used as a purely negative determination that stands for the abyss of every transcendental horizon: although nothing is given outside the symbolic horizon, this horizon is in itself finite and contingent. In short, 'dialectical materialism' is a negative reminder that the horizon of historical-symbolic practice is 'not-all', that it is inherently 'decentred', founded upon the abyss of a radical fissure – in short, that the Real as its Cause is forever absent.

19. As to this vicious circle, see Chapter 5 of Slavoj Žižek, *For They Know Not What They Do*, London: Verso 1991.

20. What opens up here is the possibility of 'secondary perverse resexualization' (Deleuze): at a meta-level, such an instrumental, non-sexualized relationship to sexuality can 'turns us on'. One way of enlivening our sexual practice is to pretend that we are dealing with an ordinary instrumental activity – with our partner, we approach the sexual act as a difficult technical task, we discuss every step in detail and establish the exact plan of how we shall proceed. . . .

21. In order to exemplify this logic of sexual connotation, let us take the signifier 'commerce', whose predominant meaning is 'trade, merchandising', yet which is also an (archaic) term for sexual act. The term is 'sexualized' when the two levels of its meaning intermingle. Let us say that 'commerce' evokes in our mind the figure of an elderly merchant who delivers tedious lessons on how we are to conduct commerce, on how we must be careful in our dealings, mind the profit, not take excessive risks, and so on; or let us suppose that the merchant actually talks about *sexual* commerce – all of a sudden, the entire affair acquires an obscene superego dimension, the poor merchant changes into a dirty old man who gives ciphered advice on sexual enjoyment, accompanied by obscene smiles. . . .

22. For an unsurpassed presentation of this problematic, see Jean-François Marquet, *Liberté et existence. Étude sur la formation de la philosophie de Schelling*, Paris: Gallimard 1973.

23. This withdrawal also implies a radical change in the political attitude: in the *Weltalter*-fragments, the State is denounced as Evil incarnate, as the tyranny of the external machine of Power over individuals (as such, it has to be abolished), whereas the late Schelling conceives of the State as the embodiment of man's Sin – precisely in so far as man can never fully recognize himself in it (in so far as the State remains an external, alienated force that crushes individuals) it is a divine punishment for man's conceit, a reminder of man's sinful origins (as such, it has to be obeyed unconditionally). See Jürgen Habermas, 'Dialektischer Idealismus im Übergang zum Materialismus – Geschichtphilosophische Folgerungen aus Schellings Idee einer Contraction Gottes', in *Theorie und Praxis*, Frankfurt: Suhrkamp 1966, pp. 108–61.

24. The effort to formulate this 'impossible' intersection between (symbolic) negativity and the body seems also to be the driving force of Jacqueline Rose's 'return to Melanie Klein' (see her *Why War?*, Oxford: Blackwell 1993). For that reason, although the author of these lines considers himself a pure 'dogmatic' Lacanian, he feels a deep solidarity with her enterprise.

25. Deleuze, *The Logic of Sense*, New York: Columbia University Press 1990, p. 41.

26. Is not Deleuze's oversight, therefore, correlative to Althusser's? Deleuze confines himself to the axis Imaginary–Real and forecloses the Symbolic, whereas the Althusserian duality of the 'real object' (i.e. the experienced reality, object of imaginary experience) and the 'object of knowledge' (the symbolic structure produced through the process of knowledge) fits the axis Imaginary–Symbolic. Lacan is the only one to thematize the axis Symbolic–Real, which underlies the other two axes. Furthermore, does not this opposition of Deleuze and Althusser account for the uncanny closeness and fundamental difference of their respective readings of Spinoza? Althusser's Spinoza is the Spinoza of symbolic structure, of subjectless knowledge, freed from imaginary affects; whereas Deleuze's Spinoza is the Spinoza of the real, of 'anarchic' bodily mixtures.

6

Otto Weininger, or, 'Woman Doesn't Exist'

'Let us hope that the public will not deem it unworthy of a philosopher and beneath him to concern himself with coitus ...' (237[1]) – this statement could be taken as a motto to Weininger's work: he elevated sexual difference and the sexual relationship to the central theme of philosophy. The price he paid for it was terrible: suicide at twenty-four, only months after his great book *Sex and Character* came out. Why?

The first thing that strikes us about Weininger is the unmitigated *authenticity* of his writing – we are not dealing with an 'objective' theory; the writer is utterly, unreservedly *engaged in* his subject matter. It is no accident that in the first decades of our century, *Sex and Character* headed the reading lists of troubled adolescents: it provided an answer to all the questions that tormented their stormy inner lives. It is easy to denigrate this answer as a combination of contemporary anti-feminist and anti-Semitic prejudices, with some rather shallow philosophical common-places mixed in. But what gets lost in such a dismissal is the effect of *recognition* brought about by reading Weininger: it was as if he 'called by name' all that the 'official' discourse silently presupposed, not daring to pronounce publicly. In short, Weininger hauled into the light of the day the 'sexist' phantasmic support of the dominant ideology.

'Woman is only and thoroughly sexual ...'

For Weininger, sexual difference is grounded in the very ontological opposition of subject and object, of active spirit and passive matter. Woman is a passive, impressionable object, which means that she is entirely dominated by sexuality:

> Woman is only and thoroughly sexual, since her sexuality extends to her entire body and is in certain places, to put it in physical terms, only more dense than in others – *she is sexually affected and penetrated* by every thing –

always and on the entire surface of her body. What we usually call coitus is merely a special case of the highest intensity. ... Fatherhood is for that reason a miserable deception: we have always to share it with innumerable other things and people.... An entity which can be at every point sexually penetrated by all things can also get pregnant everywhere and by all things; *mother is in herself a receptacle*. In her, all things are alive, since physiologically everything acts upon her and forms her child.

(258–9)

(Here we already encounter the source of all Weininger's difficulties: his confounding of phallic enjoyment with the feminine Other enjoyment: the latter is not centred on the phallus, and bombards the body from all directions. Weininger's entire theoretical edifice hinges on the possibility of reducing the Other enjoyment to phallic enjoyment.)

For that reason,

the idea of pairing is the only conception that has positive worth for women. ... Pairing is the supreme good for the woman; she seeks to effect it always and everywhere. Her personal sexuality is only a special case of this universal, generalized, impersonal instinct.

(260)

This universality is to be conceptualized in two ways. First, coitus colours woman's entire activity with its specific tonality. Woman is not capable of a pure spiritual attitude, she cannot aim at truth for the sake of truth itself, at the fulfilment of duty for the sake of duty; she cannot sustain a disinterested contemplation of beauty. When she seems to assume such a spiritual attitude, closer observation never fails to discern a 'pathological' sexual interest lurking in the background (a woman speaks the truth in order to make an impression on man and thus facilitate her seduction of him, etc.). Even suicide *qua* absolute act is accomplished with narcissistic-pathological considerations: 'such suicides are accompanied practically always by thoughts of other people, what they will think, how they will mourn over them, how grieved – or angry – they will be' (286).

It goes without saying that the same holds even more strongly in the case of love, which always conceals the motive for sexual intercourse: woman is never capable of pure, disinterested admiration of the beloved person. Furthermore, for a woman, the idea of coitus is the only way to overcome her egoism, the only ethical idea available to her – 'ethical' in the sense of expressing an ideal towards which woman strives irrespective of her particular 'pathological' interest:

Her wish for the activity of her own sexual life is her strongest impulse, but

138

it is only a special case of her deep, her only vital interest, the interest that sexual unions shall take place; the wish that as much of it as possible shall occur, in all cases, places, and times.

(257–8)

Coitus is therefore the only case apropos of which woman is capable of formulating her own version of the universal ethical imperative: 'Act so that your activity will contribute to the realization of the infinite ideal of general pairing.'

In contrast to woman, who is thoroughly dominated by sexuality – that is, by the notion of coitus – man, in his relationship to woman, is split between the mutually exclusive poles of sexual coveting and erotic love:

Love and desire are two unlike, mutually exclusive, opposing conditions, and during the time a man really loves, the thought of physical union with the object of his love is insupportable. ... The more erotic a man is the less he will be troubled with his sexuality, and vice versa ... *there is only 'platonic' love, because any other so-called love belongs to the kingdom of the senses.*

(239–40)

If, however, by the very nature of woman, the scope of her interest is limited to coitus, where does woman's beauty come from? How can she function as an object of purely spiritual love? Here Weininger draws a radical conclusion: the nature of woman's beauty is 'performative' – that is to say, it is man's love that creates woman's beauty:

The love bestowed by the man is the standard of what is beautiful and what is hateful in woman. The conditions are quite different in aesthetics from those in logic or ethics. In logic there is an abstract truth that is the standard of thought; in ethics there is an ideal good that furnishes the criterion of what ought to be done.... In aesthetics beauty is created by love.... *All beauty is really more a projection, an emanation of the requirements of love*; and so the beauty of woman is not apart from love, it is not an objective to which love is directed, but woman's beauty is the love of man; they are not two things, but one and the same thing.

(242)

A further inevitable conclusion is that man's love for a woman – his very 'spiritual', 'pure' love as opposed to sexual longing – is a thoroughly *narcissistic* phenomenon: in his love of a woman, man loves only himself, his own ideal image. Man is well aware of the gap that forever separates his miserable reality from this ideal, so he projects, transfers, it on to another, on to the idealized woman.[2] This is why love is 'blind': it hinges

139

on the illusion that the ideal we are striving for is already realized in the other, in the object of love:

> In love, man is only loving himself. Not his empirical self, not the weaknesses and vulgarities, not the failings and smallnesses which he outwardly exhibits; but all that he wants to be, all that he ought to be, his truest, deepest, intelligible nature, free from all fetters of necessity, from all taint of earth. . . . *He projects his ideal of an absolutely worthy existence, the ideal that he is unable to isolate within himself, upon another human being, and this act, and this alone, is none other than love and the significance of love.*
>
> (243–4)

Love, no less than hate, is therefore a phenomenon of cowardice, an easy way out: in hate, we externalize and transfer on to the other the evil that dwells in ourselves, thereby avoiding any confrontation with it; whereas in love, instead of taking pains to realize our spiritual essence, we project this essence upon the other as an already realized state of being. On this account, love is cowardly and treacherous not only in relationship to man himself but also, and above all, in relationship to its object – it utterly disregards the object's (woman's) true nature, and uses it only as a kind of empty projection screen:

> Love of a woman is possible only when it does not consider her real qualities, and so is able to replace the actual psychical reality by a different and quite imaginary reality. The attempt to realize one's ideal in a woman, instead of the woman herself, is a necessary destruction of the empirical personality of the woman. And so the attempt is cruel to the woman; it is the egotism of love that disregards the woman, and cares nothing for her real inner life. . . . Love is murder.
>
> (249)

Here, of course, Weininger speaks aloud the hidden truth of the idealized figure of the Lady in courtly love.[3] The key enigma of love is therefore: why does man choose *woman* as the idealized object in which he (mis)perceives the realization of his spiritual essence? Why does he project his *salvation* upon the very being responsible for his *Fall*, since – as we have already seen – man is split between his spiritual-ethical essence and the sexual longing aroused in him by woman's standing invitation to sexual intercourse? The only way to solve this enigma is to accept that man's relationship towards woman as object of erotic love and his relationship towards woman as object of sexual coveting are both 'performative'. Strictly speaking, woman is not the *cause* of man's Fall: it is man's Fall into sexuality itself that *creates* woman, conferring existence upon her:

It is only when man accepts his own sexuality, denies the absolute in him, turns to the lower, that he gives woman existence.
When man became sexual he formed woman. That woman is at all has happened simply because man has accepted his sexuality. Woman is merely the result of this affirmation; she is sexuality itself. . . . Therefore woman's one object must be to keep man sexual ... she has but one purpose, that of continuing the guilt of man, for she would disappear the moment man had overcome his sexuality.
Woman is the sin of man.

(298–9)

Here the normal relationship between cause and effect is inverted: *woman is not the cause of man's Fall, but its consequence.*[4] For that reason, one need not fight woman actively, since she possesses no positive ontological consistency whatsoever: '*Woman therefore does not exist*' (302). For woman to cease to exist, it is enough for man to overcome the sexual urge in himself. We can see, now, precisely why man has chosen woman as the object of his love: the unbearable fault of creating woman by way of acknowledging his sexuality weighs heavily upon him. Love is but a cowardly, hypocritical attempt by man to compensate for his guilt towards woman:

The crime man has committed in creating woman, and still commits in assenting to her purpose, he excuses to woman by his eroticism. ... Woman is nothing but man's expression and projection of his own sexuality. Every man creates himself a woman, in which he embodies himself and his own guilt. But woman is not herself guilty; she is made so by the guilt of others, and everything for which woman is blamed should be laid at man's door. *Love strives to cover guilt, instead of conquering it*; it elevates woman instead of nullifying her.

(300)

Woman's existence bears witness to the fact that man 'compromised his desire', that he betrayed his true nature as an autonomous ethical subject by giving way to sexuality. Consequently, her true nature consists of the boundless craving for sexual intercourse, an expression of how the phallus 'entirely – although often only unconsciously – dominates woman's entire life'. On account of this constitutive submission to the phallus, woman is heteronomous in the strict Kantian sense – that is, unfree, at the mercy of external Fate:

The male organ is to a woman the Id whose name she doesn't know; her destiny resides in it, something she cannot escape from. For that reason, she does not like to see a naked man and she never expresses a need to see him:

141

she feels she is lost at that moment. The phallus *thus deprives woman completely and irrevocably of her freedom.*

(269)

Woman is not free: ultimately, the urge to be raped by man in one or another way always prevails in her; woman is governed by the phallus.

(274)

Consequently, when a woman resists her sexual urge and is ashamed of it, she suppresses her true nature. Internalizing male spiritual values can go so far as to shove awareness of a woman's true nature out of her consciousness – however, this nature fights back violently, returning in the guise of hysterical symptoms. What the hysterical woman experiences as a foreign, evil and immoral urge is thus simply her innermost nature, her subordination to the Phallus. The ultimate proof of woman's amoral character is that the more desperately she endeavours to assume male spiritual values, the more hysterical she becomes. When a woman acts in accordance with moral precepts, she does so in a heteronomous way, out of fear of the male Master or in efforts to fascinate him: woman's autonomy is feigned, it is an externally imposed imitation of autonomy. When she speaks the truth, she does so not out of true veracity but in order to impress man, to seduce him in a more subtle way: 'So that woman always lies, even if, objectively, she speaks the truth' (287). Herein resides the '*ontological* untruthfulness of woman' – that is, in this sense, woman's 'love for truth is only a special *case of her mendaciousness*' (291). The highest insight a woman can achieve is an obscure premonition of her constitutive enslavement, which leads her to strive for salvation through self-annihilation.

For the reader who is familiar with Lacan's theory of feminine sexuality, it is not difficult to discern in this brief outline a whole series of Lacan's fundamental propositions. Cannot we see in Weininger's 'Woman therefore does not exist' the herald of Lacan's 'la femme n'existe pas'? Does not the notion that woman gives body to man's fault – that her very existence hinges on man's betrayal of his spiritual-ethical posture – present a variation on Lacan's thesis on 'woman as a symptom of man'? (According to Lacan, the symptom as a compromise-formation bears witness to how the subject 'gave up his desire'.) When Weininger insists that woman can never be fully integrated into the spiritual universe of Truth, Good and Beauty, since this universe remains for her a heteronomous order externally imposed upon her, does he not point towards Lacan's assertion that woman is not fully integrated into the symbolic order? And finally, as to the motif of woman's total subordination to the

Phallus (in contrast to man, who is only partially submitted to its rule): do not Lacan's 'formulas of sexuation' also assert that no part of woman is exempt from the phallic function, whereas the masculine position involves an exemption, an X that is *not* submitted to the phallic function?

The Feminine 'Night of the World'

Unfortunately, a closer examination soon unsettles this apparent homology, without thoroughly devalorizing it. The great merit of Weininger, which must be taken into account by feminism, is his complete break from the ideological problematic of 'woman's enigma', of femininity *qua* Secret that supposedly eludes the rational, discursive universe. The assertion 'Woman does not exist' does not in any way refer to an ineffable feminine Essence beyond the domain of discursive existence: *what does not exist is this very unattainable Beyond.* In short, by playing upon the somewhat worn-out Hegelian formula, we can say that the 'enigma of woman' ultimately conceals the fact that there is nothing to conceal.[5] What Weininger fails to accomplish is a Hegelian reflexive reversal of *recognizing in this 'nothing' the very negativity that defines the notion of the subject.*

Let us recall here the well-known joke about a Jew and a Pole, in which the Jew extracts money from the Pole under the pretext of imparting to him the secret of how Jews succeed in extracting from people their very last penny.[6] Weininger's violent anti-feminist outburst – 'There is no feminine secret at all; behind the mask of the Enigma, there is simply nothing!' – remains at the level of the Pole's fury which wells up when he finally grasps how the Jew, by endlessly postponing the final revelation, was merely extracting more and more money from him. What Weininger fails to perform is a gesture that would correspond to the Jew's answer to the Pole's outburst: 'Well, now you see how we, the Jews, extract money from people...' – that is, a gesture that would reinterpret, reinscribe, the failure as a success – something like 'Look, this nothingness behind the mask is the very absolute negativity on account of which woman is the subject *par excellence*, not a limited object opposed to the force of subjectivity!'.[7]

The status of this Nothing can be explained by means of the Lacanian distinction between the subject of the enunciation and the subject of the enunciated. Far from being dismissable as a meaningless paradox, the statement 'I don't exist' can acquire an authentic existential weight in so far as it signals the contraction of the subject into the empty vanishing point of enunciation that precedes every imaginary or symbolic identification: I can easily find myself excluded from the intersubjective symbolic network, so that I lack the identificatory feature which would enable me to declare victoriously: 'That's me!'. That is to say, in a far from simply metaphorical sense, 'I am' only what I am for others, in so far as I am inscribed into the network of the big Other, in so far as I possess a social-symbolic existence – outside of such an inscribed existence I am nothing, nothing but the vanishing point of 'I think', devoid of any positive content. However, 'It's me who thinks' is already an answer to the question 'Who is the one who thinks?' – that is, it already accounts for a minimal positive identity of the thinking subject. This same distinction underlies Wittgenstein's assertion that 'I' is not a demonstrative pronoun:

> When I say 'I am in pain,' I do not point to a person who is in pain, since in a certain sense I don't know at all *who* is in pain. . . . I did not say that such-and-such a person is in pain, but 'I am'. . . .[8]

> The word 'I' does not mean the same as 'L.W.' even if I am L.W.[9]

It is against the background of this gap that assertions of symbolic authority are to be conceived: when I assert pathetically: 'I, Ludwig Wittgenstein, the president of this society, hereby nominate . . .', I evoke my symbolic mandate, my place within the socio-symbolic network, in order to legitimate my act of nomination and ensure its performative power. Lacan's point here is that an unsurmountable gap forever separates what I am 'in the real' from the symbolic mandate that procures my social identity: the primordial ontological fact is the void, the abyss on account of which I am inaccessible to myself in my capacity as a real substance – or, to quote Kant's unique formulation from his *Critique of Pure Reason*, on account of which I never get to know what I am as 'I or he or it (the thing) which thinks [*Ich, oder Er, oder Es (das Ding), welches denkt*]'. Every symbolic identity I acquire is ultimately nothing but a supplementary feature whose function is to fill out this void. This pure void of subjectivity, this empty form of 'transcendental apperception', has to be distinguished from the Cartesian *Cogito* which remains a *res cogitans*, a little piece of substantial reality miraculously saved from the destructive force of universal doubt: it was only with Kant that the distinction was made between the empty form of 'I think' and the thinking substance, the 'thing which thinks'.[10]

Here, then, Weininger falls short: when, in his ontological interpretation of woman's seduction of man as the 'infinite craving of Nothing for Something', he conceives of woman as *object*. In this endeavour of Nothing to become Something, he fails to recognize *the*

OTTO WEININGER, OR, 'WOMAN DOESN'T EXIST'

very striving of the subject for a substantial support. Or, in so far as the subject is a 'being-of-language', Weininger fails to recognize in this striving the constitutive motion of the subject *qua* void, lack of the signifier – that is, the striving of a hole, a missing link in the signifying chain, ($) for a signifying representative (S_1). In other words, far from expressing the subject's fear of a 'pathological' stain, of the positivity of an inert object, Weininger's aversion to woman bears witness to the fear of the most radical dimension of subjectivity itself: of the Void which 'is' the subject.

In a manuscript for the *Jenaer Realphilosophie* (1805–06), Hegel characterized this experience of pure Self *qua* 'abstract negativity', this 'eclipse of (constituted) reality', this contraction-into-self of the subject, as the 'night of the world':

> The human being is this night, this empty nothing, that contains everything in its simplicity – an unending wealth of many representations, images, of which none belongs to him – or which are not present. This night, the inner of nature, that exists here – pure self – in phantasmagorical representations, is night all around it, in which here shoots a bloody head – there another white ghastly apparition, suddenly here before it, and just so disappears. One catches sight of this night when one looks human beings in the eye – into a night that becomes awful.[11]

And the symbolic order, the universe of the Word, *Logos*, can emerge only from the experience of this abyss. As Hegel puts it, this inwardness of the pure self 'must enter also into existence, become an object, oppose itself to this innerness to be external; return to being. This is language as name-giving power. ... Through the name the object as individual entity is born out of the I.'[12]

What we must be careful not to miss here is how Hegel's break with the Enlightenment tradition can be discerned in the reversal of the very metaphor for the subject: the subject is no longer the Light of Reason opposed to the non-transparent, impenetrable Stuff (of Nature, Tradition ...); his very kernel, the gesture which opens up the space for the Light of *Logos*, is absolute negativity *qua* 'night of the world'. And what are Weininger's infamous 'henids' – the confused feminine representations that had not yet achieved the clarity of the Word, the self-identity of Notion – if not the very 'phantasmagorical representations' mentioned by Hegel – that is, the fantasy formations that emerge where the Word fails, since their function is precisely to fill out the void of this failure? Herein resides the paradox of Weininger's anti-feminism: far from being a result of his obscurantist anti-Enlightenment attitude, his anti-feminism attests to his adherence to the ideal of the Enlightenment – to his avoidance of the abyss of pure subjectivity.[13]

The same goes for Weininger's notorious anti-Semitism, which also cannot obliterate its indebtedness to the Enlightenment – notwithstanding Weininger's ethical voluntarism, the fact remains that his principal philosophical reference is Kant, the philosopher of the Enlightenment *par excellence* (this link between anti-Semitism and a certain kind of Enlightenment thinking was already suggested by Adorno and Horkheimer in their *Dialectic of Enlightenment*). At the most fundamental level, anti-Semitism does not associate Jews with corruption as a positive feature, but rather with shapelessness itself – with the lack of a definite and delimited ethnic disposition. In this vein, Alfred Rosenberg, Hitler's chief ideologue, asserted that all European nations possess a well-defined 'spiritual shape [*Gestalt*]' which gives expression to their ethnic character – and this 'spiritual shape' is precisely what is missing in Jews. And – again – is not this very 'shapelessness [*Gestaltlosigkeit*]' the constitutive feature of subjectivity? Does not subjectivity, by definition, transcend every positive spiritual shape? It should be clear, now, precisely how anti-Semitism and Fascist corporatism form the two sides of one and the same coin. In its repudiation of Judaeo-democratic 'abstract universalism', as opposed to the notion of society *qua* harmonious organic form in which every individual and every class has its own well-defined place, corporatism is inspired by the very insight that many a democrat prefers to shirk: *only an entity that is in itself hindered, dislocated – that is, one that lacks its 'proper place', that is by definition 'out of joint' – can immediately refer to universality as such.*

Or – to put the question in terms of the relationship between the Universal and the Particular: how does the Particular participate in the Universal? According to the traditional ontology, the Universal guarantees the Particular its identity: particular objects participate in their universal genus in so far as they 'truly are what they are' – that is, as far as they realize or fit their notion. A table, for example, participates in the notion of table in so far as it is 'truly a table'. Here universality remains a 'mute', indifferent feature connecting particular entities, an In-itself that is not posited as such – that is to say, the Particular does not relate to the Universal as such, in contrast to the subject *qua* 'self-consciousness', who participates in the Universal precisely and only in so far as his identity is truncated, marked by a lack; in so far as he is not fully 'what he is' – this is what Hegel has in mind when he speaks of 'negative universality'.[14] Let us recall an examplary case from political dialectics: when does some particular (ethnic, sexual, religious, etc.) minority make an appeal to the Universal? Precisely when the existing framework of social relations fails to satisfy that minority's needs, and prevents it from realizing its potential. At this precise point, the minority is compelled to ground its demands in the universal and universally acknowledged principles, claiming that its members are prevented from participating in education, job opportunities, free expression, public political activity, and so on, to the same extent as others.

An exemplary case of this For-itself of the Universal – that is, of the dialecticized relationship towards the Universal – is offered by Malcolm X's infamous claim that *white man as such is evil.* The meaning of this pronouncement is not that all whites are evil but rather that, because of the wrongs committed by white men against black people, evil pertains to the very universal notion of a white man. This, however, does not prevent me, an individual white man, from becoming 'good' by achieving awareness of the Evil that defines the very substance of my being, and by fully assuming this guilt and working to overcome it. (The same goes for the Christian notion of the sinfulness inscribed into the very core of human nature in so far as we are all 'sons of Adam': the way to salvation lies in reflectively assuming this guilt.)

Let us quote here Ernesto Laclau's apposite formulation (thoroughly Hegelian, notwithstanding Laclau's declared anti-Hegelianism):

> ... the universal is part of my identity insofar as I am penetrated by a constitutive lack – that is, insofar as my differential identity has failed in its process of constitution. The universal emerges out of the particular not as some principle underlying and explaining it, but as an incomplete horizon suturing a dislocated particular identity.[15]

In this precise sense 'the universal is the symbol of a missing fullness':[16] I can relate to the Universal as such only in so far as my particular identity is thwarted, 'dislocated'; only in so far as some impediment prevents me from 'becoming what I already am'. And as we have already pointed out, proof *per negationem* is provided by the interconnection of the two features that distinguish Fascist corporatism: its obsession with the image of society as an organic community whose every constituent is supposed to 'occupy its proper place'; its pathological resistance against abstract universality as a force of social disintegration – that is, against the idea that an individual can directly, irrespective of his or her place within the social organism, participate in the Universal (the idea, for example, that I possess inalienable rights simply as a human being, and not only in my capacity as a member of a certain class, corporation, etc.).

In a passage from *Phenomenology* whose 'Weiningerian' undertones are unmistakeable, Hegel formulates this negative relationship between the Universal and the Particular precisely apropos of woman as the ethical community's 'inner enemy':

> Since the community gets itself subsistence only by breaking in upon family

147

happiness and dissolving self-consciousness into the universal, it creates itself on what it represses [*erzeugt es sich an dem, was es unterdrückt*] and what is at the same time essential to it – womankind in general, its inner enemy. Womankind – the eternal irony of the community – alters by intrigue the universal purpose of government into a private end.[17]

The relationship of the Particular (family) to the Universal (community) is therefore not that of a harmonious incorporation of the family into the wider community, but is mediated by negativity: an individual ('self-consciousness') can relate to the Universal beyond family only through his negative relationship towards the family – that is, his 'betrayal' of the family, which entails the family's dissolution (this negativity is exactly what the corporatist metaphor of society *qua* large family strives to obliterate). In this precise sense, the universal community, its public space, 'creates itself on what it represses', on the debris of the family. What further strikes us about the passage quoted above is that Hegel himself presents as an integral part of the dialectical movement the very thing that his critics labour to denounce as its fatal weakness – namely, that the gesture of sublation [*Aufhebung*] never occurs without a certain remainder: after the 'sublation' of the family in the universal community, not only does the family continue to exist as the immediate foundation of the universal society, but *the negative relationship between the family and the universal community is further reflected back into the family itself*, in the guise of the woman who negatively reacts to the universal community with her 'eternal irony'. Woman is the cynic capable of discerning, in portentous statements about public welfare, the private motives of those who propagate these statements.

It may seem that Hegel simply ascribes to woman the narrowness of a private point of view: woman is the community's 'inner enemy' in so far as she misapprehends the true weight of the universal purposes of public life, and is able to conceive of them only as a means of realizing private ends. This, however, is far from being the entire picture: it is this same position of society's 'inner enemy' that renders possible the sublime ethical act of exposing the inherent limitation of the standpoint of social totality itself (Antigone).

Beyond the Phallus

In this duality of private and public sphere is rooted woman's splitting into Mother and Whore. Woman is not Mother and Whore, but *the same woman* is Mother in the private sphere and Whore in the public sphere – and the more she is Mother in the private sphere, the more she is

Whore in the public one. In other words, contrary to appearances, the division Mother/Whore does not concern the difference of content (positive characteristics that oppose the two figures), but is of a purely formal nature – that is to say, it designates the two inscriptions, the two modalities, of one and the same entity. Its ideological co-ordinates become clear the moment we relate them to the male's splitting into Adventurer, destroyer of the family in the private sphere, and Ethical Hero in the public sphere: woman *qua* Mother (the reliable support of the family) involves the opposition to man *qua* dislocated Adventurer (in contrast to feminine substantial inertia and steadiness, man is active, reaching outside, transcending himself, the family frame restricts him, he is ready to put everything at risk – in short, he is Subject); whereas woman *qua* dislocated Whore (superficial, unsteady, unreliable, a being of delusive appearance) involves the opposition to man *qua* agency of ethical reliability (man's word is his bond, he is the very embodiment of reliable symbolic commitment, he possesses the proper spiritual depth in contrast to feminine prattle ...). We thus obtain a double opposition: female Substance against male Subject and female Appearance against male Essence. Woman stands for substantial fullness *and* for the fickleness of Appearance; man stands for the disruptive force of negativity *and* for the uprightness of Essence. These four terms, of course, form a Greimasian semiotic square:

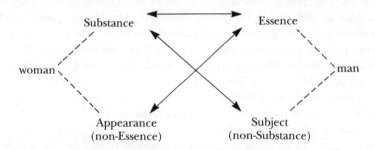

How does Weininger displace these traditional ideological co-ordinates? Here again, he is closest to feminism precisely where he appears to be more anti-feminist than 'official' ideology. In opposition to such ideology, Weininger denies even the (limited) ethical value of Mother, the pillar of the family, and reformulates the traditional splitting: man is divided into autonomous spiritual attitude and phallic sexuality (fall into heteronomy); woman is divided into her 'true nature' (which consists of her very lack of proper nature: she 'is' nothing but craving for man, she exists only in so far as she attracts his gaze) and heteronomous, externally imposed, morality. If, however, we recognize in the onto-logical Void of the woman the very void that defines subjectivity, this double division changes into Lacan's 'formulas of sexuation':

• Woman's division is of a hysterical nature, it assumes the form of the *inconsistency* of her desire: 'I demand that you refuse my demand, since this is not *that*' (Lacan). When, for example, Wagner's Kundry seduces Parsifal, she actually wants him to resist her advances – does not this obstruction, this sabotage of her own intent, testify to a dimension in her which resists the domination of the Phallus? (Weininger himself speaks of an obscure longing in woman for deliverance, for shaking off the yoke of the Phallus through self-annihilation.) The male dread of woman, which so deeply branded the *Zeitgeist* at the turn of the century, from Edvard Munch and August Strindberg up to Franz Kafka, thus reveals itself as the dread of feminine inconsistency: feminine hysteria, which traumatized these men (and also marked the birthplace of psycho-analysis), confronted them with an inconsistent multitude of masks (a hysterical woman immediately moves from desperate pleas to cruel, vulgar derision, etc.). What causes such uneasiness is the impossibility of discerning behind the masks a consistent subject manipulating them: behind the multiple layers of masks is nothing; or, at the most, nothing but the shapeless, mucous stuff of the life-substance.

Suffice it to mention Edvard Munch's encounter with hysteria, which left such a deep mark upon him. In 1893 Munch was in love with the beautiful daughter of an Oslo wine merchant. She clung to him, but he was afraid of such a tie and anxious about his work, so he left her. One stormy night a sailing-boat came to fetch him: the report was that the young woman was on the point of death and wanted to speak to him for the last time. Munch was deeply moved and, without question, went to her home, where he found her lying on a bed between two lighted candles. But when he approached her bed, she rose and started to laugh: the whole scene was nothing but a hoax. Munch turned and began to leave; at that point, she threatened to shoot herself if he left her; and drawing a revolver, she pointed it at her breast. When Munch bent to wrench the weapon away, convinced that this too was only part of the game, the gun went off and wounded him in the hand....[18] Here we encounter hysterical theatre at its purest: the subject is caught in a masquerade in which what appears to be deadly serious reveals itself as fraud (dying), and what appears to be an empty gesture reveals itself as deadly serious (the threat of suicide).[19] The panic that seizes the (male) subject confronting this theatre expresses a dread that behind the many masks, which fall away from each other like the layers of an onion, there is nothing, no ultimate feminine Secret.

150

Here, however, we must avoid a fatal misunderstanding. In so far as these hysterical masks are the way for a woman to captivate the male gaze, the inevitable conclusion seems to be that the feminine Secret inaccessible to the male phallic economy – the 'eternally Feminine [*das ewig Weibliche*]' (Goethe) beyond symbolic masks – consists of the feminine substance that eludes the reign of 'phallogocentrism'. The complementary conclusion is that in so far as there is nothing behind the masks, woman is wholly subordinated to the Phallus. According to Lacan, however, the exact opposite is true: the pre-symbolic 'eternally Feminine' is a retroactive patriarchal fantasy – that is, it is the Exception which grounds the reign of the Phallus (like the anthropological notion of an original matriarchal Paradise, which was ruined by the Fall into patriarchal civilization and which, from Bachofen onwards, firmly supports patriarchal ideology, since it relies on the notion of teleological evolution from matriarchy to patriarchy). It is thus the very lack of any exception to the Phallus that renders the feminine libidinal economy inconsistent, hysterical, and thereby undermines the reign of the Phallus. When, therefore, as Weininger puts it, woman is 'coited by every object', this very boundless extension of phallus undermines Phallus as the principle of the Universal and its founding Exception.

Lacan's 'Subversion of the subject ...' ends with the ambiguous 'I won't go any further here'.[20] Ambiguous, since it can be taken to imply that later, somewhere else, Lacan *will* 'go further'. This lure enticed some feminist critics of Lacan to reproach him for coming to a halt at the very point where he should accomplish the decisive step beyond Freud's phallocentrism: although Lacan does talk about feminine *jouissance* eluding the phallic domain, he conceives of it as an ineffable 'dark continent' separated from (the male) discourse by a frontier that is impossible to traverse. For feminists like Irigaray or Kristeva, this refusal to traverse the frontier, this 'I won't go any further here', signals the continued tabooing of women; what they want is to 'go further' – to deploy the contours of a 'feminine discourse' beyond the 'phallic' symbolic order.

Why does this operation – which, from the standpoint of common sense, cannot but appear fully justified – miss its mark? In traditional terms, the Limit that defines woman is not epistemological but onto-logical – that is to say, *beyond it there is nothing*. 'Feminine' is this structure of the limit as such, a limit that *precedes* what may or may not lie in its Beyond: all that we perceive in this Beyond (the Eternal Feminine, for example) are our own fantasy projections.[21] Woman *qua* Enigma is a spectre generated by the inconsistent surface of multiple masks – the secret of 'Secret' itself is the inconsistency of the surface.[22] And the Lacanian name for this inconsistency of the surface (for a convoluted topological space like the Moebius band) is simply *the subject.*

• In the case of man, on the contrary, the split is, as it were, externalized: man escapes the inconsistency of his desire by establishing a line of separation between the domain of the Phallus – that is, sexual enjoyment, the relationship with a sexual partner – and the non-Phallic – that is, the domain of ethical goals, of non-sexual 'public' activity (Exception). Here we encounter the paradox of 'states that are essentially by-products': man subordinates his relationship to a woman to the domain of ethical goals (forced to choose between woman and ethical duty – in the guise of professional obligation, etc. – he immediately opts for duty), yet he is simultaneously aware that only a relationship with a woman can bring him genuine 'happiness' or personal fulfilment. His 'wager' is that woman will be most effectively seduced precisely when he does not subordinate all his activity to her – what she will be unable to resist is her fascination with his 'public' activity – that is, her secret awareness that he is actually doing it for her. What we have here is the inverted libidinal economy of *courtly love*: in courtly love I devote myself directly to the Lady, I posit my serving her as my supreme Duty, and for that reason woman remains a cold, indifferent, capricious Despot, an 'inhuman partner' (Lacan) with whom a sexual relationship is neither possible nor really desirable, whereas here I render the sexual relationship possible precisely by *not* positing it as my explicit goal. . . . [23]

This paradox emerges in almost every melodrama that interprets the man's readiness to sacrifice his beloved for the (public) Cause as the supreme proof of his love for her – that is, of how 'she is everything to him'. The sublime moment of recognition occurs when the woman finally realizes that the man has left her for the sake of his love for her. An interesting variation on this theme is offered by Vincente Minnelli's version of *The Four Horsemen of the Apocalypse*: Glenn Ford plays Julio, a wealthy Argentinian who leads a merry life in Paris during the German occupation, socializing with German officers and living with the beautiful wife of an absent Resistance leader (Ingrid Thulin). Although the woman is passionately in love with Julio, she has an uneasy feeling that the man she is living with is a weakling, taking refuge in private pleasures, whereas the husband whom she left for her lover is a true hero. Suddenly this entire scenario is exposed as masquerade: in an emergency, Julio is urgently contacted by a man whom she knows to be part of the Resistance, so she guesses that Julio was pretending to be a man of pleasure in order to socialize with German high officers and thereby gain access to precious information about the enemy. Formally, Julio betrayed her love, yet in spite of this betrayal she lets him go forward into his last, probably suicidal, action: she is well aware that in a deeper sense he is doing it for her, in order to become worthy of her love....[24]

What Lacan designates as the 'phallic function' is this very splitting between the domain of phallic enjoyment and the desexualized 'public' field that eludes it – that is to say, *'phallic' is this self-limitation of the Phallus, this positing of an Exception.* In this precise sense the phallus is the signifier of castration: 'symbolic castration' is ultimately another name for the paradox of 'states that are essentially by-products': *if we are to achieve fulfilment through phallic enjoyment, we must renounce it as our explicit goal.* In other words, true love can emerge only within a relationship of 'partnership' that is animated by a different, non-sexual goal (see the novels of Marguerite Duras). Love is an unforeseeable answer of the real: it (can) emerge(s) 'out of nowhere' only when we renounce any attempt to direct and control its course. (Here, of course, as with every instance of the Real, opposites coincide: love is at the same time the foreseeable product of an absolute mechanism – as evidenced by the absolutely predictable character of transference love in psychoanalysis. This love is produced 'automatically' by the very analytic situation, irrespective of the actual characteristics of the analyst. In this precise sense the analyst is the *objet petit a*, not another subject: because of its 'automatic' character, transference love dispenses with the illusion that we fall in love on account of the beloved person's positive properties – that is, on account of what he or she is 'in reality'. We fall in love with the analyst *qua* the formal place in the structure, devoid of 'human features', not with a flesh-and-blood person.[25])

The 'Formulas of Sexuation'

Such a notion of sexual difference opens up a series of philosophical connections; the first thing that strikes the eye is the structural homology between Lacan's 'formulas of sexuation' and the Kantian duality of mathematical and dynamic antinomies.[26] In contemporary philosophy, one of the possible tie-ins is offered by the opposition of objectal *signification* (the universal meaning of terms) and the incorporeal effect of *sense*, articulated by Deleuze in *The Logic of Sense*. Deleuze associates this opposition to the two types of paradox that perfectly fit the Kantian duality of antinomies:

The paradoxes of signification are essentially that of the *abnormal set* (which includes itself as a member or which includes members of different types) and that of the *rebel element* (which forms part of a set whose existence it presupposes and belongs to two sub-sets which it determines). The paradoxes of sense are essentially that of the *subdivision ad infinitum* (always past-future

153

and never present), and that of the *nomadic distribution* (distributing in an open space instead of distributing a closed space).[27]

Is not the Kantian free subject precisely such a 'rebel element': in its capacity as a phenomenal entity it is part of the causal enchainment, wholly subject to natural laws, whereas as a noumenal entity it is free – that is, it interrupts the chain of causes and starts a new series out of itself? Is not the problem of God that he is, in a sense, both part of the world and its cause? And is not the problem of the second antinomy of pure reason, on the other hand, precisely the problem of the infinite divisibility of the stuff?

At a more general level, this notion of sexual difference enables us to locate properly Lacan's seemingly paradoxical assertion that the subject of psychoanalysis is none other than the Cartesian subject of modern science. This subject emerges by way of the radical *desexualization* of man's relationship to the universe. That is to say, traditional Wisdom was thoroughly anthropomorphic and 'sexualized'; its comprehension of the universe was structured by oppositions bearing an indelibly sexual connotation: yin–yang, Light–Darkness, active–passive.... This anthropomorphic foundation made possible the metaphorical correspondence, the mirror-relationship, between micro- and macrocosm: the establishment of structural homologies between man, society and universe (society as an organism with the monarch as its head, workers as its hands ...; the birth of the universe through the coupling of Earth and Sun, etc.). In the modern world, on the contrary, reality confronts us as inherently non-anthropomorphic, as a blind mechanism which 'speaks the language of mathematics' and consequently can be expressed only in meaningless formulas – every search for a 'deeper meaning' of phenomena is now experienced as the leftover of traditional 'anthropomorphism'. The modern subject is thus no longer 'at home' in the universe; the difficulty of sustaining this solitude is attested to by the recurrent returns of the anthropomorphic-sexualized world-view in the guise of pseudo-ecological Wisdom ('new holism', 'new paradigm', etc.).

And it is against this background that we can measure the extent of Lacan's achievement: he was simply the first to outline the contours of a non-imaginary, non-naturalized theory of sexual difference – of a theory that radically breaks with anthropomorphic sexualization ('male' and 'female' as the two cosmic principles, etc.) and, as such, is appropriate to modern science. The problem that confronted Lacan was: how do we pass from animal coupling led by instinctual knowledge and regulated by natural rhythms to human sexuality possessed by a desire which is eternalized and, for that very reason, insatiable, inherently perturbed, doomed to fail, and so on? (Even the lesson of an idyllic pastoral novel like *Daphnis and Chloe* is that one cannot achieve a 'normal' sexual relationship by following natural urges or imitating animal sexual behaviour: what is needed is the instruction of an experienced woman – that is, the reference to symbolic tradition. Herein lies also the point of Freud's doctrine on the Oedipus complex: what we (or at least, most of us) experience as the most 'natural' sexual relationship is something learned, internalized through a series of traumatic cuts, interventions of the symbolic Law.) So the answer to Lacan's problem is: we enter human sexuality through the intervention of the symbolic order *qua* heterogeneous parasite that disrupts the natural rhythm of coupling.

Apropos of the two asymmetrical antinomies of symbolization (the 'masculine' side that involves the universality of the phallic function grounded in an exception; the 'feminine' side that involves a 'non-all' field which, for that very reason, contains no exception to the phallic function) a question imposes itself with a kind of self-evidence: what constitutes the link that connects these two purely logical antinomies with the opposition of female and male, which, however symbolically mediated and culturally conditioned, remains an obvious biological fact? The answer to this question is: *there is no link*. What we experience as 'sexuality' is precisely the effect of the contingent act of 'grafting' the fundamental deadlock of symbolization on to the biological opposition of male and female. The answer to the question: isn't this link between the two logical paradoxes of universalization and sexuality illicit?, therefore, is: *that's precisely Lacan's point*. What Lacan does is simply to transpose this 'illicit' character from the epistemological level to the ontological level: sexuality itself, what we experience as the highest, most intense assertion of our being, is a *bricolage*, a montage of two heterogeneous elements. Herein resides Lacan's 'deconstruction' of sexuality.

This parasitic 'grafting' of the symbolic deadlock on to animal coupling undermines the instinctual rhythm of animal coupling and confers on it an indelible brand of failure: 'there is no sexual relationship'; every relationship between the sexes can take place only against the background of a fundamental impossibility, and so on. This 'graft' is radically contingent in the sense that it hinges on the homology between the penis in the male and the fact that in the 'masculine' formulas we are dealing with the exception that grounds universality: the short circuit between the two changes the penis into a material support of the phallic signifier, the signifier of symbolic castration. How, then, on closer inspection, are the 'masculine' and the 'feminine' side structured?

A standard example of a 'non-all' field is provided by the Marxist notion of class struggle: every position we assume towards the class struggle, including a theoretical one, is already a moment of the class struggle; it involves 'taking sides' in it, which is why there is no impartial objective standpoint enabling us to delineate class struggle. In this precise sense, 'class struggle doesn't exist', since 'there is no element that eludes it' – we cannot apprehend it 'as such', what we are dealing with are always the partial effects whose absent cause is the class struggle. (In the Stalinist discursive universe, on the contrary, class struggle *does* exist, since there is an exception to it: technology and language are conceived of as neutral instruments at the disposal of everybody and, as such, external to class struggle.)

Let us, however, turn to a more abstract example, that of philosophy. A quick glance at any philosophy manual makes it clear how every universal, all-encompassing notion of philosophy is rooted in a particular philosophy, how it involves the standpoint of a particular philosophy. There is no neutral notion of philosophy to be divided into analytical philosophy, hermeneutical philosophy, and so on; every particular philosophy encompasses itself and (its view on) all other philosophies. Or – as Hegel put it in his *Lessons on the History of Philosophy* – every epochal philosophy is in a way the whole of philosophy, it is not a subdivision of the Whole but this Whole itself apprehended in a specific modality. What we have here, therefore, is not a simple reduction of the Universal to the Particular but, rather, a kind of *surplus* of the Universal: no single Universal encompasses the entire particular content, since each Particular has *its own* Universal – that is, it contains a specific perspective on the entire field.

And the masculine position designates precisely the endeavour to resolve this impasse of 'too many Universals' by way of excluding one paradoxical Particular; this exceptional Particular immediately gives body to the Universal as such, and simultaneously negates its constitutive feature. *This is how Universal 'as such', in its opposition to particular content, comes to exist.* An exemplary case is the figure of the Lady in courtly love, which belongs completely to the masculine symbolic economy. In the figure of the Lady, woman *qua* sexual object reaches existence – yet at the price of being posited as the inaccessible Thing, that is to say, desexualized, transformed into an object which, precisely in so far as it gives body to Sexuality as such, renders the masculine subject impotent.[28]

One privileged way of maintaining the fiction of Woman's existence as the Exception that immediately gives body to the Universal is the operatic aria: its climactic moment, when the soprano 'puts herself entirely into the voice' – perhaps the neatest exemplification of what Lacan calls *jouis-sense*, enjoy-meant, the moment at which sheer self-consuming enjoyment of the voice eclipses meaning (the words of the aria). At this moment, one can briefly entertain the illusion that the woman 'has it in herself', *objet petit a*, the voice-object, the cause of desire; and, consequently, that she exists.

The key to these paradoxes of the Universal grounded in an Exception is provided by the Hegelian notion of the 'For-itself' of the Universal – that is, of the difference between a 'mute' Universal that constitutes an impassive tie linking individual terms together and the reflexive turn by means of which this Universal is posited as such. In his Introduction to *Grundrisse*, Marx asserts that it is possible to formulate the abstract-universal notion of labour only when the 'real indifference' towards particular forms of labour reigns in the actual social life itself, when actual individuals experience their particular labour as something contingent, ultimately indifferent to their essence – in short, as a (freely chosen) 'profession'. Or, with reference to Eurocentrism: actual multi-culturalism can emerge only in a culture within which its own tradition, communal heritage, appears as contingent; that is to say, in a culture that is indifferent towards itself, towards its own specificity. For that reason multiculturalism is, *stricto sensu*, 'Eurocentric': only within modern-age subjectivity is it possible to experience one's own tradition as a contingent ingredient to be methodologically 'bracketed' in the pursuit of truth. Herein resides the paradox of the Universal and its constitutive exception: the universal notion of the multiplicity of peoples, each embedded in its particular tradition, presupposes an exception, a tradition that experiences *itself* as contingent.

In Hegel himself, this paradox is articulated in an exemplary way apropos of the state, of the inherent tension that pertains to the very notion of the State in so far as it is split between the 'mute' universality (the neutral-abstract notion of State whose examples are particular states) and the emphatic notion of State as the Idea of Reason that gradually realizes itself and to which no existing, positive state is fully adequate.[29] In so far as the notion of State is 'posited as such', becomes 'for itself', it necessary enters into a negative relationship towards particular, actually existing states – that is to say, these particular states appear as inadequate, deficient with regard to their Notion. (Perhaps this same tension also provides the matrix of what Heidegger designated the onto-theological structure of metaphysics: *onto-* stands for the neutral universality of the abstract notion of State and *theo-* for the fully realized State as opposed to imperfect existing States.) To put it differently: the 'catch' of the Universal resides in what it secretly excludes. The 'man' of universal human rights excludes those who are considered 'not fully human' (savages and non-civilized barbarians, madmen, criminals, children, women ...) – this logic was brought to its extreme in the Jacobinical Terror, where *every* concrete individual was at least potentially excluded: every individual is branded by some 'pathological' stain (of corruption, egotism, etc.) and, as such, does not fit the notion of Man, so that guilt ultimately pertains to individual existence as such.

A few years ago, *Mad* magazine published a series of caricatures exemplifying the four possible levels at which a subject can relate to a symbolic norm adopted in his community. Let us limit ourselves to the norm of fashion. At the lowest level are the poor, whose attitude towards fashion is indifference – their sole aim is simply to avoid looking shabby; that is, to maintain a standard of decency. Next are the lower middle classes, who desperately strive to follow fashion; due to financial constraint, however, they always come 'too late' and wear what was fashionable a season ago. The upper middle classes, who actually can afford the latest fashion, do not yet represent the highest level: above them are the trendsetting rich, who are again (as are those at the lowest level) indifferent towards fashion, but for a very different reason – they have no external norm to comply with, since they themselves set the norm. What they wear *is the fashion*.

Of special significance to the theory of the signifier is this fourth and last level, which, as a kind of paradoxical surplus, supplements perfect compliance with the latest fashion. This level involves a kind of reflective reversal of the preceding one: as to content, the last two levels are exactly the same; the difference between them is of a purely formal nature – the trendsetting rich are dressed the same as the upper middle classes, but not for the same reason: not, that is, because they want to follow the latest fashion, but simply because whatever they wear *is* the latest fashion.

We encounter the same four levels apropos of legal power: beyond those who are indifferent to laws, those who break laws while remaining integrated into the system of law and order, and those who stick strictly to the letter of the law, there are those at the very top whose acts are always in accordance with the law, not because they obediently follow the law but because their activity *determines* what is law in a performative way – what(ever) they do simply *is* the law (the King in an absolute monarchy, for example). This point of inversion is the exception that founds the Universal.[30]

Hegel's thesis that every genus has only one species, the other species being the genus itself, aims at the same paradoxical point of inversion. When, for example, we say 'Rich people are poor people with money', this definition is not reversible – we cannot say 'Poor people are rich people without money'. We do not have a neutral genus 'people', divided into its two species, 'poor people' and 'rich people': the genus is 'poor people', to whom we must add the *differentia specifica* (money) in order to obtain its species, 'rich people'. Psychoanalysis conceives of the sexual difference in a somewhat homologous way: 'Woman is a castrated man'. Here also, the proposition cannot be inverted into 'Man is woman with phallus'. It would be wrong, however, to conclude from this that man *qua* male possesses a kind of ontological priority. The properly Hegelian paradox is that the *'cut' of the specific difference is constitutive of the genus itself.* In other words, castration defines the genus of man; the 'neutral' universality of Man unmarked with castration is already an index of the disavowal of castration.

Lacan's achievement here is to conceive of the sexual difference at the transcendental level in the strict Kantian sense of the term – that is to say, without reference to any 'pathological' empirical content. At the same time, his definition of sexual difference avoids the pitfall of 'essentialism' by conceiving of the 'essence' of each of the two sexual positions as a specific form of inconsistency, of antagonism. The 'essence of woman' is not some positive entity but an impasse, a deadlock that prevents her from 'becoming woman'. In this respect Lacan simply follows Hegel, whose answer to the reproach of essentialism would have been that *essence itself is a non-essentialist notion* – the 'essence of essence' resides in its inconsistency, in its inherent splitting; or, as Derrida would have put it, essence itself can assert its 'essential' character only by having recourse to inconsistent strategies *à la* Freud's argument about the borrowed umbrella from his dream about Irma's injection (I returned the umbrella to you in good condition; it was already damaged when I borrowed it from you ...) . An exemplary case of such 'deconstruction' is provided by Hegel's critique of Kant in his *Phenomenology of Spirit*: Hegel demonstrates how Kant, in order to assert his 'ethical formalism', is compelled to accomplish a whole series of 'illegitimate' *Verstellungen* (to change the signification of key concepts in the midst of a deduction, etc.).

This is why the parallel between Lacan's 'formulas of sexuation' and Kant's antinomies of pure reason is fully justified: in Lacan, 'masculine' or 'feminine' is not a predicate providing positive information about the subject – that is, designating some of its phenomenal properties; rather, it is a case of what Kant conceives of as a purely negative determination which merely designates, registers, a certain limit – more precisely: a specific modality of how the subject failed in his or her bid for identity which would constitute him or her as an object within phenomenal reality. On that account Lacan is as far as it is possible to be from the notion of sexual difference as the relationship of two opposite poles which supplement each other and together form the whole of Man: 'masculine' and 'feminine' are not the two species of the genus Man but, rather, the two modes of the subject's *failure* to achieve the full identity of Man. 'Man' and 'woman' together do not form a Whole, since *each of them is already in itself a failed Whole.*

It should also be clear, now, why Lacan's conceptualization of sexual difference avoids the trap of the infamous 'binary logic': in it, 'masculine' and 'feminine' are not opposed in the guise of a series of contrary predicates (active/passive, cause/effect, reason/sentiment; etc.); rather, 'masculine' and 'feminine' involve a different modality of the very antagonistic relationship between these opposites. 'Man' is not a cause of the woman-effect but a specific modality of the relationship between cause and effect (the linear succession of causes and effects with an excepted unique element, the Last Cause), in contrast to 'woman', who implies a different modality (a kind of convoluted 'interaction' where the cause functions as an effect of its own effects). Within the domain of sexual pleasures proper, masculine economy tends to be 'teleological', centred on phallic orgasm *qua* pleasure *par excellence*, whereas feminine economy involves a dispersed network of particular pleasures that are not organized around some teleological central principle. As a result, 'masculine' and 'feminine' are not two positive substantial entities but two different modalities of one and the same entity: in order to 'feminize' a masculine discourse it is enough to change – sometimes almost imperceptibly – its specific 'tonality'.

It is here that Foucauldian 'constructionists' and Lacan part company: for the 'constructionists', sex is not a natural given but a *bricolage*, an artificial unification of heterogeneous discursive practices; whereas Lacan rejects this view without returning to naive substantialism. For him, sexual difference is not a discursive, symbolic construction; instead, it emerges at the very point where symbolization fails: we are sexed beings because symbolization always comes up against its own inherent impossibility. What is at stake here is not that 'actual', 'concrete' sexual beings can never fully fit the symbolic construction of 'man' or 'woman': the point is, rather, that this symbolic construction itself supplements a certain fundamental deadlock. In short, *if it were possible to symbolize sexual difference, we would have not two sexes but only one.* 'Male' and 'female' are not two complementary parts of the Whole, they are two (failed) attempts to symbolize this Whole.

The ultimate result of our reading of Weininger is thus a paradoxical yet inevitable inversion of the anti-feminist ideological apparatus espoused by Weininger himself, according to which women are wholly submitted to phallic enjoyment, whereas men have access to the desexualized domain of ethical goals beyond the Phallus: it is man who is wholly submitted to the Phallus (since positing an Exception is the way to maintain the universal domination of the Phallus), whereas woman, through the inconsistency of her desire, attains the domain 'beyond the Phallus'. Only woman has access to the Other (non-phallic) enjoyment.

The traumatic element that Weininger absolutely refused to acknowledge, although it followed from his own work, was this inherent reversal of his 'official' position: woman, not man, can reach 'beyond the Phallus'. Weininger opted instead for suicide – for this sole example of a successful repression, a repression without the return of the repressed. By means of his suicide, Weininger confirmed two things: that somewhere 'deep in himself', in his unconscious, *he knew it*; and, simultaneously, that this knowledge was absolutely unbearable for him. The choice for him was neither 'life or death' nor 'money or death' but, rather, 'knowledge or death'. The fact that death was the only possible escape from this knowledge bears witness to the unquestionable *authenticity* of his subjective position. In other words, does not the unbearable tension in Weininger's subjective position attest to the *hysterical* nature of his speech? For that reason, Weininger is still worth reading.

Notes

1. Numbers in brackets refer to the pages of the (extremely unreliable) English translation *Sex and Character. Authorized translation from the sixth German edition*, London: William Heinemann/New York: G.P. Putnam's Sons (no date). All emphasis original.
2. This is perhaps the proper place to denounce one of the crucial misapprehensions about Lacan: Lacan in no way claims that love can be reduced to an imaginary phenomenon, to a narcissistic obsession with one's own ideal ego. At a more radical level, love *qua* passion aims at the real kernel of the other beyond imaginary and/or symbolic identifications – in loving you, I love what is 'in you more than yourself'.
3. As for the figure of the Lady in courtly love, see Chapter 4 above.
4. As for this reversal in the relationship between cause and effect, see Chapter 5 above.
5. For an exemplary refusal of this logic of the 'feminine Secret' from a feminist standpoint, see Mary Ann Doane, 'Veiling over Desire: Close-ups of the Woman', in *Femmes Fatales*, New York: Routledge 1991.
Incidentally, a homologous mystification is at work in so-called 'Orientalism', the Western admiration for and elevation of Oriental wisdom as a cure for our Western obsession with production and domination. The infamous 'enigma of the East' follows the same logic as the 'enigma of the Woman'. In short, the first step in breaking with Eurocentrism must be to repeat *mutatis mutandis* Lacan's 'Woman doesn't exist' and to assert that 'the Orient doesn't exist'.
6. For an interpretation of this joke, see Chapter 2 of Slavoj Žižek, *The Sublime Object of Ideology*, London: Verso 1989.
7. Here, apropos of this joke with the double dénouement, we should recall that the process of *la passe* (the passage of the analysand into the analyst) is characterized by the same scansion of the double dénouement. Apropos of *la passe*, Lacan distinguishes between *passeur* and *passant* as its two successive moments. The analysand becomes a *passeur* upon assuming his *non-being* as a subject – that is, upon renouncing the support of imaginary and/or symbolic identifications and fully assuming the void of subjectivity (\$); he becomes a *passant* upon undergoing the 'subjective destitution' – upon identifying with *objet a*, the non-symbolizable remainder of the process of symbolization; upon recognizing in this

'excrement' the sole support of his *being*. And in the joke about the Jew and the Pole we encounter the same supplementary 'turn of the screw' from 'I am nothing' to 'I am that object which gives body to my nothingness': first, the Pole becomes aware of how the Jew is deceiving him – behind all the Jew's talk there is nothing, no secret; the Jew is just procrastinating in order to get more money out of him; what follows thereupon is the crucial experience of how the Jew, *through this very deception*, delivered the promised good (*a*) – that is to say, fulfilled his promise of disclosing how the Jews....

8. Ludwig Wittgenstein, *Philosophical Investigations*, Oxford: Blackwell 1976, para. 404.

9. Ludwig Wittgenstein, *The Blue and The Brown Book*, Oxford: Blackwell 1958, para. 67. For a more detailed account of this Wittgensteinian distinction, see Chapter 4 of Slavoj Žižek, *For They Know Not What They Do*, London: Verso 1991.

10. As to this shift from Descartes to Kant, see Chapter 1 of Slavoj Žižek, *Tarrying with the Negative*, Durham, NC: Duke University Press 1993.

11. Quoted from Donald Phillip Verene, *Hegel's Recollection*, Albany, NY: SUNY Press 1985, pp. 7–8.

12. Ibid., p. 8.

13. The link between *la femme n'existe pas* and her status as pure subject can also be ascertained through a precise reference to Kant. That is to say, in Kant's philosophy the passage from subject to substance takes place via 'schematization': 'subject' is a purely logical entity (subject of a judgement), whereas 'substance' designates the schematized subject, subject *qua* real entity that persists in time. Only substance exists in the precise meaning of an entity that is part of empirical-phenomenal reality; a being that is a pure subject – that is to say, is not schematized, caught in the causal-temporal continuum of reality – *stricto sensu* does not exist.

14. We are dealing here with the difference between Universal-in-itself – the 'mute' universal feature which brings elements of a genus together – and the Universal posited as such; that is to say, the Universal to which the subject relates in its opposition to the Particular. According to Hegel, this difference is what distinguishes the dialectical approach:

... a primary task is always to distinguish clearly between what is simply *in itself* and what is *posited*: between how the determinations are when in the concept, and how they are when posited or when there for another. This is a distinction which belongs only to the dialectical development, and which the metaphysical way of philosophizing (and that includes the critical) knows not.

(*Hegel's Science of Logic*, Atlantic Highlands, NJ: Humanities Press 1969, p. 122)

This crucial distinction between In-itself and For-itself enables us to elucidate the Hegelian logic of self-reflection – of reflection-into-other as reflection-into-self. Let us recall Hegel's critique of representative democracy: its illusory, false presupposition is that, prior to the act of elections, individuals already know what they want, what is their true interest – as if, by means of their electoral vote, they choose somebody who could transmit this interest of which they are already fully aware to the political sphere proper. In opposing this notion, Hegel points out that the (political) representative, far from simply carrying out an already-conscious interest, brings this interest to self-consciousness. In other words, the political representative accomplishes the conversion of my interest from 'In-itself' to 'For-itself': by providing a clear public formulation of my interest, he serves as a medium of its recognition by me ('It is only now that it is quite clear to me what I always really wanted!'). When I choose my representative I therefore, in a sense, *choose myself*, my own political identity. In this precise sense, the choice of my representative is not only my reflection-into-other, the mirroring of my interest in the political sphere, but simultaneously my self-reflection.

An example of this For-itself of the Universal from a totally different domain is the reflected relationship of a literary work towards its genre. What we have in mind here is not primarily the explicit playing with the rules of the genre but rather more refined cases such as, for example, Patricia Highsmith's *The Tremor of Forgery*, the portrait of a lonely American woman on vacation in Tunis. The identification of Highsmith with psycho-thrillers totally changes our perception of what would otherwise be received as a standard psychological study: the reader is far more attentive to signs of madness, to the terrifying potentials of different intersubjective constellations, and so on.

15. Ernesto Laclau, 'Universalism, Particularism, and the Question of Identity', *October* 61, p. 89.

16. Ibid.

17. G.W.F. Hegel, *Phenomenology of Spirit*, Oxford: Oxford University Press 1977, p. 496.

18. See J.P. Hodin, *Edvard Munch*, London: Thames & Hudson 1972, pp. 88–9.

19. Hitchcock's *Murder* offers an exemplary case of the same double movement in which reality proves fictitious and fiction proves real. In the last shot of the film we see the couple happily united in a drawing-room – but then the camera moves back and it becomes clear that what we have just seen was taking place on a stage. The suicide of the murderer Fane ten minutes before involves the opposite movement: we witness a theatrical scene (the act of a trapeze artist) that suddenly turns deadly – Fane commits suicide in public, hanging himself on the rope of the trapeze.

20. Jacques Lacan, *Écrits: A Selection*, New York: Norton 1977, p. 324.

21. In Wagner's *The Twilight of the Gods*, the moment of the intrusion of the superego in its sociopolitical obscenity occurs with Hagen's 'call to men [Männerruf]' and the ensuing chorus: a scene of raw violence previously unheard of in an opera.... Yet when he proceeds to legitimize the violence he is instigating, Hagen makes an appeal to the goddess Fricka. Fricka, the protectress of family and household, is of course a phantasmic projection of male discourse. This, however, does not mean that we should oppose woman as she is 'for the other', for man ('male narcissistic projection', etc.) and the 'true' woman-in-herself. One is almost tempted to assert the exact opposite: 'Woman-in-herself' is ultimately a male fantasy, whereas we get much closer to the 'true' woman by simply following to their conclusion the inherent deadlocks of the male discourse on woman.

22. Here one should reread Mary Ann Doane's essay on *Gilda* (in *Femmes Fatales*): Gilda's striptease is supported by a male fantasy that after she has thrown off all her clothes, we – men – shall find her unspoiled kernel, a 'good wife' who was only 'pretending' to be a debauchee. In contrast, the basic feature of what Lacan calls 'subject' is precisely that *there is no such kernel*: the subject is like an onion whose layers conceal nothing....

23. One of the apocryphal versions of the myth of Tristan and Isolde brings this paradox to the point of self-reference: the relationship between duty and woman overlaps with that between Lady and the 'ordinary' woman. Tristan, married to the fair-haired Isolde, whom he does not love, erects a stone fetish in the wood near his castle – a statue of the true Isolde, his Lady. He visits the statue regularly at night; this veneration of the fetish restores his sexual prowess with the fair-haired Isolde, and thus enables him to maintain the appearance of a normal married life. Perhaps the inaccessible Ideal (Dante's Beatrice, etc.) as such is a purely negative instance whose function is to render possible the 'normal' sexual relationship with another, 'ordinary' woman. This version of the myth of Tristan and Isolde also confirms that fetish *qua* non-genital partial object, far from being a simple hindrance to a 'normal' sexual relationship, can even function as a condition of its possibility.

24. In general, the crucial reversal of almost every melodrama occurs when the agency which stands in for the big Other *recognizes the truth about the subject* and thus undoes the wrong. Let us take a (perhaps surprising) example, *Alyosha's Love*, a Soviet film from the early sixties (the time of the so-called 'Khrushchev's thaw'): its sublime reversal occurs when the hero's passionate love is finally publicly acknowledged by the seemingly ignorant and cynical big Other; what is thereby confirmed is the fact that the big Other's cynicism was feigned, that it functioned from the very beginning as the Ordeal to which the big Other submitted the hero.

Alyosha's Love is set among a group of geologists camping near a small town in the middle of the Siberian wilderness. The young Alyosha falls in love with a girl from the town; despite all the troubles attendant upon his love (at first the girl is indifferent towards him; her ex-boyfriend's companions give him a brutal beating; his own elder colleagues deride him cruelly, etc.) Alyosha saves all his free time for long walks to the town, so that he can cast a quick and distant glance at the girl. At the end of the film, the girl gives way to the force of his love: she changes from the beloved to the loving one, takes the long walk herself and joins him in the camp. Alyosha's colleagues, who are working on the hill above the camp, stop their digging, stand up and silently follow the girl, who approaches Alyosha's tent: the cynical distance and derision are over; the big Other itself is compelled to recognize its defeat, its fascination with the force of love. . . .

25. The automatism of love is set in motion when some contingent, ultimately indifferent, (libidinal) object finds itself occupying a pre-given fantasy-place. This role of fantasy in the automatic emergence of love hinges on the fact that 'there is no sexual relationship', no universal formula or matrix guaranteeing a harmonious sexual relationship with the partner: because of the lack of this universal formula, every individual has to invent a fantasy of his own, a 'private' formula for the sexual relationship – for a man, the relationship with a woman is possible only inasmuch as she fits his formula. The formula of the Wolf Man, Freud's famous patient, consisted of 'a woman, viewed from behind, on her hands and knees, and washing or cleaning something on the ground in front of her' – the view of a woman in this position automatically gave rise to love. In the case of John Ruskin, the formula which followed the model of old Greek and Roman statues led to a tragicomic disappointment when Ruskin, on his wedding night, caught sight of the pubic hair that is not found on statues – this discovery made him totally impotent, since he was convinced that his wife was a monster. In Jennifer Lynch's film *Boxing Helena*, the fantasy ideal is none other than Venus de Milo herself: the hero kidnaps the beloved girl and performs an operation on her in order to make her fit the ideal, and thus to render a sexual relationship possible (he cuts off her hands, makes a scar to match the place where the statue is truncated, etc.).

26. For a detailed development of this homology, see Chapter 2 of Žižek, *Tarrying with the Negative*; and Joan Copjec, *Read My Desire*, Cambridge, MA: MIT Press 1994.

27. Gilles Deleuze, *The Logic of Sense*, New York: Columbia University Press 1990, p. 75.

28. For that reason, man as the love object in the songs of woman troubadours is never posited in a symmetrical way as the inaccessible Ideal-Thing, but obeys a thoroughly different economy.

29. A fatal misunderstanding must be avoided here: Hegel's 'concrete universal' does not designate a particular, 'concrete' state that finally fits the universal notion of State, but the totality of the failed attempts to realize the notion of State.

30. Another example here is the most notorious case of universal judgement: 'All men are mortal'. In its implicit libidinal-symbolic economy, such a judgement always excludes *me* – that is, the absolute singularity of the speaker *qua* subject of enunciation. It is easy to ascertain, from the observer's safe distance, that 'everybody' is mortal; however, this very statement involves the exception of its subject of enunciation – as Lacan puts it, in the unconscious, nobody truly believes that *he* is mortal; this knowledge is disavowed, we are dealing with a fetishistic splitting: 'I know very well that I am mortal, but still. . .'.

Appendix

Taking Sides:
A Self-Interview

The dialogue that follows is a game in which I, in the guise of the questioner, endeavour to assume the role of the Lacanian 'big Other': to look at myself through the eyes of 'common knowledge', raising all the questions that seem to bother 'common knowledge' apropos of Lacanian theory.

Subjective Destitution

In what consists the most elementary impact of psychoanalysis, of the psychoanalytic treatment, as a specific subjective experience? It is customary to maintain that psychoanalysis undermines the subject's Narcissism by way of enabling him to experience his decentrement, his dependence on the Other....

All this takes place even before psychoanalysis proper, in the so-called preliminary encounters. This 'correction of the subjective attitude', as Lacan calls it, is double: the subject has to recognize an inherent impossibility in what appears to him as a contingent obstacle, a result of unfortunate circumstances, *and* – the same operation in reverse – to recognize success in what appears as his failure. Suffice it to recall the rhetorical figures that abound in theoretical texts: 'The constraints of the present book do not allow for a more detailed account...'; 'Here, we can only delineate the contours of what must be fully substantiated in a more thorough conceptual development...'; and so on – in all such cases one can rest assured that this reference to external, empirical limitations is an excuse concealing the inherent impossibility: the 'more detailed account' is a priori impossible – or, more precisely, it would undermine the very thesis it is supposed to account for. An exemplary case of such a symptomatic postponement is the titles of numerous Marxist books from the sixties that display an obsessive fear of confronting the 'thing itself' – never directly 'Theory of Ideology' but always '*Towards* a Theory of

Ideology', '*Elements For a Future* Theory of Ideology', and so forth.

As for the opposite act of recognizing success in apparent failure rather than relying on the standard example of a slip in which the subject's true desire manifests itself, let us turn to the politico-ideological domain. Officially, the goal of 'socialist education' in Communist Eastern Europe was to produce a new Socialist Man – honest, dedicated to the well-being of society, sacrificing his narrow personal interests for the sake of the future, and so on. Its actual result, of course, was a cynical individual who, while publicly partaking in the official ideological ritual, maintained his inner distance, mocked the imbecility of Socialist ideology and confined his true interest to private pleasures. So, measured by its proclaimed goals, 'socialist education' was a dismal failure. What, however, if its true goal was precisely such a de-politicized cynical individual, since he fitted the reproduction of the existing power relations perfectly? Much more dangerous than the cynic was somebody who naively believed in the system and who, since he was prone to take it at its word, was already halfway to being a dissident. I personally knew a woman in ex-Yugoslavia who lost her job at the Central Committee because of her sincere belief in self-management: the cynical Party bureaucrats felt threatened by her. . . .

Is not this Narcissistic loss – or, more radically, 'subjective destitution' – a sublime version of the utter humiliation, 'de-subjectivization', described by Orwell – among others – in Nineteen Eighty-four, *whose exemplary case in 'reality' was the Stalinist monster-trials? Does it not designate the shift that forces the subject to renounce the inner kernel of his or her dignity?*

Why not? In a very precise way, things are *even worse* in psychoanalysis than in Stalinism. Yes, we do have to renounce the secret treasure in ourselves, the *agalma* that confers on us our innermost dignity – all those things so dear to personalism; we do have to undergo the conversion of this treasure into a 'piece of shit', into a stinking excrement, and identify with it. However – and this is why things get even worse in psychoanalysis – the analysand has to accomplish this conversion *by himself*, without the alibi of monstrous circumstances that can be blamed for it.

The 'subjective destitution' involved in the position of the analyst *qua objet a* may be illustrated by a story from the American antebellum South. In the whorehouses of old New Orleans, the black servant was not perceived as a person, so that the white couple of the prostitute and her client was not at all disturbed when the servant entered the room to deliver drinks – they simply went on with their copulation, since the servant's gaze did not count as the gaze of another person. And in a sense, it is the same with the analyst: we rid ourselves of all our shame when we talk to him, we are able to confide in him the innermost secrets of our loves and hatreds, although our relationship with him is entirely 'impersonal', lacking the intimacy of true friendship.

This dialectics of intimacy is in general extremely interesting: true sexual intimacy is not achieved when, in the moonlit darkness, my partner and I yield to sensual passion – I expose myself far more radically to my partner when I disclose the intimacy of my enjoyment to his or her gaze that maintains a distance towards me. *Vulgari eloquentia,* far greater trust in my partner is needed when I let him or her observe me during masturbation than when I perform the act of copulation with him or her. Perhaps this is why Brecht had a preference for non-simultaneous orgasm: first you, so that I can observe you, and then you can observe me reaching my climax. . . . Trust is needed here, since I expose myself to the danger that in the eyes of the observing partner I shall all of a sudden become *ridiculous* – to an indifferent observer, the sexual act cannot but appear a meaningless repetition of mechanical gestures, accompanied by painful sighing. For the sexual act to appear ridiculous, it is enough to assume a Formanesque distance towards it – what I have in mind here is the procedure of 'extraneation' applied by Miloš Forman in his early Czech films, the procedure that relies on the 'malevolent neutrality of the camera'. Forman himself evoked the shift in our reception that occurs when, all of a sudden, the sound of a TV set fails due to some mechanical malfunction: the impassioned speech of a politician or the dazzling operatic aria changes into an absurd, comic twisting and waving of hands. . . .

Let us, however, return to the unique figure of the analyst. The analyst is also 'impersonal' in that he is *absolutely responsible for the effects of his words.* When the outcome of our action is the opposite of what we had in mind, we, ordinary people, each with his or her own limitations, have the right to say, 'Oh my God, this is not what I wanted!'; the analyst, on the contrary, is somebody who is *never* allowed to take refuge in saying 'This is not what I had in mind!'. For that reason the analytic discourse – social link – is something exceptional and extremely surprising. What is so unusual about it is not that it might well disappear; far more unusual is the fact that it emerged at all.

How does this 'subjective destitution' affect the position of the Master?

In one of the recent 'corporate nightmare' thrillers, *The Virtual Boss,* a company is actually (and unbeknownst to the employees) run by a computer that suddenly 'runs amok', grows beyond control and starts to implement measures against the top managers (it instigates conflicts among them, gives orders for them to be fired, etc.); finally, it sets in motion a deadly plot against its own programmer. . . . The 'truth' of this plot is that a Master is, in a sense, always virtual – a contingent person who fills out a preordained place in the structure, while the game is actually run by the 'big Other' *qua* impersonal symbolic machine. This is what a Master is forced to take note of via the experience of 'subjective destitution': that he is by definition an impostor, an imbecile who misperceives as the outcome of his decisions what actually ensues from the automatic run of the symbolic machine.

And ultimately, the same holds for every subject: in his autobiography, Althusser writes that he has been persecuted all his adult life by the notion that he does not exist, by the fear that others will become aware of his non-existence – that is, of the fact that he is an impostor who is only pretending to exist. His great fear after the publication of *Reading Capital*, for example, was that some perspicacious critic would reveal the scandalous fact that the main author of this book does not exist. . . .

In a sense, this is what psychoanalysis is about: the psychoanalytic cure is effectively over when the subject loses this fear and *freely assumes his own non-existence*. Thus psychoanalysis is the exact opposite of subjectivist solipsism: in contrast to the notion that I can be absolutely certain only of the ideas in my own mind, whereas the existence of reality outside myself is already an inconclusive inference, psychoanalysis claims that reality outside myself definitely exists; the problem, rather, is that *I myself* do not exist. . . .

In this precise sense, 'subjective destitution' is closely linked to another key Hegelian–Lacanian motif, that of the 'sacrifice of the sacrifice'. In one of Roald Dahl's macabre stories, a wife whose husband died young dedicates her entire life to him by assuming the role of the guardian of his memory, elevating him into an idealized lost object; twenty years later, however, she accidentally discovers that just before his death her husband had become involved in a passionate love affair, and had intended to leave her. . . . This void in which the wife finds herself is the Hegelian 'loss of the loss'. Herein resides the interest of Kieslowski's *Blue*, the first part of his trilogy *The Colours*, in which the wife of a famous composer (Juliette Binoche), traumatized by the loss of her husband and son in a car accident, discovers all of a sudden that her husband had a mistress whom he loved and who is now, after his death, expecting his child; the ethical beauty of the film resides in the fact that the wife, on this unexpected discovery, does not go into a fury against the mistress but becomes reconciled with her and, in a way, even rejoices at the prospect of her late husband's child. . . .

Incidentally, *Blue* is also of great interest on account of a conspicuous formal feature: the uncommon use of fade-out. That is to say, the standard use of fade-out is to mark the passage from one sequence (spatio–temporal continuity) to another. In *Blue*, however, one passes from one sequence to the next via a direct cut; in the midst of a continuous conversation the shot of the speaker fades out all of a sudden, and the following fade-in brings us back to a continuation of the *same* shot. Here we are dealing with something that resembles the Lacanian practice of the variable ending of the psychoanalytic session: the analyst's gesture of signalling that the session is over, like Kieslowski's fade-out, does not follow an externally imposed logic (the preordained fifty-minute span), it cuts all of a sudden in the midst of the scene and thus acts as an interpretative gesture *sui generis* by highlighting an element in the analysand's speech-flow (or, in Kieslowski, in the speech of a person on the screen) as especially significant.

So there is, in this Lacanian 'subjective destitution', at least a distant echo of the renunciation of the 'little fly of subjectivity' – that is, of the demand for complete self-instrumentalization – that the Stalinist Party addressed to the subject? After all, most of the Lacanians around Jacques-Alain Miller, at least the first generation of his fellow-combatants, are ex-Maoists. . . .

One should acknowledge openly what many a critique of the alleged 'totalitarian', 'Stalinist' nature of Lacanian communities makes a big deal of by allusion: yes, the 'spirit', the structuring principle, which expressed itself distortedly in the Stalinist Party, found its proper form in the Lacanian community of analysts, in the reversal of the *travail du transfert*, the work of transference that occurs during a psychoanalytic cure, into the *transfert du travail*, the 'transference of work' *qua* the absolute externalization of the result of the analysand's self-analysis in 'mathem', in a theoretical formulation that is released from the last shadow of 'initiation' and, as such, wholly transparent to the community of analysts. In this precise sense, *passe* equals the dissolution of transference. While he is in transference, the analysand recognizes in every analyst's utterance or gesture a *de te fabula narratur*: 'he is really speaking about myself, what he is aiming at is my *agalma*, the ineffable secret of my being'. The analytic cure reaches its conclusion when the analysand is able to formulate the result of his analysis in a mathem that no longer 'speaks about himself' but is, in a radical sense, impersonal. Therein resides the wager of *passe*: to confer upon the most intimate kernel of our being the form of an anonymous 'meaningless' formula in which no unique subjectivity resounds.

The choice here is unavoidable – that is to say, what occurs after *passe*, when the psychoanalysis is over? On the one side is the 'obscurantist' choice: *passe* as an intimate experience, an ecstatic moment of authenticity that can only be transmitted from person to person in an initiating act of communication. On the other is the 'Stalinist' choice: *passe* as an act of total externalization through which I irrevocably renounce the ineffable precious kernel in me that makes me a unique being, and leave myself unreservedly to the analytic community. This homology between

171

the Lacanian analyst and the Stalinist Communist can be unfolded further: for example, the Lacanian analyst, like the Stalinist Communist, is in a sense 'infallible' – in contrast to ordinary people, he does not 'live in error', the error (the ideological delusion) is not an inherent constituent of his speech. So when he is empirically 'wrong', the causes are purely external: 'fatigue', 'nervous overcharge', and so on. What he needs is not theoretical enlightenment of his error but simply to 'take a rest' and restore his health. . . .

Does not this 'infallibility' of the Lacanian analyst imply that Lacanian discourse is totally dominated, permeated, by the Master-Signifier?

Quite the contrary: paradoxical as it may sound, it implies that the analytic community is the only community capable of passing by the Master-Signifier. What is the Master-Signifier, strictly speaking? The signifier of transference. Its exemplary case occurs when, while reading a text or listening to a person, we assume that every sentence harbours some hidden profound meaning – and since we assume it in advance, we usually also find it. Let us take the following passage from M.O'C. Drury's memoirs of Wittgenstein:

> The next day being fine and sunny, we walked over the hill to Tully sands.
>   WITTGENSTEIN: *The colours of the landscape here are marvellous. Why even the surface of the road is coloured.*
>   When we reached the sands we walked up and down by the sea.
>   WITTGENSTEIN: *I can well understand why children love sand.*[1]

Quite ordinary, everyday remarks – yet the way they are quoted leads us to search them for some undreamt-of depth. . . . That is to say, would anybody bother to write them down if they were made by his aged, senile uncle? Such a transferential relationship is what the community of Lacanian analysts avoid via their 'infallibility': this community is not founded upon some *supposed* knowledge, it is simply a community of those who *know.*

In short: it is the 'subjective destitution', the subject's complete self-externalization, that makes the Master superfluous: a Master is a Master only in so far as I, his subject, am not completely externalized; only in so far as I contain somewhere deep in myself *agalma*, the secret treasure that accounts for the unique character of my personality – a Master becomes a Master by recognizing me in my uniqueness. The constitutive illusion of religious discourse, for example, is that God addresses each individual by name: I know God has me precisely in his mind. . . .

Why Popular Culture?

Two leitmotivs of your approach to Lacan are already discernible in what you have said. The first is that you do not conceal Lacan's inconsistencies: you seem always to be on the lookout for unexpected shifts in his position. Your Lacan is a theoretician engaged in continuous polemics against himself, his own previous statements. . . .

True, the fundamental presupposition of my approach to Lacan is the utter incongruity of a 'synchronous' reading of his texts and seminars: the only way to comprehend Lacan is to approach his work as a work in progress, as a succession of attempts to seize the same persistent traumatic kernel. The shifts in Lacan's work become manifest the moment one concentrates on his great negative theses: 'There is no Other of the Other', 'The desire of the analyst is not a pure desire'. . . . Upon encountering such a thesis, one must always ask the simple question: who *is* this idiot who is claiming that *there is* an Other of the Other, that the desire of the analyst *is* a pure desire, and so on? There is, of course, only one answer: *Lacan himself a couple of years ago.* The only way to approach Lacan, therefore, is to read 'Lacan contre Lacan' (the title of the 1993–4 Jacques-Alain Miller seminar).

Apropos of the first thesis, 'There is no Other of the Other', for example, one should bear in mind that it appears in Lacan's work rather late, at the beginning of the 1960s, as a correlative to the notion of the inconsistent Other: 'There is no Other of the Other' since the big Other, the symbolic order, lacks the ultimate signifier that would guarantee its consistency. In clear contrast, the fundamental thesis of Lacan's Seminar III on Psychoses (1954–5) is precisely that there *is* an Other of the Other, namely the Name-of-the-Father *qua* the central signifier that guarantees the consistency of the symbolic field. And the same goes for the thesis 'The desire of the analyst is not a pure desire' from the very last page of Seminar XI on The Four Fundamental Concepts: this thesis implicitly argues against Seminar VII on the Ethics of Psychoanalysis, in which Antigone's desire is determined precisely as a pure desire, as a desire purified of all 'pathological' imaginary content, as a desire whose sole impetus is the signifier's cut [*coupure*]. Consequently, the desire of the analyst is here also determined as a purely symbolic desire (purity is, of its very nature, always symbolic) – that is, the analyst stands here for the big Other, not yet for the 'small other', *objet a*, the foreign body, the stain, within the symbolic order.

The tension internal to Seminar VII on the Ethics of Psychoanalysis concerns the relationship between desire and law. On the one hand, we have the 'Pauline' notion of the antagonistic or 'transgressist' relationship between Law and desire: via a reference to Saint Paul, Lacan claims that an object becomes the object of desire only in so far as it is prohibited (there is no incestuous desire prior to the prohibition of incest, etc.) – desire itself needs Law, its prohibition, as the obstacle to be transgressed. At a deeper level, however, there is the far more radical notion of a direct identity of desire and Law – the claim that Kantian moral Law *is* desire in its pure state. In both cases we find ourselves 'beyond the pleasure principle', in the domain of a drive that persists and forces its way irrespective of the subject's well-being.

Herein resides the sense of Lacan's 'Kant avec Sade': Sade's assertion of a boundless desire involves an imperative that fully meets Kant's rigorous criteria of an ethical act. This is how Lacan subverts the opposition that provides the axis of the entire history of psychoanalysis: either the resigned-conservative acceptance of Law/Prohibition, of renunciation, of 'repression', as the *sine qua non* of civilization; or the endeavour to 'liberate' drives from the constraints of Law. There is a Law which, far from being opposed to desire, is the Law of desire itself, the imperative that sustains desire, that tells the subject not to give up his or her desire – the only guilt this law acknowledges is the betrayal of desire.

Yet another crucial shift in Lacan's teaching concerns the relationship between the unconscious and language. One of the classical *topoi* of 1950s and 1960s Lacan is 'ça parle', it speaks: the unconscious is 'structured like a language', the procedures of the dream work (condensation, displacement) correspond to metaphor and metonymy as the two fundamental rhetorical figures. It is deeply significant, however, that Lacan never develops this homology in full detail – all we get is the usual unspecified claim that we are dealing with a fact that is obvious to anyone who approaches the problem with an open mind, accompanied by a vague reference to the example of Signorelli....

In Seminar XX (*Encore*), Lacan radically shifts his position all of a sudden (probably under the influence of Lyotard's *Figures, Discours*): in *lalangue* ('llanguage'), 'it' does not speak, 'it' enjoys; in psychoanalytic decipherment of the formations of the unconscious, we are dealing not with an interpretation that aims at attaining the hidden meaning, but with the display of the ciphers of enjoyment – Rat Man's formula 'Gleisamen', for example, clearly provides the matrix of his enjoyment in relationship to his Lady. *Lalangue* operates not at the level of a differential signifying structure, but at the level of wordplays, homonymies, and so on, which is why Lacan is on the lookout for new terms that would differentiate *lalangue* from the order of the signifier – witness his unexpected reaffirmation of 'sign', his use of 'letter' as opposed to 'signifier'....

Incidentally, one should not confuse enjoyment with pleasure here. If their opposition seems unclear, suffice it to recall the difference between the Protestant and the Catholic attitude towards adultery. In Catholic countries, adultery – in so far as it remains concealed from the public eye – provides pleasure without any guilt; the only problem is to keep it secret, since 'what you don't know doesn't hurt'. In Protestant countries, on the contrary, adulterous partners feel terribly guilty; they experience their act as a monstrosity that threatens to upset the balance of the natural order itself – and this very feeling of guilt increases their enjoyment immensely. . . .

The second leitmotiv of your approach to Lacan is your obsession with providing examples from the domain of popular culture. . . .

I resort to these examples above all in order to avoid pseudo-Lacanian jargon, and to achieve the greatest possible clarity not only for my readers but also for myself – the idiot for whom I endeavour to formulate a theoretical point as clearly as possible is ultimately myself. For me an example from popular culture has the same functional role as the two *passeurs* in the Lacanian procedure of *passe*: in the psychoanalytic cure, I can effectively claim that I have gained access to the truth about my desire only when I am able to formulate this truth in such a way that when I pass it to the two *passeurs* – two idiots, two average men who stand for the inherent imbecility of the big Other – they in turn are able to transmit it to the *comité de la passe* without losing any ingredient of the message. In a somewhat homologous way, I am convinced of my proper grasp of some Lacanian concept only when I can translate it successfully into the inherent imbecility of popular culture. Therein – in this full acceptance of the externalization in an imbecilic medium, in this radical refusal of any initiating secrecy – resides the ethics of finding a proper word.

Let us take the Kantian notion of infinite judgement – how much more enlightening than a pure conceptual exposition is a simple reference to the scene from *Citizen Kane* in which Kane answers the reproach that he incites the lower classes to disobedience, and arouses their low passions, by claiming that he merely speaks for them and articulates their grievances – to which he adds, significantly: 'I have means and wealth to speak for them – if I don't do it, *then somebody else without means and wealth will do it for them!*' In short, the determinate negation would have been: 'If I don't do it, they will have nobody to speak for them and articulate their grievances', whereas the infinite negation denies the very common presupposition of positive and negative judgement – that one has to have adequate means and wealth if one is to speak for the underprivileged; so the infinite negation announces the uncanny spectre of revolution. . . . Or let us take the other crucial Kantian notion, that of radical Evil – does it not offer the key to *Macbeth*? That is to say, the main enigma of *Macbeth* is the motivational void of its main character: why does Macbeth accomplish the terrible act of regicide, although he lacks the proper psychological motivation? At the beginning of this century, A.C. Bradley solved this mystery when he observed that Macbeth commits his crime as if it were 'an appalling duty'.[2]

One of the common prejudices about theory and examples from high art or popular culture is that too much knowledge somehow damages our enjoyment. If we go to watch a film with an excessive baggage of theoretical preconceptions about what we are about to see, does this not spoil our spontaneous enjoyment of the show?

The most persuasive argument against this prejudice is provided by the way we relate to *film noir* or to Hitchcock's films: this nostalgic enjoyment is always-already theoretically mediated. Today, it is only theory that can teach us how to enjoy them – if we approach them directly, they necessarily strike us as naive, ridiculous, 'inedible'....

Another worn-out reproach concerns the alleged incapacity of psychoanalytic interpretation of works of art to explain their specificity – 'Even if Dostoevsky was really an epileptic with an unresolved paternal authority complex, not every epileptic with an unresolved paternal authority complex was Dostoevsky'....

It is somewhat strange to consider this worn-out commonplace as a reproach against Lacan, since apropos of courtly love and troubadour poetry, Lacan says exactly the same thing: the crucial thing to bear in mind is that in the era of troubadours the subject had at his disposal the medium of poetry and courtly love as a social *institution* by means of which he was able to articulate, to symbolize, his traumatic relationship to the Lady *qua* Thing. True, every epileptic with an unresolved paternal authority complex is not Dostoevsky; however, we search in vain for the answer to the enigma of why it was precisely the epileptic Dostoevsky who became such a great artist in Dostoevsky's unique psyche; this answer is to be found 'outside', in the radically non-psychological symbolic network that formed the space of inscription of his activity. This network decided that Dostoevsky's way of articulating his psychic traumas should function as great art – it is easy to imagine how, in a different symbolic space, this same Dostoevsky would be considered a confused, foolish scribbler.

Fantasy and the *objet petit a*

*OK, so we have to renounce the fetish of the hidden Treasure responsible for my
uniqueness, and to accept radical externalization in the symbolic medium.
However, does not the uniqueness of my personality find an outlet in* fantasy, *in
the absolutely particular, non-universalizable way I stage desire* . . . ?

Yes, but *whose* desire? Not *mine*. What we encounter in the very core of
fantasy is the relationship to the desire of the Other, to the latter's
opacity: *the desire staged in fantasy is not mine but the desire of the Other.*
Fantasy is a way for the subject to answer the question of what object he
is in the eyes of the Other, in the Other's desire – that is, what does the
Other see in him, what role does he play in the Other's desire? A child,
for example, endeavours to dissolve, by means of his fantasy, the enigma
of the role he plays as the medium of the interactions between his
mother and his father, the enigma of how mother and father fight their
battles and settle their accounts through him. In short, fantasy is the
highest proof of the fact that the subject's desire is the desire of the
Other. It is at this level that we have to locate the obsessional neurotic's
version of *Cogito ergo sum*: 'What I *think* I am, that is, what I am in my own
eyes, for myself, I also *am* for the Other, in the discourse of the Other,
in my social-symbolic, intersubjective identity.'[3] The obsessional neurotic
aims at complete control over what he is for the Other: he wants to
prevent, by means of compulsive rituals, the Other's desire from
emerging in its radical heterogeneity, as incommensurable with what he
thinks he is for himself.

The key ingredient of obsessional neurosis is the conviction that the
knot of reality is held together only through the subject's compulsive
activity: if the obsessive ritual is not properly performed, reality will
disintegrate. We encounter this economy among the ancient Incas, who
believed that their negligence in performing human sacrifices would
result in a disturbance of the natural circuit (the sun would not rise
again, etc.); and in the caring mother, pillar of the family, convinced
that, after her death, family life will break apart. (The 'catastrophe' they
are all trying to avoid is, of course, nothing but the emergence of desire.)
We escape the obsessional economy the moment we become aware that
eppur si muove: everything is not dependent on me, life goes on even if
I don't do anything. . . . In this respect, the obsessional neurotic is the
very opposite of the hysteric: he believes that everything hinges on him,
he cannot accept the fact that his disappearance would not change much
in the normal run of things; whereas the hysteric perceives himself as a
neutral observer, a victim of unfortunate circumstances that are independent of his will – what he cannot accept is the fact that the

circumstances whose victim he is can reproduce themselves only through his active participation.

Back to the notion of fantasy: the first thing to do here is to get rid of the simplified notion of fantasy as an idealized image that conceals the underlying horrendous reality – the 'corporatist fantasy of a harmonious society free of antagonisms', for example. The 'fundamental fantasy' is, on the contrary, an entity that is exceedingly traumatic: it articulates the subject's relationship towards enjoyment, towards the traumatic kernel of his being, towards something that the subject is never able to acknowledge fully, to become familiar with, to integrate into his symbolic universe. The public disclosure of this phantasmic kernel entails an unbearable shame that leads to the subject's *aphanisis*, self-obliteration.

The object of fantasy is the famous objet petit a . . .

One should always bear in mind that *objet petit a* emerges to solve the deadlock of how the subject is to find support in the big Other (the symbolic order). The first answer, of course, is: in a signifier – that is, by identifying himself with a signifier in the big Other, a signifier that then represents him for the other signifiers. However, in so far as the big Other is in itself inconsistent, not-all, structured around a lack, a constitutive failure, a further possibility opens up for the subject to find a niche in the Other by identifying with this very void in its midst, with the point at which the Other fails. And *objet petit a* positivizes, gives body to, this void in the big Other: we encounter the object where the word fails.

Lacan's concept of the *objet a* thus inverts the standard notion of the symbolic order (signifier) as the agency that mediates, interposes itself, between the subject and the reality of objects: for Lacan, the subject and the Other overlap in the object (or, to put it in the terms of set theory: object is the intersection of $ and the big Other). 'Object' gives body to the void that is the subject *qua* $, and to the void that gapes in the midst of the big Other. Here again we are dealing with the topology of 'curved' space in which the inside coincides with the outside: identification with the object is not external to the Symbolic, it is an identification with the ex-timate kernel of the Symbolic itself, with that which is in the symbolic more than symbolic, with the void at its very heart.

The first thing one should always bear in mind apropos of *objet petit a* is that, as is often the case with Lacan's categories, we are dealing with a concept that *comprises itself and its own opposite and/or dissimulation. Objet a* is simultaneously the pure lack, the void around which the desire turns and which, as such, causes the desire, *and* the imaginary element which conceals this void, renders it invisible by filling it out. The point, of course, is that there is no lack without the element filling it out: *the filler sustains what it dissimulates.*

Rather than a pure 'this', the object without properties, *a* is a bundle of properties that lacks existence. In a brilliant essay, Stephen Jay Gould – a Lacanian biologist if ever there was one – extrapolates *ad absurdum* the long-term tendency in the relationship between price and quantity of Hershey chocolate bars. For some time the price stays the same, while the quantity gradually diminishes; then, all of a sudden, the price goes up and, with it, the quantity, yet the new quantity is still less than what we had gained with the previous rise.... The quantity of chocolate bar over a temporal span thus follows a zigzag: it gradually declines, then it suddenly jumps up, then it gradually declines again, and so on, with the long-term tendency towards decline. By extrapolating this tendency to the senseless extreme, we can calculate not only the exact moment when the quantity will reach zero – that is, when we will get a nicely wrapped void – but also how much this void will cost. This void – which, none the less, is nicely wrapped and has a definite price – is an almost perfect metaphor for the Lacanian *objet petit a*.

In this precise sense *objet a* is the anal object. In Lacanian theory, one usually conceives of the anal object as a signifying element: what effectively matters is the role of shit in the intersubjective economy – does it function as proof to the Other of the child's self-control and discipline, of his complying with the Other's demand, as a gift to the Other ...? However, prior to this symbolic status of a gift, and so on, the excrement is *objet a* in the precise sense of the non-symbolizable surplus that remains after the body is symbolized, inscribed into the symbolic network: the problem of the anal stage resides precisely in how we are to dispose of this leftover. For that reason, Lacan's thesis that animal became human the moment it confronted the problem of what to do with its excrement is to be taken literally and seriously: in order for this unpleasant surplus to pose a problem, the body must already have been caught up in the symbolic network.

It is no less crucial to avoid confusing *objet a* with an ordinary material object. Even in the late 1950s, Lacan distinguished between ordinary and sublime body – a distinction that is perhaps best exemplified by the subjective position of a *nun*. A nun radically refuses the status of the sexual object for another human being – this refusal, however, concerns only her ordinary, material body, while enabling her to offer all the more passionately her sublime body, that which is 'in her more than herself', to God *qua* absolute Other.

One should also take into account the radically *intersubjective* status of *objet a: objet a* is something 'in me more than myself' that *the other* sees in me. In Fritz Lang's *Secret Beyond the Door*, this is how Joan Bennett describes her traumatic experience of Michael Redgrave's gazing at her: 'Suddenly I felt that someone was watching me. ... I felt eyes touching me like fingers. There was a current flowing between us. Warm and sweet. And frightening too. Because he saw behind my make-up what no one had ever seen. Something I didn't know was there.' She did not know it, and was able to discern it only *through the mediation of the other's gaze.*

Is not the ultimate example of objet petit a *the Hitchcockian object . . .*

. . . that is found not only in Hitchcock, but also where one would not expect to find it – say, in *Jurassic Park. Jurassic Park* was dismissed by most critics as a techno-spectacle whose sole interest resides in special effects, whereas the intersubjective relations between the characters remain wholly flat and undeveloped. However, is this really true? What if, here also, evil resides in the very gaze that perceives evil – that is to say, what if the dismissal of *Jurassic Park* as techno-*kitsch* expresses not so much the quality of the film as, rather, the limitation of the critical gaze itself?

The first feature that should make us more attentive is the film's unusually static character: the action soon 'gets stuck' in one place with the dinosaurs' repeated attacks. If *Jurassic Park* is a spectacle, then, it represents the paradox of a chamber spectacle. That is to say: my thesis is that *Jurassic Park* is a chamber drama about the trauma of fatherhood in the style of the early Antonioni or Bergman. This dimension becomes visible the moment we direct our attention to the Hitchcockian object in the film: the tiny dinosaur bone used by Sam Neill in the first scene to strengthen his verbal bash against a kid who is plaguing him with questions. This bone, in its role as Hitchcockian object (it is not in Crichton's novel; it was added by Spielberg), condenses Neill's parenthood trauma, his refusal to assume the paternal function. And what are the attacking dinosaurs if not this same object, overblown into a resuscitated monster that materializes the paternal superego – that is, the father's destructive fury directed at his offspring (analogous to Hitchcock's *The Birds*, in which the birds materialize the maternal superego)?

For that reason, the other key scene of the film occurs when, after the fight with the evil, carnivorous dinosaurs, Neill and the two children take refuge in a huge tree. Up there, in the safe haven of the branches, Neill becomes reconciled with them and accepts his parenthood, his symbolic role of father – his conversion is signalled by the fact that once the three of them fall asleep, the tiny bone, the evil object, falls from his pocket to the ground, and is lost to their view. No wonder, then, that the next morning the atmosphere changes miraculously into one of blissful peace: the dinosaurs that now approach the tree are good, herbivorous, since the paternal fury has passed away. In terms of its intersubjective symbolic economy, the film is now over – all that follows is an inconsistent mixture of fragments from different genres that lacks any coherent libidinal impact.

It is also by no means difficult to establish the link with Spielberg's other films, since most of them, from *Empire of the Sun* up to *Schindler's List*, are centred on the trauma of fatherhood. *ET*, for example: what is ET itself if not a kind of 'vanishing mediator' that enables the fatherless family to reconstitute itself into a complete family (ET shows up in a family deserted by the father, who eloped to Mexico; at the film's end, the 'good' scientist clearly assumes the role of the future father – he already has his arm round the mother's shoulders ...)?

How does objet petit a differ from the primordial Thing?

Perhaps the best way to distinguish them is via a reference to the philosophical distinction between ontological and ontic levels. The status of the Thing is purely ontic, it stands for an irreducible excess of the ontic that eludes *Lichtung*, the ontological clearance within which entities appear: the Thing is the paradox of an ontic X in so far as it is not yet an 'inner-worldly' entity, appearing within the transcendental-ontological horizon. In contrast, the status of *a* is purely ontological – that is to say, *a* as the fantasy-object is an object that is an empty form, a frame that determines the status of positive entities. (This is how we are to interpret Lacan's statement according to which fantasy is the ultimate support of our 'sense of reality'.) Therein resides the enigma of the relationship between the Thing and *a*: how can the surplus of the ontic over its ontological horizon convert into the surplus of the ontological; how can the plenitude of the Real convert into a pure lack, into an object that coincides with its own absence and, as such, keeps open the clearing within which ontic entities can emerge?

Psychoanalysis, Marxism, Philosophy

We have now reached the theme of philosophy. The first impression aroused by your work is that it endeavours to resuscitate Freudo–Marxism – clearly an outdated, superseded enterprise. ...

The link that connects Marxism and psychoanalysis is sufficiently justified by the parallel between the Marxist political movement and the psychoanalytic movement. In both cases, we are dealing with the paradox of an enlightened (non-traditional) knowledge founded in the transferential relationship to the unsurpassable figure of the founder (Marx, Freud): knowledge does not progress through gradual refutation and reformulation of the initial claims, but through a series of 'returns to ... (Marx, Freud)'. In both cases, we are dealing with a field of knowledge that is *inherently antagonistic*: errors are not simply external to the true knowledge, they are not something that we can cast off once we reach the truth, and as such of purely historical interest – that is, irrelevant for the present state of knowledge (as is the case in physics, biology, etc.). In Marxism, as in psychoanalysis, truth literally emerges through error, which is why in both cases the struggle with 'revisionism' is an inherent part of the theory itself. The entire 'structure' of the relationship between the field of knowledge and the subjectivity of the 'scientist' involved in it differs radically from contemporary positive science as well as from traditional forms of knowledge (initiating wisdom, etc.).

In short, in Marxism as well as in psychoanalysis we encounter what Althusser calls *topique*, the topical character of thought. This topicality does not concern only or even primarily the fact that the object of thought has to be conceived as a complex Whole of instances that cannot be reduced to some identical underlying Ground (the intricate interplay of base and superstructure in Marxism; of Ego, Superego and Id in psychoanalysis). 'Topicality', rather, refers to *the topical character of the 'thought' itself*: theory is always part of the conjunction into which it intervenes. The 'object' of Marxism is society, yet 'class struggle in theory' means that the ultimate theme of Marxism is the 'material force of ideas' – that is, the way Marxism itself *qua* revolutionary theory transforms its object (brings about the emergence of the revolutionary subject, etc.). This is analogous to psychoanalysis, which is also not simply a theory of its 'object' (the unconscious) but a theory whose inherent mode of existence involves the transformation of its object (via interpretation in the psychoanalytic cure).

Both theories, therefore, are fully justified in answering their critics with what an external gaze necessarily misperceives as a case of *petitio principii*: opposition to Marxism is not a simple refutation of a mistaken theory that makes use of the neutral tools of rational argumentation but is itself part of the class struggle, and expresses the resistance of the ruling ideology to the revolutionary movement – like resistance to psychoanalysis, which itself partakes in the mechanisms of repression....

In short, a 'topic' theory fully acknowledges the short circuit between the theoretical frame and an element within this frame: theory itself is a moment of the totality that is its 'object'. For that reason, Marxism and psychoanalysis are two exemplary cases of a thought that endeavours to grasp its own limitation and dependence, a thought that continually raises the question of its own position of enunciation. In contrast to the comfortable evolutionary position – always ready to admit the limitation and relative character of its own propositions, yet speaking from a safe distance that enables it to relativize every determinate form of knowledge – Marxism and psychoanalysis are 'infallible' at the level of the enunciated content, precisely in so far as they continually question the very place from which they speak.

My only reproach to Althusser here is that he remains blind to the inherent link between this notion of the 'topicality' of thought and the Hegelian problematic of 'self-consciousness' *qua* reflective inscription of the subject's own activity into his object: Althusser is clearly the victim of a ridiculously inadequate conception of self-consciousness (total self-transparence of the subject, etc.).

The relationship between Marxism and psychoanalysis is none the less marked by an irreducible tension. So, from the point of view of Lacanian psychoanalysis, what is still alive in Marxism?

The first thing to do here is to *invert* the standard form of the question 'What is still alive today of the philosopher X?' (as Adorno has already done apropos of Croce's dull and patronizing title-question 'What is alive and what is dead in Hegel?'). Far more interesting than the question of what of Marx is still alive today, of what Marx still means to us today, is the question of *what our contemporary world itself means in Marx's eyes.*

So Marx's key theoretical achievement, which allowed him to articulate the constitutive imbalance of capitalist society, was his insight into how the very logic of the Universal, of formal equality, involves material inequality – not as a remainder of the past to be gradually abolished, but as a structural necessity inscribed into the very formal notion of equality. There is no 'contradiction' between the bourgeois principle of equality in the eyes of the law, the equivalent exchange between free individuals, and material exploitation and class domination: domination and exploitation are contained in the very notion of legal equality and equivalent exchange; they are a necessary ingredient of *universalized* equivalent exchange (since at this point of universalization, the labour force itself becomes a commodity to be exchanged on the market). This is what Lacan has in mind when he claims that Marx discovered the symptom.

How does (Lacanian) psychoanalysis relate to philosophy at a more general level? Why – if at all – does it need to relate to philosophy?

What Lacan is aiming at is neither a 'philosophical foundation of psychoanalysis' nor the reverse operation of a psychoanalytic 'uncovering' of philosophy as a paranoiac-megalomaniac delusion, but something much more precise: analytic discourse is a kind of 'vanishing mediator' between the traditional, pre-philosophical universe of *mythos* and the philosophical universe of *logos*. In his Seminar VIII, on Transference, Lacan unfolds this in an exemplary way apropos of Socrates as the starting point of philosophy. Socrates – at least, the Socrates of Plato's early dialogues, who claims to know only that he does not know anything, and to be truly versed only in the matter of love – provides the first embodiment of the position of the analyst: far from supplying his dialogical partner – the subject who claims to know or believes he knows – with the true knowledge, he only confronts him with the inconsistency of his position, with the fact that his pretension to knowledge was a mere semblance; more precisely, he forces his partner to acknowledge that his desire (for Truth) has no guarantee in Truth itself, so that the responsibility for his claims falls entirely on him.

Socrates' 'ignorance' is therefore not a simple ignorance of a mortal human to whom eternal Truth-*Logos* is inaccessible, it stands for the inconsistency of the field of *Logos* itself: Socrates does not speak from the place of complete Truth; the place he occupies is that of the inconsistency, the hole in *Logos*. This passing, intermediate experience of what – much later – Lacan called the 'non-existence of the big Other', this experience of the 'barred Other', becomes invisible as soon as the big Other, as it were, heals its wounds and presents itself as the guarantee of Truth. Psychoanalysis – more precisely, the position of the analyst – thus stands in for the ex-timate kernel of philosophy, for its disavowed founding gesture.

In contemporary philosophy, 'metaphysics' is usually conceived as a kind of closure – one has to go beyond it, or at least 'pass through' it and pierce it to its roots. Even when one readily admits that a simple exit is not feasible (Derrida), the aim is still a continuous traversing of the closure. . . .

What if, perhaps, the fundamental metaphysical impetus is preserved in this very drive to traverse the metaphysical closure – what, that is, if this impetus consists in the very striving towards meta-, beyond the given domain perceived as a closure? In other words, is not the only way effectively to step out of metaphysics, perhaps, precisely to renounce the transgressive impulse and to *comply with the closure without restraint*?

The Decentred Subject

Why does Lacan, in spite of all the 'deconstructive' work accomplished by Heidegger, Derrida, and others, maintain the concept of subject?

The entire tradition from pre-philosophy (Parmenides: 'thinking and being are the same') to Heidegger's post-philosophy ('being-in-the-world') relies on a kind of primordial 'accordance' between thought ('man') and world – even in Heidegger, *Dasein* is always-already 'in' the world (or, as Heidegger puts it in his famous reversal of Kant: the scandal is not that the problem of how we can pass from ideas or representations in our mind to objective reality remains unresolved; the true scandal is that this passage is perceived as a problem at all, since it silently presupposes that an unbridgeable distance separates the subject from the world ...).

Lacan, however, insists that our 'being-in-the-world' is already the outcome of a certain primordial choice: the psychotic experience bears witness to the fact that it is quite possible not to choose the world – a psychotic subject is not 'in the world', it lacks the clearance [*Lichtung*] that opens up the world. (For that reason Lacan establishes a link between Heidegger's *Lichtung* and the Freudian *Bejahung*, the primordial 'Yes', the assertion of being, as opposed to the psychotic *Verwerfung*.) In short, 'subject' designates this primordial impossible-forced choice by means of which we choose (or not) to be 'in the world' – that is, to exist as the 'there' of being.

Where, within philosophy, do we encounter the 'decentred', 'barred' subject for the first time?

In Kant's philosophy. The key to this 'decentrement' of the Kantian subject is provided by his notion of the transcendental object. As is well known, the transcendental object – this empty form of the object's unity, a reference to which converts the multitude of sensible affections into a determinate and self-identical object – is possible only against the background of the unity of the apperception of the pure I: the transcendental object is in a sense identical to the I, it is the I itself – the primordial synthesis that 'is' the I – in its externality, in the guise of the objectivity opposed to the I – or, as Hegel would have put it, in its otherness. If, however, we are to dispel the enigma of the transcendental object, it is not sufficient to evoke the fact that the transcendental object is built upon the model of the unity of the I; the true – Hegelian – enigma is, rather, why the transcendental object emerges in the first place – that is to say, why does the I oppose himself to himself in the guise of an external object, why does he project his own shadow outside himself?

The only consistent answer involves a radical splitting of the I: contrary to what Kant himself occasionally claims, one has to maintain unconditionally the difference between the I of pure apperception and his noumenal support, the subject *qua* Thing – the relationship of the transcendental I of pure apperception to the phenomenal I is not the

185

relationship of a noumenal to a phenomenal entity. And it is for that very reason – because the I is not accessible to himself *qua* Thing – that he is, as it were, constitutively predisposed to project his own unity outside himself. In other words, the primordial *Objekt* is not a *Gegen-Stand* but the I itself as a Thing.

Is this problem not solved already, however, in Kant's refutation of (empirical) idealism, by means of which he demonstrates that inner intuition necessarily, in its very notion, comes after *external intuition: if I am to arrive at the intuition of myself* qua *phenomenal I, I must already relate to 'external' reality via my sensible intuition . . . ?*

No, because we are dealing here with the relationship between inner and external intuition – that is to say, between two empirical-phenomenal entities. Fichte, Kant's immediate continuator and critic, would have pointed out that the empirical/finite I, of course, depends on external objectivity, on the non-I opposed to him, yet the absolute I is defined by the very fact that he transcends this opposition. Kant's problem, on the contrary, is how and why the transcendental object *qua* intelligible entity is a necessary correlative not to the empirical I but to the I of pure apperception. My thesis here is that Kant gains the insight into this correlation – into the fact that there is no I of pure apperception without its objectal correlative – precisely on account of his refusal of intellectual intuition: that is, on account of his insistence that in self-consciousness, the I does not gain access to itself *qua* Thing.

To common knowledge, such a notion of self-consciousness cannot but appear strange – why? Because most of us are still victims of the persistent prejudice that reduces self-consciousness in German Idealism to the later, nineteenth-century, problematic of self-consciousness *qua* 'introspection' – that is, of the subject turning his gaze inward and making himself the object of his intuition. It must be pointed out again and again that Kantian self-consciousness consists of an empty formal gesture of reflection that has nothing whatsoever in common with psychological introspection.[4]

Is the transcendental object, then, Kant's version of the Lacanian objet petit a *?*

Yes – the supreme proof is the enigma of Kant's theory of schematism: why must the a priori categories be 'schematized' through their relation to time, if they are to structure the multitude of sensible affects into reality? In other words, the enigma of schematism resides in the fact that, in a sense, it is *superfluous*: if our experience is always-already structured through transcendental categories, if it is never given in a 'pure' state (since without the intervention of categories it would not be experience at all), does not Kant's gesture – which consists first in opposing sensible experience and categories and then in trying to solve the problem of how we can apply categories to experience – amount to an exemplary case of getting entangled in a pseudo-problem?

And yet – in order to convince oneself of the inevitability of schematism, it is enough to draw our attention to the parallel between schematism as the mediator between categories of reason and experience in Kant and fantasy as the mediator between the purely formal symbolic order and reality in Lacan. That is to say, the enigma of the fantasy is strictly homologous to the enigma of schematism: if our experience of reality is always-already structured by the symbolic order, if it is never given in its pure pre-symbolic 'innocence' (since as such it would be the experience not of *reality* but of the impossible Real), then to oppose our experience of reality to the symbolic order and to address the problem of the 'application' of the symbolic network on to reality means to engage oneself in an artificial, self-created pseudo-problem. . . .

Lacan, however, provides the key to this enigma when he conceives of fantasy as strictly correlative to the inconsistency, 'faultiness', of the big Other, the symbolic order. Schematism is needed on account of the 'faultiness' of the transcendental frame; its necessity proves that the transcendental frame itself is bound to the horizon of the subject's finitude and/or temporality. Far from functioning as a kind of auxiliary ladder enabling us to cross the gap that separates our finite sensible experience from the kingdom of the suprasensible categories of pure reason, schematism bears witness to a far more radical splitting: the gap that separates the very a priori transcendental order from the noumenal domain. In other words, schematism attests to the fact that what we experience as the suprasensible domain of pure reason is radically heterogeneous with regard to the inaccessible noumenal order: we, finite subjects, are always dealing with the Suprasensible in the way it appears within the horizon of our finitude/temporality.

You always insist on a close relationship between Kant and Hegel, on how Hegel is 'more Kantian than Kant himself', that which is 'in Kant more than Kant himself'; why, then, do Hegel's appraisals of Kant combine the highest praise (Kant as the first philosopher who formulated the true speculative principle, etc.) with the worst abuse?

Hegel rails at Kant more than at any other philosopher, be it a pre-critical metaphysician or Fichte and Schelling, for the same reason that propels a true Stalinist to rail at the Trotskyites more than at bourgeois liberals – because a Trotskyite is, in a sense, infinitely closer to him. Hegel grows furious precisely because Kant was already there, within the speculative principle, yet radically misrecognized the true dimension of his own act, and espoused the worst metaphysical prejudices.

Lacan and Hegel

Let us now pass over to Hegel. One naive yet difficult-to-answer objection to Hegel is: What 'sets in motion' the dialectical process? Why does the 'thesis' not simply persist in its positive self-identity? Why does it dissolve its self-complacent identity, and expose itself to the dangers of negativity and mediation? In short, is not Hegel caught in a vicious circle here; does he not succeed in dissolving every positive identity only because he conceives of it in advance as something mediated by negativity?

What is wrong here is the implicit presupposition of this objection: that there is something akin to the full immediacy of the 'thesis'. Hegel's point, on the contrary, is that there is no 'thesis' (in the sense of the full self-identity and organic unity of a starting point). That is to say: one of the illusions that characterize the standard reading of Hegel concerns the notion that the dialectical process somehow progresses from what is immediately given, from its fullness, to its mediation – say, from the naive, non-reflected consciousness that is aware only of the object opposed to it, to self-consciousness that comprises the awareness of its own activity as opposed to the object.

Hegelian 'reflection', however, does not mean that consciousness is followed by self-consciousness – that at a certain point consciousness magically turns its gaze inward, towards itself, making itself its own object, and thus introduces a reflective distance, a splitting, into the former immediate unity. Hegel's point is, again, that consciousness *always-already is self-consciousness*: there is no consciousness without a minimal reflective self-relating of the subject. Here Hegel turns against Fichte and Schelling and, in a sense, goes back to Kant, for whom the transcendental apperception of the I is an inherent condition of the I's being conscious of an object.

The passage of consciousness to self-consciousness thus involves a kind of failed encounter: at the very moment when consciousness endeavours to establish itself as 'full' consciousness of its object, when it endeavours to pass from the confused foreboding of its content to its clear representation, it suddenly finds itself within self-consciousness – that is to say, it finds itself compelled to perform an act of reflection, and to take note of its own activity as opposed to the object. Therein resides the paradox of the couple of 'in-itself' and 'for-itself': we are dealing here with the passage from 'not yet' to 'always-already'. In 'in-itself', the consciousness (of an object) is not yet fully realized, it remains a confused anticipation of itself; whereas in 'for-itself' consciousness is in a way already passed over, the full comprehension of the object is again blurred by the awarenes of the subject's own activity that simultaneously

renders possible and prevents access to the object. In short, consciousness is like the tortoise in Lacan's reading of the paradox of Achilles and
the tortoise – Achilles can easily outrun the tortoise, yet he cannot catch
up with her.

Another way to make the same point is to emphasize that *the passage
from consciousness to self-consciousness always involves an experience of failure*,
of impotence – consciousness turns its gaze inside, towards itself, it
becomes aware of its own activity, only when the direct, unproblematic
grasp of its object fails. Suffice it to recall the process of knowledge: the
object's resistance to the grasp of knowledge forces the subject to admit
the 'illusory' nature of his knowledge – what he mistook for the object's
In-itself are actually his constructions.

*What about Hegel's teleology, his notion of Telos as the inherent impetus of the
dialectical process? Is not his idealism quite explicit here?*

Rather than repeat parrot-fashion the worn-out phrases on the Hegelian
teleology of the Notion that dominates the process of its own actualization, it is worth taking the trouble to read closely the section on teleology
in Part II of Hegel's 'Subjective Logic'. The first surprise that awaits us
there is that in the triad of Ends, Means and Object, the effective unity,
the mediating agency, is not the End but the *Means*: the means effectively
dominate the entire process by mediating between the End and the
external Object in which the End is to be realized-actualized. The End
is thus far from dominating the means and the Object: the End and the
external Object are the two objectivizations of means *qua* the movable
medium of negativity.

In short, Hegel's result is that the End is ultimately a 'means of means
themselves', a means self-posited by means to set in motion its mediating
activity. (It is similar with the *means* of production in Marx: the
production of material goods is, of course, a means whose aim is to satisfy
human needs; at a deeper level, however, this very satisfaction of human
needs is a means self-posited by the means of production to set in motion
its own development – the true End of the entire process is the
development of the means of production as the assertion of man's
domination over nature – or, as Hegel puts it, as the 'self-objectivization
of the Spirit'.)

A further point that deserves mention here is how Hegel passes from
means to the object: 'means' designates an external objectivity that is
already subjectivized, in the service of an inner subjective End; however,
since the End here is a merely subjective, 'inner' notion opposed to the
external, actual objectivity, it follows from the inherent logic of this
structure that the End does not yet pervade and dominate the entire
objectivity – otherwise it would not be a merely subjective End.

189

Consequently, there must exist, besides Means – an external objectivity that is already under the domination of the End – another, indifferent-external objectivity that is not yet under the domination of the End: this indifferent-external objectivity is the Object *qua* material that the End endeavours to transform through the use of means, and thus to confer upon it a form in which it finds a suitable expression.

A very precise speculative conclusion follows from this – namely, *the ultimate identity of End and Object*: they are one and the same entity, their difference is merely formal and concerns the modality – that is, the Object is in-itself what the End is for-itself. It is crucial to bear in mind this coincidence of the End (the subjective inwardness not yet exter-nalized in the object via Means) and the Object (the indifferent external objectivity not yet internalized, transformed into an expression of the inner End, via Means): Means is literally just a means, a mediator, the medium of the purely formal conversion of the End into the Object by means of which the object 'becomes what it always-already was'.

Yet, again, is not Hegel's regular use of the syntagm 'return to itself' (following its loss in self-alienation, the Spirit returns to itself, etc.) an unmistakeable sign of the 'metaphysics of presence'?

This is where we must be on the lookout for the most perfidious trap of the commonsensical reading of Hegel. Yes, in the 'negation of negation' the Spirit does 'return to itself'; it is absolutely crucial, however, to bear in mind the 'performative' dimension of this return: the Spirit changes in its very substance through this return-to-itself – that is, *the Spirit to whom we return, the Spirit that returns to itself, is not the same as the Spirit that was previously lost in alienation.* What occurs in between is a kind of transubstantiation, so that this very return-to-itself marks the point at which the initial substantial Spirit is definitely lost.

Suffice it to recall the loss, the self-alienation, of the Spirit of a substantial community that takes place when its organic links dissolve with the rise of abstract individualism: at the level of 'negation', this dissolution is still measured by the standard of organic unity, and therefore experienced as a loss; the 'negation of negation' occurs when the Spirit 'returns to itself' – not by means of the restitution of the lost organic community (this immediate organic unity is lost for ever), but by the full consummation of this loss – that is, by the emergence of the new determination of society's unity – no longer the immediate organic unity but the formal legal order that sustains the civil society of free individuals. This new unity is *substantially* different from the lost immediate organic unity.

To put it in another way: 'castration' designates the fact that the 'full' subject immediately identical with the 'pathological' substance of drives

(S) has to sacrifice the unimpeded satisfaction of drives, to subordinate this substance of drives to the injunctions of an alien ethico-symbolic network – how does this subject 'return to himself'? By fully consummating this loss of substance – that is, by shifting the 'centre of gravity' of his being from S to $, from the substance of drives to the void of negativity: the subject 'returns to himself' when he no longer recognizes the kernel of his being in the substance of drives but identifies with the void of negative self-relating. From this new standpoint, drives appear as something external and contingent, as something that is not 'truly himself'.

This is also one way of reiterating the difference between Derrida and Hegel: Derrida endlessly varies the motif of how return to itself is always doomed to fail, how the gesture of externalization involves a dissemination that can never be sublated-reappropriated; whereas Hegel asserts that return to itself is quite possible, the problem being, rather, that the 'self' to whom we return is no longer the same as the self that was previously lost. . . .

As for Lacan himself, does not his emphatic assertion that 'a letter always arrives at its destination' involve a certain kind of teleology? See Derrida's elaborate reading of Lacan. . . .

A letter does not 'arrive at its destination' because of some hidden teleology that regulates its wandering: what we are dealing with here is always a retroactive construction founded upon the fortuitous erring of the letter. Take A.S. Byatt's novel *Possession*: when Maud, a young literary historian who has discovered unknown letters by the Victorian poetess Christabel LaMotte, finds out that Christabel was her great-great-great-grandmother, she recognizes herself as the addressee of Christabel's last letter to her great love, the poet Randolph Ash:

> '. . . he can't ever have read it, can he? She wrote all that for no one. She must have waited for an answer – and none can have come –'
> [. . .]
> 'She didn't know what to do, perhaps. She didn't give it to him, and she didn't read it – I can imagine that – she just put it away –'
> 'For Maud,' said Blackadder. 'As it turns out. She preserved it, for Maud.'[5]

Incidentally, the principal charm of *Possession* resides in the typical postmodern gesture of redoubling: the two heroes of the novel (Maud and her fellow-literary historian Roland) can constitute themselves as a sexual couple only by means of reference to the past romance between Christabel and Randolph: direct love is not possible; we always need the phantasmic frame of Another Couple to be imitated. . . .

A further unexpected variation on the theme of the letter that 'arrives at its destination' is in Jane Campion's film *The Piano*, when the small daughter (Anna Paquin) transmits the piano key that her mother Ada (Holly Hunter) asked her to deliver to her lover Baines (Harvey Keitel) to her stepfather Stewart (Sam Neill), thereby setting in motion the tragic aggravation of their relationship: for the girl, determined by the fantasy-image of a happy family that she, her mother and her stepfather could have constituted, Stewart *is* its true addressee. However, is this fantasy simply and only the wishful thinking of a daughter blind to her parents' actual libidinal tensions? Things are far more ambiguous. The proof that *The Piano* is truly a *woman's* picture, not just an illustration of politically correct 'feminist' notions, is provided by its successful avoidance of the simplistic condemnation of male patriarchal violence: the film is very sensitive to the libidinal impasse that underlies the outburst of male violence.

The most complex figure is the unfortunate Stewart; the opposition of him and Baines definitely cannot be reduced to a trivial opposition between a 'bad' white patriarchal male chauvinist and a 'good' white-man-turned-native who is, for that reason, more susceptible to feminine enjoyment. When Stewart observes the sexual interplay of Ada and Baines through a fissure in the wall, he in a sense breaks down – that is, his reaction is by no means simple patriarchal fury directed at the feminine enjoyment. Quite the contrary: it is only now, through this discovery of a new awesome, venerable dimension in Ada, that he starts to respect her and to treat her as a subject of her own, so that when, later at home, he endeavours to approach her sexually, we are witnessing a desperate attempt to get in touch with this dimension, whose intensity overwhelms him.

Stewart's subsequent violent outburst (he cuts off Ada's little finger) is thus far from simple male-chauvinist woman-bashing: rather, it expresses his impasse, his despair at being unable to make contact with this 'other enjoyment'. He somehow has a hunch of this dimension of the 'other enjoyment', yet he wants to capture it into the phallic enjoyment; consequently, Ada spurns him when, unable to accept her sensuality of a floating touch, he starts to pull his trousers down in order to jump on her. The scornful glance she casts at him at this precise moment tells all: in spite of his real violence, she defeats him, which is why he withdraws in shame. So when the daughter 'delivers the letter to its addressee', she does this out of the utopian hope and/or foreboding that Ada and Stewart will be able to meet at the level of the 'other enjoyment'....

Lacan, Derrida, Foucault

Let us, then, bite at this apple of discord – the traumatic relationship between Derrida and Lacan. . . .

I still maintain that Derrida's criticism of Lacan is a case of prodigious misreading. If, however, we set aside major confrontations and tackle the problematic nature of their relationship *en détail*, as befits Freudians, a series of unexpected connections opens up. Suffice it to mention the fundamental characteristic of the Lacanian notion of the symbolic order: this order of symbolic *exchanges* is based upon a constitutive surplus-gesture that *eludes* the balance of exchanges – this is what 'symbolic castration' is ultimately about; this is what Freud himself was eventually aiming at apropos of the 'economic paradox of masochism'.

An excessive act that disturbs the symbolic balance is the condition of the very emergence of the economy of exchanges: *the first move is, by definition, superfluous.* (And perhaps the problem of a certain kind of pragmatic-enlightened utilitarianism resides in the fact that it endeavours to get rid of this excess without being prepared to pay the price for it – to acknowledge that once we obliterate the excess, we lose the very 'normal', balanced field of exchanges by reference to which the excess is excessive. . . .) This excessive gesture that sets the circle of exchanges in motion while remaining external to it does not simply 'precede' the symbolic exchange: there is no way of grasping it as it is 'in itself', in its naked innocence; it can only be reconstructed retroactively as the inherent presupposition of the Symbolic. In other words, this gesture is 'real' in the precise Lacanian sense: the traumatic kernel 'secreted' by the process of symbolization.

The same point could also be made in the terms of the dialectic of Good and Evil, as the coincidence of the Good with the supreme Evil. The 'Good' stands for the balanced order of symbolic exchanges, whereas the supreme Evil designates the excessive gesture (the expenditure and/or loss) of disruption, disjunction, which is not simply the opposite of the Good – rather, it sustains the network of symbolic exchanges precisely in so far as it becomes invisible once we are 'within' the symbolic order.[6] From within the symbolic order, spectres, apparitions, the 'living dead', and so on, signal the unsettled (symbolic) accounts; as such, they disappear the moment these accounts are settled by way of symbolization. There is, however, a debt that can never be honoured, since it sustains the very existence of a system of exchange-indemnification. At this more radical level, 'ghosts' and other forms of revenants bear witness to the virtual, fictional character of the symbolic order as such, to the fact that this order exists 'on credit'; that, by definition, its accounts are never fully settled.

This is what Lacan has in mind when he asserts that the truth has the structure of a fiction – one has to distinguish strictly between *fiction* and *spectre*: fiction is a symbolic formation that determines the structure of what we experience as reality, whereas spectres belong to the Real; their appearance is the price we pay for the gap that forever separates reality from the Real, for the fictional character of reality. In short, *there is no Spirit* (mind, reason, etc.) *without spirits* ('ghosts', revenants, living dead), no pure, rational, self-transparent spirituality without the accompanying stain of an obscene, uncanny, spectral pseudo-materiality.[7] Or, with reference to the distinction between the public symbolic Law and its nightly obscene superego underside:[8] superego is the annoying 'ghost', the shadowy double that always accompanies the public Law.

It seems to me that at this specific level it is possible to establish the link between Lacan and the problematic articulated by Derrida in *Given Time*,[9] the problematic centred around the motif of the gift *qua* 'impossible', unaccountable act, the act that subverts the 'closed economy' of symbolic exchanges and is, as such, 'eternally past' – its time is never present, since it 'always-already took place' once we are within the symbolic economy. The pure gift not only precludes any counter-gesture, allows of no compensation, no return thanks; it even cannot and/or must not be acknowledged as a gift – the moment a gift is recognized as such, it gives rise to a symbolic debt in the recipient, it becomes entangled in the economy of exchange, and thus loses the characteristic of pure gift. The gift, therefore, *is not*; all we can say is that 'there is [*il y a/es gibt*] one'; as such, it also cannot be attributed to any positive subject alleged to perform it – all that befits it is the impersonal '*es*'.

Derrida, of course, reads this *es gibt* against the background of Heiddegger's *es gibt Zeit*, of the 'event [*Ereignis*]' – the gift 'just happens', we might say. Perhaps the most interesting feature of Derrida's approach to Heidegger is the way he 'combines the incompatible' – here Derrida is postmodern in the best sense of the term. As Fredric Jameson pointed out, one of the key features of the 'postmodern sensitivity' consists in bringing face to face entities which, although contemporary, belong to different historical epochs.

One of the mythical figures of the old American South is the pirate Jean Lafitte: his name is associated with his and General Andrew Jackson's defence of New Orleans, with the buccaneer romantic, and so on – what is less known is that in his old age, when he retired to England, Lafitte made friends with Marx and Engels, and even financed the first English translation of the *Communist Manifesto*. This image of Lafitte and Marx walking together in Soho, a nonsensical short circuit of two entirely different universes, is eminently postmodern. What Derrida does to Heidegger is, in a way, quite similar: he often brings Heidegger face to face with the 'vulgar', 'ontic' problematic – he links the Heideggerian gift of *es gibt* with the 'economic' problematic of the gift in Marcel Mauss (*Essai sur le don*), with the modalities of its functioning in intersubjective relations (Baudelaire's prose poem *La fausse monnaie*), and so on. In this way, Heidegger is delivered from the 'jargon of authenticity' in which the only suitable examples are those taken from Hölderlin's poems or German rural life.

With Lacan, however, things get complicated. As usual, Derrida opposes this *il y a* of the pure gift to the Lacanian symbolic order that allegedly remains within the confines of the 'closed economy' of symbolic exchange – there is no place in it for the excess of a gift. According to Derrida, Lacan's fundamental gesture is to enlarge the domain of symbolic exchange, not to render visible its limitation and dependence on an excess. Lacan is at his best when he succeeds in demonstrating how, on the unconscious Other Scene, some symbolic exchange is already at work in what, from the standpoint of consciousness and its imaginary experience, appears as a non-economical expenditure (for example, in the unconscious economy an 'irrational' *acting out* can function as the repayment of a symbolic debt).

It seems, however, that Derrida pays a price for his reduction of the Lacanian Symbolic to the balanced economy of exchange, for his refusal to recognize in the notion of an excessive 'first move' that founds the symbolic order a key ingredient of the Lacanian Symbolic: this price is his inability fully to take note of how, in his own theoretical edifice, the notion of gift, of a primordial 'there is' (*il y a/es gibt*: 'it gives'), introduces an aspect that is heterogeneous to the standard 'Derridean' problematic of *différance*-trace-writing. This 'there is' *qua* event names the *counterpart* to the movement of *différance*, of the irreducible dissemination-deferral: presence itself in its ultimate inaccessibility. (Significantly, in his attempt to determine the paradoxical status of this excessive gift, Derrida is obliged to resort to a quasi-transcendental language: gift as 'the indeconstructible condition of every deconstruction'.) The 'there is' of the gift consists of the gesture of a pure *Yes!*, of an accordance that precedes the movement of dissemination-deferral. What forever eludes the subject's grasp or the *Logos* is eventually presence itself in its non-mediated, pre-discursive 'there is'. The ultimate excess is that of the event of presence itself.

Or, to approach this same problem via the Derridean motif of the voice-phenomenon *qua* medium of the illusory self-presence to be deconstructed and denounced as an effect of the process of *différance*, of the interplay of traces, and so on: what Derrida remains blind to is the radical ambiguity of the voice. The voice-phenomenon, in its very presence, is simultaneously the Lacanian Real, the non-transparent stain that puts an irreducible obstacle in the way of the subject's self-transparency, a foreign body in his midst. In short, the greatest hindrance to the self-transparency of *Logos* is the voice itself in its inert presence.

Correlative to this refusal to take note of the impenetrability of the voice is Derrida's failure to acknowledge fully the *ultimate identity of supplement and Master-Signifier*. On the one hand, Derrida varies endlessly the motif of the excessive element which functions simultaneously as a lack and as a surplus, which is indecidable, unlocalizable, simultaneously within and without, part of the text and maintaining a distance towards it, completing the text and opening it towards its externality, and so on. On the other hand, Derrida's 'deconstruction' aims at undermining the authority of the central signifier that pretends to totalize the texture of traces, and thus to restrain its dissemination – again and again, he emphasizes how this central signifier is always subverted, displaced, by what it is supposed to dominate; how it depends structurally on its effects, and so forth.

It might seem, therefore, that the supplement and the Master-Signifier are opposites whose tension provides the contours of the textual process: the supplement is the undecidable margin that eludes the Master-Signifier. Lacan, however, locates this undecidability in the very heart of the Master-Signifier: with reference to the series of 'ordinary' elements, the Centre is by definition an excessive, supplementary element whose place is structurally ambiguous, neither within nor without. Lacan's name for the supplement is *le plus-un*, the excessive element, the stand-in for the lack, which performs the operation of *suture*; the Master-Signifier proper emerges through the 'neutralization' of the supplement, through the obliteration of its constitutive indecidability.

What, then, is the status of Derrida's insistent reference to an 'indeconstructible condition of deconstruction'?

Far from bearing witness to an inconsistency, this motif of the indestructible condition of deconstruction brings to the light the vow/promise, the engagement, that sustains the very procedure of deconstruction: the openness to the event, to the otherness in its alterity, prior to the circle of exchanges between me and the other, prior to justice *qua* settlement of accounts. This idea of justice is 'unrealizable' in so far as it demands simultaneously the recognition of the other in its uniqueness *and* the formulation of a universal medium within which the other and I can meet as equals. For that reason, every positive determination of the idea of justice is by definition deficient and inadequate, since no positively defined universality is ever truly neutral with regard to its particular content – it always introduces an imbalance by privileging a part of its particular content. (Here Derrida is effectively close to Marx, to the Marxian insight into the complicity between universal form of equality and material inequality.) Consequently, the idea of justice that sustains our interminable work of deconstruction must forever remain a form without content, the form of a promise that always transcends its content – in short, it must remain *spectral*, it should not be 'ontologized' into a positive agency:

> ... what remains irreducible to every deconstruction, as indeconstructible as the very possibility of deconstruction, is perhaps a certain experience of the emancipatory promise; is perhaps even the formality of a structural messian-ism, a messianism without religion, even a messianic without messianism, an idea of justice – that we distinguish always from right and even from human rights – and an idea of democracy – that we distinguish from its actual concept and from the predicates that determine it today.[10]

Notwithstanding all denials, does not Derrida follow here the Kantian logic of the regulative Idea? Is not this surplus of form over content Kantian in its very essence, as the surplus of the regulative promise over the constitutive principle, over the positive determinations of material content? Does not Derrida's insistence that this messianic promise of justice must remain spectral, that it must not be 'ontologized' into a self-present Entity (the supreme Good, the promise of Communism as an effective future world order, etc.) repeat Kant's injunction that the regulative Idea must not be misperceived as a constitutive principle? (In Kant already, this distinction is of crucial political importance: for Kant, the horror of the French Revolution resides precisely in the attempt to assert the idea of freedom as the constitutive, positive, structuring principle of social life.)

This, then, would be Derrida's minimal determination of ideology: the ontological misreading of the spectral ethical injunction. What one should do here is to 'deconstruct' this very opposition of the spectral and the ontological in a Hegelian way. Derrida demonstrates triumphantly that there is no ontology without the spectral, that there is no way of drawing a clear line of distinction between the spectral and the positive effectivity-actuality-reality. The question to be asked, however, is: *Where does the imminent, incessant, danger of the 'ontologization' of the spectral promise-idea come from?* The only logical answer to this question is: from the fact that there is also no spectre without the ontological, without *le peu de réel* of some inert-opaque stain whose presence sustains the very spectre in its opposition to the ontological. Or – to put it in Hegelese – *no spirit without a bone. . . .*

Kant, of course, aimed at maintaining the gap that forever separates the ethical Idea of justice from justice *qua* positive legal order – yet the more he purified the Idea of all empirical, positive, ontological features, the greater was the danger of the fall, the more 'totalitarian' was the system brought about by the fall. His formal definition of ethical activity delivered the field of ethics from all 'pathological' content; yet simultaneously it opened up the space for a radical Evil incomparably worse than ordinary 'empirical' Evil.[11] True, Kant provided a precise definition of the short circuit that led to the Terror of the French Revolution – the 'ontologization' of freedom into a positive principle of social life – yet simultaneously we are obliged to assert that in a sense there is no revolutionary Terror without Kant, prior to the Kantian revolution.

Here we are dealing with a kind of knot, a concatenation, a 'the more you are pure (non-ontological, formal), the more you are dirty', which culminates in the radical ambiguity of *out of joint*, of this central motif of Derrida's *Spectres de Marx*. On the one hand, 'the world is out of joint' stands for 'all that is wrong in the world', for all that causes suffering and feeds the emancipatory promise of messianic deliverance. On the other hand, however, the most traumatic eruption of the *out of joint* is the very emergence of the messianic promise – is not this promise the ultimate *skandalon* that disrupts the routine way of all flesh? If, however, the supreme disruption, the supreme *out of joint*, is that of the messianic Idea itself, then – as Hegel would have put it – 'in fighting the evils of the world that appear to prevent its realization, the messianic Idea is fighting itself, its own offspring' (or, with reference to the relationship between Centre and supplement: 'in endeavouring to control/master the supplement, the Centre is fighting its own founding gesture').

Let us tackle another philosopher who is commonly considered close to Lacan: Foucault. Foucault's (implicit) critique of Lacan in the first volume of The History of Sexuality *is that Lacan remains within the traditional notion of Law that is characterized by two features: it is 'negative' – Law as the agency of prohibition – and 'emanational' – Law draws its authority from some unique centre and transmits it downwards. To this, Foucault opposes his notion of Power as productive and constituted 'from below' . . .*

. . . I know, Foucault is never tired of repeating how power constitutes itself 'from below', how it does not emanate from some unique summit: this very semblance of a Summit (the Monarch or some other embodiment of Sovereignty) emerges as the secondary effect of the plurality of micro-practices, of the complex network of their interrelations. The real problem, however, is how we are to combine this problematic of micro-power with the way Foucault himself (in *Discipline and Punish*) uses the notion of Panopticon – as a uniform matrix, a structuring model that can be applied to different domains, from prisons to schools, from hospitals to barracks, from factories to offices. The only way to avoid the reproach of inconsistency is to introduce the notion of *fantasy* as the common matrix that confers consistency upon the plurality of social practices. In other words, 'actual' social relations are plural, they consist of the intricate network of micro-relations that run in all directions, up and down, left and right ... what 'holds together' this plurality is not some underlying Essence or Foundation but precisely the pure surface of fantasy as a 'non-lieu' (Foucault apropos of Panopticon), a formal matrix which, although it is not to be found anywhere in 'reality', provides its structuring principle. What causes Foucault so much trouble is therefore again the spectre, the spectral nature of Panopticon: Derrida's spectre perfectly fits the psychoanalytic notion of fantasy whose emergence, by definition, bears witness to an unsettled symbolic debt.

'Phallocentrism'

A critical reproach of your work that imposes itself from Foucauldian historicist premisses runs as follows: If we conceive of the lack as 'castration', if we posit the phallus as its signifier, do we not nevertheless eternalize a historically specified, limited logic of symbolization?

The crucial point here is to distinguish historicity proper from evolutionary historicism. Historicity proper involves a dialectical relationship to some unhistorical kernel that stays the same – not as an underlying Essence but as a rock that trips up every attempt to integrate it into the symbolic order. This rock is the Thing *qua* 'the part of the Real that suffers from the signifier' (Lacan) – the real 'suffers' in so far as it is the trauma that cannot be properly articulated in the signifying chain. In Marxism, such a 'real' of the historical process is the 'class struggle' that constitutes the common thread of 'all history hitherto': all historical formations are so many (ultimately failed) attempts to 'gentrify' this kernel of the real.

We must be careful here to distinguish between *Verwerfung* and *Verdrängung*, between foreclosure and 'ordinary' repression. The Real *qua* Thing is not 'repressed', it is foreclosed or 'primordially repressed [*ur-verdrängt*]' – that is, its repression is not a historical variable but is constitutive of the very order of symbolic historicity. In other words, the Real *qua* Thing stands for that X on account of which every symbolization fails – in its very unhistoricity, it sets in motion one new symbolization after another. For that reason, Lacan is as far as it is possible to be from any 'tabooing' of the Real, from elevating it into an untouchable entity exempted from historical analysis – his point, rather, is that the only true ethical stance is to assume fully the impossible task of symbolizing the Real, inclusive of its necessary failure. The intersection of pornography and 'normal' realist narrative, for example, is by definition impossible, an empty set: the moment we 'show it all', our belief in diegetic reality is suspended, the narrative is experienced as a ridiculous pretext for showing 'that'.[12] Yet it was undoubtedly for this very reason that Lacan was so fascinated by *The Empire of Senses*, a film that endeavours to realize this impossible intersection – to offer a consistent narrative and (almost) hard-core sex....

There is another aspect to this anti-historicist 'sting' of Lacan. In his classical Marxist analysis of Stendhal's *Le Rouge et le Noir*, Georg Lukács argues as follows. Stendhal was clearly aware of the alienated character of early-capitalist social reality; however, due to the fact that, in his time, the proletariat did not yet assert itself as a historical subject, he was unable to gain insight into the historical possibility of the abolition of alienation through the socialist revolution; consequently, he was able to conceive of protest against the difficult social conditions only in the form of a suicidal, self-destructive individualistic outburst of 'irrational' aggression. What is wrong with this argument? According to Lukács, the distinction between 'ourselves' and Stendhal hinges on the difference in our respective objective situations: objective historical conditions prevented Stendhal from gaining an insight (into the historical role of the proletariat), while changed conditions enable 'us' to gain this insight....

If there is anything to be learned from psychoanalysis, it is the falsity of such a distinction: historical epochs are not divided into those that render an insight possible and those that prevent it. Such a 'possibility of insight' concerns only 'ontic', positive knowledge (for example, it is clear that prior to our age it was not possible to formulate the relativity of time and space); on the other hand, each epoch has its own direct 'access to the Absolute' via the experience of its inherent limitation and failure. This failure – the breakdown, the disintegration of a certain historical horizon of meaning – is never simply the failure of a specific epochal constellation; it always renders possible, for a brief moment, the experience of what Lacan calls the 'lack in the Other', the inconsistency and/or non-existence of the big Other – of the fact that there is no Other of the Other, no ultimate guarantee of the field of meaning. As soon as the contours of the new epoch assert themselves, the 'non-existence of the big Other' again becomes invisible.

A phenomenological counterpart to this Marxist historicism is the predominant historicist reading of Heidegger, according to which each epoch is constrained by the ontological horizon of the understanding of

Being that is its fate – a hundred years ago Europe reached the peak of the epoch of subjectivity, whereas today it is possible to have a presentiment of the metaphysical closure as such.... Such a reading is belied by Heidegger himself apropos of Hölderlin who, in the midst of the epoch of modern-age subjectivity, articulated Being as *Ereignis*; the same goes for Schelling who, in his *Treaty on Freedom*, already gained an insight into the dimension beyond metaphysics, yet blurred this insight by articulating it in traditional ontological categories.

On an entirely different level, this notion of 'access to the Absolute' via the experience of the disintegration of one's own horizon of meaning allows us to realize the greatness of a figure like Geronimo: in pursuing the lost cause of the battle against white men, Geronimo clearly experienced the limitation of the Native American horizon; although he was fully aware of the fragility of his universe, he persisted in it, thereby displaying a true ethical attitude.

But there is still the standard argument apropos of the phallic signifier: 'Why phallus? By calling the quasi-transcendental signifier 'phallus', do we not legitimize the elevation of a contingent bodily part into the transcendental condition of the very symbolic system? Do we not subscribe to an 'illegitimate' short circuit between a purely formal structural function and the empirical, contingent organ that symbolizes it? Do we not thereby constrain the essential, irreducible 'openness' of the signifying process – the possibility of endless rearticulations of the symbolic field?'

The moment we oppose the finitude/closure of the given symbolic texture to the endless horizon of its possible rearticulations, language is reduced to an ordinary natural entity and its development to a gradual evolution of such an entity. What differentiates language from a natural entity or system is the presence in it of the element designated by Lévi-Strauss the mana-signifier: the 'reflective' signifier that holds the place, within the system, of what eludes the system, of its *not-yet-signified*. The 'openness' of a symbolic system has nothing whatsoever to do with the pressure of the ever-changing external circumstances that compel the system to transform; in the case of a symbolic system proper, this openness has to be inscribed into the 'closed' system itself in the guise of a paradoxical signifier that represents non-sense within the field of Sense – what Lacan calls the phallic signifier. Hegel, in his 'idealist' way, says the same when he asserts that Spirit, in contrast to nature, contains negativity in itself: negativity is not an external force that decomposes spiritual formations from outside, since Spirit is capable of sustaining a negative relationship towards itself, of 'tarrying with the negative'.

Again, the phallic signifier is none other than this purely negative signifier, a 'signifier without signified'. Consequently, the feminist critique of the 'phallocentric' logic of castration is guilty of condensing two different gestures: while it is fully justified in emphasizing the ultimately *contingent* character of the fact that the signifier elevated into the stand-in for the lack is precisely the phallus, it tends to obscure the fact that this paradoxical function of the signifier that stands for its own lack is constitutive of symbolic order. In other words, the phallus suspends, renders inoperative, the opposition of fixed identity and the process of its subversion or 'liquefaction': the 'identity' of the phallus resides in its own displacement – 'phallic' is the element in the structure that stands for its own opposite, an identity that marks pure difference, a presence that marks pure absence.

What about the seemingly Hegelian argument that Lacan's famous formulas of phallus qua signifier (neither bodily organ nor an image but a signifier) are to be read as a denial or 'determinate negation' bearing witness to the fact that phallus qua signifier remains attached to, dependent on, marked by penis qua its positive support: the phallic signifier emerges as a sublation-mediation of penis qua image that stands for the unattainable totality of the body. . . .

I think Judith Butler (who develops this argument) is here the victim of a non-dialectical obsession with content, which is why she leaves out of consideration what is always crucial for Hegel, the 'formal aspect'. When Lacan claims, in 'The Signification of Phallus', that phallus is the signifier of the very gesture of *Aufhebung*, one has to take this literally: 'phallus' is the form of mediation-sublation as such. 'Phallus' is not what remains of penis after penis is submitted to the process of mediation-sublation; rather, it stands for this very process of mediation-sublation. In short, 'phallus' designates the form of symbolization as such.

With reference to Deleuze, this difference between 'form' and 'content' can be conceived of as the difference between the 'phallus of co-ordination' and the 'phallus of castration'. On the one hand, there is the 'pre-castrative' phallus, phallus as the organ that endeavours to co-ordinate all erogenous zones into a unified global field; this phallus is undoubtedly built upon the model of the unity of the Ego-image in the mirror stage – that is to say, its emergence merely repeats the operation of imaginary identification with an idealized organ. At this level, 'everything has a sexual meaning', and the phallus guarantees the unity of this meaning. This phallus, however, necessarily converts into the 'phallus of castration', into the phallus as the signifier of loss and/or desexualization: what the child experiences through the 'castration complex' is that phallus – *qua* crossing-point of meaning and sexuality – can guarantee 'normal' sexuality only by acting as the operator of *desexualization*, that it can perform its function of the guarantor of (literal, desexualized) meaning only by acting as the signifier-*without*-signified.

Butler passes in silence over this crucial dimension, and this neglect of the 'phallus of castration' leads her to formulate as a *reproach* to Lacan, as the 'unthought' of his concept of phallus, what is actually the fundamental feature of his concept of the phallic signifier. That is to say, in her critical analysis of the notion of castration anxiety, Butler demonstrates conclusively how 'the having of phallus as a site of anxiety is already the loss it fears'[13] – what she fails to notice is that *it is this very short circuit between possibility and actuality that defines the phallic signifier as the signifier of SYMBOLIC castration*: the subject's 'real' anxiety that he will lose the phallus, at the symbolic level, is 'already the loss it fears'. In other words, the distinctive feature of symbolic castration, in contrast to real and/or imaginary castration, is that the fear of possible castration is already castration itself.

Power

In the background of this feminist critique of Lacan lurks the problematic of power, of the psychoanalytic theory of power, of the complicity of psychoanalysis in power mechanisms. Psychoanalysis – or at least, the Lacanian version of it – emphasizes the symbolic mechanisms, the symbolic nature of power – does not this emphasis lead us to neglect the difference between 'effective' and 'symbolic' power?

No, it leads us only to conceive of this difference as the intra-discursive difference between performatively effective social link and the empty symbolic gestures that legitimize this link. Here the case of Stalin is very instructive: recent historical research arrived at the paradoxical conclusion that Stalin lost most of his 'effective' power in 1939, at the end of the period of the great purges – that is, at the very moment when the 'cult' of his personality was finally fully established – as if his symbolic elevation to the 'fourth classic of Marxism' served as a kind of recompense for the loss of 'effective' power. Until 1938, Stalin effectively concentrated an enormous amount of executive power in his own hands by means of a very precise strategy: he used NKVD cadres, elevated from the lower strata of society, for continuous purges among the ruling bureaucracy, thus enabling them to 'act out' their frustration at the privileges of the New Class. Finally, in 1938, the ruling bureaucracy that had been unable to stabilize itself into a counterforce to Stalin's personal authority (even members of the Politburo were randomly arrested) struck back and compelled Stalin to transfer most of the actual executive power to the Politburo *qua* collective body. The purges after the World War II (anti-Semitic campaign, the affair of the doctors, etc.) were thus Stalin's last desperate attempt to concentrate 'effective' power in his own hands again – an attempt that ended in his death.

In the exercise of power, one usually distinguishes between direct repression (violence or its threat) and ideological hegemony. What has Lacanian theory to say about political violence, about the opposition of violence and non-violent consent?

The well-known paradox of (social-symbolic) violence is that supreme violence is no longer experienced as violence, since it determines the 'specific colour' of the very horizon within which something is to be perceived as violence. The task of dialectical analysis, therefore, is to render visible the violence that maintains the very neutral, 'non-violent' framework that is subsequently perturbed by the eruptions of (empirical) violence, the very standard by means of which we measure the extent of violence. When we are able to perceive this fundamental violence as violence, the first step towards effective liberation is already accomplished. (The lesson of Lacanian psychoanalysis is, of course, that this coincidence of the highest form of violence with the absence of violence can occur only within the symbolic universe – that is, in an order where the very absence of a determination functions as a positive determination.)

This paradox enables us to give a precise account of the concept of *hegemony*: we are dealing with the effect of hegemony – that is, an element exerts hegemony – only when it is no longer perceived as a usurper that has violently subordinated all other elements, and thus commands the entire field, but as a neutral framework whose presence is 'a matter of course' – 'hegemony' designates usurping violence whose violent character is sublated. Democratic discourse exerts hegemony when even its opponents tacitly accept its underlying logic, and resort to it in their arguments against democracy. It is against this background that one should also approach the problem of so-called 'terrorist' *actings out*, of desperate attempts to disengage oneself from the double-bind of the hegemonic discourse in which the highest violence poses as non-violent consent and dialogue – the true target of 'terrorist' *actings out* is the implicit violence that sustains the very neutral, non-violent frame.

What opens up here is another connection with Derrida, with his motif of an 'illegitimate' performative violence constitutive of Sense itself, of the very legitimate order that retroactively renders it invisible or (which ultimately amounts to the same thing) legitimizes it. The supreme violence resides in this vicious circle of an act that establishes the order which retroactively renders invisible this very act in its dimension of constitutive violence. In other words, the supreme violence consists of the obliteration of the *double inscription of one and the same act*: of the act that founds, brings about, the symbolic Order *and* (re)appears within this Order as one of its elements, legitimized, founded by it. The question of 'origins' is therefore the traumatic point of every legal order: it is what this Order has to 'repress primordially' if it is to maintain the character of an Order. In this precise sense 'dialectics' designates the effort to unearth, to render visible again, this constitutive violence whose 'represion' is coextensive with the very existence of the Order.[14]

Furthermore, psychoanalysis makes us sensitive to the potential contrast between the manifest structure of domination and the effective relations of power. The most famous scene in *Basic Instinct* – the police interrogation of Sharon Stone with the notorious crossing of her legs when, for a brief moment, we catch (or not) a glimpse of her pubic hair – deserves this fame on account of its reversal of what appears to be a typical structure of domination, of the power relation (a woman exposed to the gaze of male interrogators who bombard her with questions): the very subject who occupies the position of victim has the situation totally under control, and plays with the interrogators like a cat with mice....

As for the analysis of the exercise of power, one often insists on the parallel between racial and sexual oppression, between racism and sexism...

... forgetting thereby their fundamental structural difference: male and female are not two 'races' of humanity in the same way as different ethnic communities are. Ethnic communities are structured according to the principle of group identification with the ethnic Thing; as such, they involve the notion of a self-contained, non-antagonistic community life; whereas sexual difference is radically 'antagonistic' – that is, the position of either sex is defined through its antagonistic relationship to the opposite sex. If there is a parallel here it is, rather, between sexual difference and some basic antagonism that splits within the community (class difference, for example). Sexual identity becomes effectively 'nationalist' only in those forms of radical feminism that count on women's capacity to reproduce themselves without male fertilization – here, women would effectively constitute themselves into a 'race' of their own. On the other hand, the anti-racist strategy that aims at the emancipation of our own ethnic community through 'apartheid', through cultural, economic, etc., separation from the dominant community (the strategy of the African-American Muslim Nation, for example), necessarily involves the patriarchal assertion of feminine subordination within our own community ('every sex in its own place').

From Patriarchy to Cynicism

One of the recurrent motifs of your work is that patriarchal-identitarian fundamentalism is today no longer the true enemy....

I am tempted to risk the hypothesis that today, in late capitalism, the hegemonic model is no longer the patriarchal *family* with children but, rather, a contractual *couple*. The child is no longer a *complement* that rounds off the family into a harmonious whole, but a disturbing *supplement* to be disposed of as quickly as possible.

The usual critique of patriarchy fatally neglects the fact that there are two fathers. On the one hand there is the oedipal father: the symbolic-dead father, Name-of-the-Father, the father of Law who does not enjoy, who ignores the dimension of enjoyment; on the other hand there is the 'primordial' father, the obscene, superego anal figure that is real-alive, the 'Master of Enjoyment'. At the political level, this opposition coincides with that between the traditional Master and the modern ('totalitarian') Leader. In all emblematic revolutions, from the French to the Russian, the overthrow of the impotent old regime of the symbolic Master (French King, Tsar) ended in the rule of a far more 'repressive' figure of the 'anal' father-Leader (Napoleon, Stalin). The order of succession described by Freud in *Totem and Taboo* (the murdered primordial Father-Enjoyment returns in the guise of the symbolic authority of the Name) is thus reversed: the deposed symbolic Master returns as the obscene-real Leader. In short, here Freud was the victim of a kind of perspective illusion: 'primordial father' is a later, eminently modern, post-revolutionary phenomenon, the result of the dissolution of traditional symbolic authority.

Today, 'primordial fathers' abound in 'totalitarian' political movements, as well as New Age sects. David Koresh, the leader of the Branch Dravidian sect killed by the FBI in Waco (Texas) in 1993, implemented the fundamental rule of the Freudian primordial father: sexual commerce with women is his exclusive prerogative – that is to say, sex is prohibited to all other men. This also throws a new light on the famous Freudian dream in which a dead son appears to his father and utters the horrible reproach 'Father, can't you see that I am burning?' – whose true meaning, of course, is 'Father, can't you see that I am enjoying?'. In other words, we are actually dealing with a *sigh of relief*: 'Thank God, father can't see it!' Only a dead-symbolic father leaves the space for enjoyment open; the 'anal' father, 'Master of Enjoyment', who can see me also where I enjoy, completely obstructs my access to enjoyment. The symbolic father *qua* dead – that is, ignorant of enjoyment – allows us to keep fantasies structuring our enjoyment at bay, to maintain a minimal distance between them and the social space; whereas the obscene 'anal' father directly animates the phantasmic support of our being which thereby immediately pervades the entire social field.

A further leitmotiv of your work, complementary to the preceding one, is that today, the true ideological enemy is the non-identitarian 'post-ideological' attitude of cynical distance. However, when we conceive of today's world as the age of cynicism, in which nobody takes the predominant ethical code seriously, do we not inevitably fall into the typical ideological trap of misperceiving the preceding age as the time of authentic mores when people still fully believed in their symbolic codes and took them seriously – in Hegelese: as the time when individuals were immediately immersed in their ethical substance? Is not such a notion of 'old times' a retroactive illusion par excellence?

As for the misperception of the former times as the age of naive 'immediacy', Edith Wharton's *The Age of Innocence* sets things in proper perspective. Although it is a canonical work of high art, *The Age of Innocence* comes close to melodrama with the reversal that takes place in the last pages of the novel, when the hero learns that his allegedly ignorant and innocent wife knew that his true love was the fatal Countess Olenska all the time.

The Age of Innocence is the story of a rich lawyer in nineteenth-century New York, engaged to the daughter of a rich family, who loves him with all the naivety of an inexperienced girl; he himself falls passionately in love with the older Countess Olenska, who has returned from Europe after her divorce and, for that reason, is not fully accepted into high society. The two lovers learn that there is no place for their love in the existing social-symbolic space of stiff etiquette and rules of the game, and that there is also no other place to escape to, no utopian place where their love could blossom without restraint, so they renounce their love: the Countess leaves again for Paris, while the hero marries his young fiancée and becomes fully integrated into his society. At the end, after the death of his wife, the hero and his son (now himself a successful young businessman) go to Paris, where they intend to visit Countess Olenska. On the way to her flat, the son tells the hero he knows they are about to visit the unfulfilled love of his father's life – his mother told him all about it long ago. . . . Upon learning this, the hero decides not to visit Countess Olenska.

Herein resided the 'innocence' of his wife: far from being an ingénue blessedly unaware of the emotional turmoils of her fiancé, she knew everything – yet she persisted in her role of ingénue, thereby safeguarding the happiness of their marriage: if the husband had known that she knew, their happiness would not have been possible. In order to understand the 'innocence' of the novel's title properly, one has therefore to introduce Lacan's notion of the big Other *qua* field of social etiquette and appearances: the 'age of innocence' was not the age of naive-immediate acceptance of social etiquette but the age in which etiquette had such a strong hold on individuals that even in the most intimate sphere of a love-relationship, appearances were maintained; one did not throw off one's mask. The wife's 'innocence' consisted in her unreserved commitment to social appearances: in a sense, she took them more seriously than inner emotional turmoil. The point is thus not that her naive trust was feigned: what she fully and sincerely trusted was the surface of social etiquette.

One of the possible misreadings of *The Age of Innocence* is that the hero, upon learning of his dead wife's knowledge, totally shifts the direction of his desire: her noble act – her feigned ignorance – elevates her retroactively into the true object of his desire, which is why he now renounces Countess Olenska, although she is finally accessible to him. In contrast to this misreading, one should insist that in a sense *it is only now that Countess Olenska is fully confirmed as the hero's absolute object of desire*; by not paying his visit to Countess Olenska, the hero repeats his wife's gesture of 'innocence' and sacrifices the object to social etiquette. In short, the object of desire is confirmed as absolute only through its sacrifice.

Let us return to cynicism: how, then, does Lacan avoid the Scylla of the cynical distance that conceives of language as a mere external means to be manipulated, without thereby getting too close to the Charybdis of the naive belief in its performative power?

Asked about their attitude towards America, the Slovene post-punk group Laibach said: 'Like Americans, we also believe in God, but unlike them *we do not trust Him*' (an allusion to the inscription on dollar banknotes, of course)! In so far as God is one of the names of the big Other, this paradoxical statement renders quite adequately the Lacanian attitude towards the big Other of language: a Lacanian is not a cynic who acknowledges only enjoyment; he counts on the efficiency of the big Other, yet he does not trust it, since he knows that he is dealing with an order of semblance. . . .

How, then, on closer inspection, are we to conceive of the 'postmodern' form of subjectivity?

In Hitchcock's *Rear Window,* James Stewart's relationship to what he sees through the window is generally referred to the centrality of his gaze: at stake is his position of domination (or impotence) with regard to what he sees in the courtyard, the fantasies he projects into that beyond, and so on. There is, however, another dimension to it, the dimension that perfectly fits what Lacan designated with the term 'the immixture of the subjects [*l'immixion des sujets*]': to the privileged gaze of James Stewart, social reality is unveiled as the coexistence of the plurality of individual or family destinies; each of these units forms its own exclusive universe of signification with its hopes and despairs, so that although they coexist as parts of the same global mechanism, they are wholly oblivious to each other – what keeps them together is not some deeper common axis of meaning but numerous contingent, 'mechanical' collisions that produce local effect of sense (the songwriter's melody saves the life of Miss Lonelyhearts, etc.). Crucial for the experience of 'immixture' is this notion of *sense as a local effect of the global nonsense*: the intermixture of individual lives is experienced as a blind mechanism in which, despite the lack of any Purpose regulating the flow of events, 'everything functions', so that the view of the totality provides an enigmatic, strangely pacifying, almost mystical experience.

At a higher technological level, a homologous effect is found in *Sliver*: an eccentric millionaire, owner of a large apartment tower, furnishes all the apartments with hidden TV cameras, so that he can observe, on the multiple screens in his hideout, the goings-on in the most intimate, private spaces of his tower: lovemaking, child molesting, financial troubles kept secret from the public eye.... As in *Rear Window*, however, the 'immixture of the subjects' remains attached to a central voyeuristic gaze that is part of the diegetic reality – the gaze of the millionaire in his safe haven.

The great revolution of Robert Altman is that he untied this effect of immixture from the privileged diegetic gaze. This tendency, which was first expressed in *Nashville*, reaches its perfect culmination in *Short Cuts*. The destinies of nine particular groups (mostly families) are held together not by the gaze of some hidden voyeur but by helicopters that spray insecticide on Los Angeles, a metaphor of the decaying megalopolis. These nine threads intermingle in totally contingent ways, so that the same event acquires absolutely incommensurable meanings through its inscription in heterogeneous series. A child hit by Lily Tomlin's car, for example: this accident sets in motion Tomlin's reconciliation with her drunken husband, tragedy in the child's family, a strange friendship between the broken parents and the baker bothering them for forgetting about the child's birthday cake (Lyle Lovett), the obscene, out-of-place confession of the child's grandfather (Jack Lemmon) to the child's father, the grandfather's unexpectedly warm contact with the African-American couple in the hospital, and so on. (In a science-fiction story, this logic of incommensurability is carried to an extreme: in the near future, scientists discover that the comet announcing the birth of Christ in the sky above Bethlehem was the trace of a gigantic cosmic catastrophe, the destruction of a noble, highly developed foreign civilization.)

The theme of *Short Cuts*, therefore, is not the failure or impossibility of communication but, rather, its utterly contingent character: there is simultaneously not enough and too much communication, since contact always occurs as an unforeseen by-product. What Altman offers is the most concise portrait hitherto of the late-capitalist, 'postmodern' immixture of subjects where collectivity is no longer experienced as a collective Subject or global Project but as an impersonal, meaningless mechanism that produces multiple and radically incommensurable meanings as its local contingent results.

What is the fate of sexuality in all this? One of today's commonplaces is that actual sexual contact with a 'real other' is losing ground more and more against masturbatory enjoyment, whose sole support is a virtual other – phone-sex, pornography, up to computerized 'virtual sex'. . . .

The Lacanian answer to this is that first we have to expose the myth of 'real sex' that is allegedly possible 'before' the arrival of virtual sex: Lacan's thesis that 'there is no sexual relationship' means precisely that the structure of the 'real' sexual act (the act with a flesh-and-blood partner) is already inherently phantasmic – the 'real' body of the other serves only as a support for our phantasmic projections. In other words, 'virtual sex' in which a glove simulates the stimuli of what we see on the screen, and so on, is not a monstrous distortion of real sex, it simply renders manifest its underlying phantasmic structure.

Bosnia

Let us now take a step from the universal to the particular case of violence: the war in Bosnia. One of the recurrent motifs in the media is compassion for the victims of the Bosnian war. . . .

In Patricia Highsmith's excellent short story 'The Terrapin' (from her first collection, *Eleven*) the mother of an eight-year-old boy brings home a live terrapin that she plans to cook for dinner. If the terrapin's meat is to taste good, he has to be boiled alive, and this is what leads to the catastrophe: in the presence of her son, the mother throws the terrapin into boiling water and covers the pot with a lid; the desperate terrapin takes hold of the pot's brim with his forelegs, raises the lid with his head, and peers out; for a brief moment, before the mother pushes the terrapin back into the boiling water with a cooking spoon, the son catches sight of the desperate gaze of the dying animal; the traumatic impact of this gaze causes him to stab his mother to death with a kitchen knife. . . . The traumatic element is thus the gaze of the helpless other – child, animal – who does not know why something so horrifying and senseless is happening to him: not the gaze of a hero willingly sacrificing himself for some Cause, but the gaze of a perplexed victim. And in Sarajevo we are dealing with the same bewildered gaze. It is not sufficient to say that the West only passively observes the slaughter in Sarajevo and does not want to act, or even to understand what is actually going on there: the true passive observers are the citizens of Sarajevo themselves, who can only witness the horrors to which they are submitted, without being able to understand how something so horrible is possible. This gaze makes us all guilty.

Compassion for the victim is precisely a way to avoid the unbearable pressure of this gaze – how? The examples of 'compassion with the suffering in Bosnia' that abound in our media illustrate perfectly Lacan's thesis on the 'reflexive' nature of human desire: desire is always desire for a desire. That is to say, what these examples display above all is that compassion is the way to *maintain the proper distance* towards a neighbour in trouble. Recently, the Austrians organized a large-scale action of collecting aid for ex-Yugoslavia under the motto '*Nachbar im Not!* (Neighbour in trouble!)' – the underlying logic of this motto was clear to everyone: we must pay so that our neighbour will remain a neighbour, at a proper distance, and will not come to us. In other words, our compassion, precisely in so far as it is 'sincere', presupposes that *in it, we perceive ourselves in the form that we find likeable*: the victim is presented so that we like to see ourselves in the position from which we stare at her. . . .

What, then, is the status of the notorious Balkan 'archaic ethnic passions' usually evoked apropos of the war in Bosnia?

In *For They Know Not What They Do*, I discussed the well-known story of an anthropological expedition trying to contact a wild tribe in the New Zealand jungle who allegedly danced a terrible war dance in grotesque death-masks. When they reached the tribe in the evening, they asked them to dance it for them, and the dance performed the next morning did in fact match the description; satisfied, the expedition returned to civilization and wrote a much-praised report on the savage rites of the primitives. Shortly afterwards, however, when another expedition reached this tribe and learned to speak their language properly, it was shown that this terrible dance did not exist in itself at all: in their discussions with the first group of explorers, the aborigines somehow guessed what the strangers wanted and quickly, in the night following their arrival, invented it especially for them, to satisfy their demand. . . . In short, the explorers received their own message back from the aborigines in its inverted, true form.

Therein consists the lure to be dispelled if one is to understand what the Yugoslav crisis is about: there is nothing autochthonous in its 'ethnic conflicts', the gaze of the West was included in them from the very beginning – David Owen and companions are today's version of the expedition to the New Zealand tribe; they act and react exactly in the same way, overlooking how the entire spectacle of 'old hatreds suddenly erupting in their primordial cruelty' is a dance staged for their eyes, a dance for which the West is thoroughly responsible.

So why does the West accept this narrative of the 'outburst of ethnic passions'?

For a long time, the 'Balkans' have been one of the privileged sites of phantasmic investments in politics. Gilles Deleuze said somewhere: 'si vous êtes pris dans le rêve de l'autre, vous êtes foutu' – if you are caught up in another person's dream, you are lost. In ex-Yugoslavia, we are lost not because of our primitive dreams and myths preventing us from speaking the enlightened language of Europe, but because we pay in flesh the price of being the stuff of *others'* dreams. The fantasy which organized the perception of ex-Yugoslavia is that of 'Balkan' as the Other of the West: the place of savage ethnic conflicts long since overcome by civilized Europe; a place where nothing is forgotten and nothing learned, where old traumas are replayed again and again; where the symbolic link is simultaneously devalued (dozens of ceasefires are broken) and overvalued (primitive warrior notions of honour and pride).

Against this background, a multitude of myths have flourished. For the 'democratic Left', Tito's Yugoslavia was the mirage of the 'third way' of self-management beyond capitalism and state-socialism; for the delicate men of culture it was the exotic land of refreshing folkloric diversity (the films of Makavejev and Kusturica); for Milan Kundera, the place where the idyll of *Mitteleuropa* meets oriental barbarism; for the Western Realpolitik of the late 1980s, the disintegration of Yugoslavia functioned as a metaphor for what might happen in the Soviet Union; for France and Great Britain, it resuscitated the phantom of the German fourth *Reich* disturbing the delicate balance of European politics; behind all this lurked the primordial trauma of Sarajevo, of the Balkans as the gunpowder threatening to set the whole of Europe alight.... Far from being the Other of Europe, ex-Yugoslavia was, rather, Europe itself in its Otherness, the screen on to which Europe projected its own repressed reverse.

How, then, can we not recall, apropos of this European gaze on the Balkans, Hegel's dictum that true Evil resides not in the object perceived as bad, but in the innocent gaze which perceives Evil all around? The principal obstacle to peace in ex-Yugoslavia is not 'archaic ethnic passions' but the very innocent gaze of Europe fascinated by the spectacle of these passions. Against today's journalistic commonplace about the Balkans as the madhouse of thriving nationalisms, where rational rules of behaviour are suspended, one must point out again and again that the moves of every political agent in ex-Yugoslavia, reprehensible as they may be, are totally rational within the goals they want to attain – the only exception, the only truly irrational factor in it, is the gaze of the West babbling about archaic ethnic passions.

Why is the West so fascinated by the image of Sarajevo, this city-victim par excellence ?

Without the *libidinal economy* of this victimization, it is not possible to account for what has gone on in the last two years in Sarajevo.

The very geographic location of the city is significant: Sarajevo is distant enough not to be perceived as part of Western Europe proper; it is tinged by the exotic Balkan mystique, yet it is close enough to make us shudder at the thought of it (a permanent theme of the European media is 'Just think, this is not some distant Third World country – here, so close to the heart of Europe, less than two hours' flight from us, such horrors occur!'). How, then, did the West proceed in this case?

As Alenka Zupančič, a member of the Slovene Lacanian inner party circle, elaborated in a perspicacious analysis, the West provided just enough humanitarian aid for the city to survive, exerted just enough pressure on the Serbs to prevent them from occupying the city; yet this pressure was not strong enough to break the siege and allow the city to breathe freely – as if the unavowed desire was to preserve Sarajevo in a kind of atemporal freeze, between the two deaths, in the guise of a living dead, a victim eternalized in its suffering. Long ago Lacan drew our attention to the fundamental feature of the Sadeian fantasy, the eternalization of suffering: the victim – usually a young, beautiful, innocent woman – is endlessly tortured by decadent aristocrats, yet she miraculously retains her beauty and does not die, as if, beyond or beneath her material body, she possesses another, ethereal, sublime body. The body of Sarajevo is treated as just such a fantasy-body, eternalized in the fixity of its suffering, outside time and empirical space.

Of special interest here is the general framework that underlies this perception of Sarajevo: Sarajevo is but a special case of what is perhaps the key feature of the ideological constellation that characterizes our epoch of the worldwide triumph of liberal democracy: the *universalization of the notion of victim.* The ultimate proof that we are dealing here with ideology at its purest is provided by the fact that this notion of victim is experienced as extra-ideological *par excellence*: the customary image of the victim is that of an innocent-ignorant child or woman paying the price for politico-ideological power struggles. Is there anything more 'non-ideological' than this pain of the other in its naked, mute, palpable presence? Does not this pain render all ideological Causes trifling? This perplexed gaze of a starved or wounded child who just stares into the camera, lost and unaware of what is going on around them – a starved Somali girl, a boy from Sarajevo whose leg has been butchered by a grenade – is today the sublime image that cancels out all other images, the ultimate scoop that all photo-reporters are after.

Victimization is thus universalized; it reaches from sexual abuse and harassment to the victims of AIDS, from the cruel fate of the homeless to those exposed to cigarette smoke, from the starving children in Somalia to the victims of the bombardment of Sarajevo, from the suffering animals in the laboratories to the dying trees in the rainforest. It is part of the public image of a movie or rock star to have his or her favoured victim: Richard Gere has the people of Tibet, victims of Communist rule; Elizabeth Taylor has AIDS victims; the late Audrey Hepburn had the starving children in Somalia; Vanessa Redgrave has children who suffer in the ex-Yugoslav civil war; Sting has the rainforest – up to the ageing Brigitte Bardot in France, concerned with the cruel fate of animals killed for their skins. . . . The case of Vanessa Redgrave is exemplary here – the diehard Trotskyite who has suddenly started to speak the language of abstract victimization, shunning, as the vampire shuns a string of garlic, a concrete analysis of the politics that led to the horrors in Bosnia. No wonder that by far the biggest classical music hit in recent years (two million CDs sold in Europe alone) is Henryk Gorecki's *Third Symphony,* a large lamentation on the fate of all possible victims quite adequately subtitled 'Symphony of Sorrowful Songs'. Philosophy itself was quick to contribute to this universal victimization: in his *Contingency, Irony and Solidarity* Richard Rorty, *the* philosopher of liberal-democratic pluralism, defines man as such as a potential victim, as 'something that can be hurt'.

So what is wrong here – what does this fantasy-image of the victim conceal?

The fantasy-image, its immobilizing power of fascination, thwarts our ability to act – as Lacan put it, we 'traverse the fantasy' by way of an *act.* The 'postmodern' ethics of compassion with the victim legitimizes the avoidance, the endless postponement, of the act. All 'humanitarian' *activity* of aiding the victims, all food, clothes and medicine for Bosnians, are there to obfuscate the urgency of the *act.* The multitude of particular ethics that thrive today (the ethics of ecology, medical ethics ...) is to be conceived precisely as an endeavour to avoid the true ethics, the ethics of the ACT as real. What we encounter here is again the genuinely dialectical tension between the universal and the particular: far from simply exemplifying the universality to which it belongs, the particular entertains an antagonistic relationship towards it. And does not the same hold for the postmodern assertion of the multitude of subject-positions against the spectre of the Subject (denounced as the Cartesian illusion)?

So the much-advertised liberal-democratic 'right to difference' and anti-Eurocentrism appear in their true light: the Third World other is recognized as a victim – that is to say, *in so far as he is a victim*. The true object of anxiety is the other no longer prepared to play the role of victim – such an other is promptly denounced as a 'terrorist', a 'fundamentalist', and so on. The Somalis, for example, undergo a true Kleinian splitting into a 'good' and a 'bad' object – on the one hand the good object: passive victims, suffering, starving children and women; on the other the bad object: fanatical warlords who care more for their power or their ideological goals than for the welfare of their own people. The good other dwells in the anonymous passive universality of a victim – the moment we encounter an actual/active other, there is always something with which to reproach him: being patriarchal, fanatical, intolerant....

This ambiguous attitude towards the victim is inscribed into the very foundations of modern American culture; it is discernible in John Ford's *Searchers* as well as Martin Scorsese's *Taxi Driver*: in both cases the hero endeavours to deliver the feminine victim from the clutches of the evil Other (American Indians, the corrupted pimp), yet the victim seems to resist her own deliverance, as if she finds an incomprehensible enjoyment in her very suffering. Is not de Niro's (Travis's) violent *passage à l'acte* in *Taxi Driver* an outburst by means of which the subject circumvents the deadlock of a victim that resists the imposed deliverance? Is not the same libidinal deadlock at the roots of the trauma of Vietnam, where the Vietnamese also somehow resisted American help? And – last but not least – is it not possible to discern the same ambiguity in the 'politically correct' male obsession with the woman as victim of sexual harassment? Is not this obsession driven by an unacknowledged fear that woman might somehow enjoy the harassment, that she might not be able to retain a proper distance towards it? Are we not thus dealing, once again, with the fear of *feminine enjoyment*? (Incidentally, one of the inherent contradictions of PC deconstructionists is that although, on the level of the enunciated content, they know very well that no subject, not even the most loathsome racist or sexist, is fully responsible (and therefore guilty) for his acts – that is to say, 'responsibility' is a legal fiction to be deconstructed – they none the less, at the level of the subjective position of enunciation, treat racists and sexists as *fully responsible* for their acts.)

The universalization of the notion of victim thus condenses two aspects. On the one hand there is the Third World victim: compassion with the victim of local warlords-fanatics-fundamentalists frames the liberal-democratic (mis)perception of today's Great Divide between those who are In (included in the law-and-order society of welfare and human rights) and those who are Out (from the homeless in our cities to starving Africans and Asians). On the other hand, the parallel victimization of the subjects of liberal-democratic societies indicates the shift in the predominant mode of subjectivity towards what is usually designated as 'pathological Narcissism': the Other as such is more and more perceived as a potential threat, as encroaching upon the space of my self-identity (by smoking, by laughing too loudly, by casting a covetous glance at me ...). It is not difficult to ascertain what this attitude desperately endeavours to elude: *desire as such*, which, as we know from Lacan, is always the desire of the Other. The Other poses a threat in so far as it is the subject of desire, in so far as it radiates an impenetrable desire that seems to encroach upon the secluded balance of my 'way of life'.

Marx distinguished 'classic' bourgeois political economy (Ricardo) from 'apologetic' political economy (Malthus and onwards): the 'classics' rendered visible the inherent antinomies of the capitalist economy, whereas the 'apologists' swept them under the carpet. *Mutatis mutandis*, the same could be claimed for liberal-democratic thought: it reaches a kind of greatness when it displays the inherent *antinomian* character of the liberal-democratic project. This antinomy concerns above all the relationship between universalism and particularism: the liberal universalist 'right to difference' encounters its limit the moment it stumbles against an *actual* difference. Suffice it to mention clitoridectomy to mark a woman's sexual maturity, a practice that pertains in parts of Eastern Africa (or – a less extreme case – the insistence of Muslim women in France on wearing the veil in state schools): what if a minority group claims that this 'difference' is an indispensable part of its cultural identity and, consequently, denounces opposition to clitoridectomy as an exercise in cultural imperialism, as the violent imposition of Eurocentric standards? How are we to decide between the competing claims of an individual's rights and group identity *when group identity accounts for a substantial part of the individual's self-identity*? The standard liberal answer, of course, is: let the woman choose whatever she wants, *on condition that she has been properly acquainted with the range of alternative choices*, so that she is fully aware of the wider context of her choice. The illusion here resides in the underlying implication that there is a neutral way of acquainting the individual with the full range of alternatives: the threatened particular community necessarily experiences the concrete mode of this acquisition of knowledge about alternative lifestyles (obligatory education, for example) as a violent intervention that threatens its identity. (For that reason, the Amish in the USA resist obligatory education for their children: they are quite justified in pointing out that state school attendance corrodes their group identity.) In short, there is no way to avoid violence: the very neutral medium of information that should enable a truly free choice is already branded by an irreducible violence.

Notes

1. M.O'C. Drury, 'Conversations with Wittgenstein', in *Recollections of Wittgenstein*, edited by Rush Rhees, Oxford: Oxford University Press 1984, p. 125.
2. A.C. Bradley, *Shakespearean Tragedy*, London: St Martin's Press 1985, p. 358.
3. See Stuart Schneiderman, *The Rat Man*, New York: NYU Press 1986, p. 115.
4. See Zdravko Kobe, 'The Unconscious within Transcendental Apperception', *The American Journal of Semiotics*, vol. 9 (1992), nos 2–3, pp. 33–50.
5. A.S. Byatt, *Possession*, London: Vintage 1991, p. 504.
6. As to this coincidence of the Good with the supreme Evil, see Chapter 3 of Slavoj Žižek, *Tarrying with the Negative*, Durham, NC: Duke University Press 1993.
7. For the Derridean approach to spectres, see Jacques Derrida, *Spectres de Marx*, Paris: Galilée 1993.
8. See Chapter 3 above.
9. See Jacques Derrida, *Given Time I: The Counterfeit Money*, Chicago and London: University of Chicago Press 1992.
10. Derrida, *Spectres de Marx*, p. 102.
11. See Chapter 4 above.
12. See Chapter 6 of Slavoj Žižek, *Looking Awry*, Cambridge, MA: MIT Press 1991.
13. Judith Butler, *Bodies That Matter*, New York: Routledge 1993, p. 127.
14. See Jacques Derrida, 'Force of Law: The "Mystical Foundation of Authority"', in *Deconstruction and the Possibility of Justice*, New York: Routledge 1992. For a different (Lacanian) articulation of a similar line of thought, see Chapter 5 of Slavoj Žižek, *For They Know Not What They Do*, London: Verso 1991.

Index

Adorno, Theodor 131
 Dialectic of Enlightenment (with
  Horkheimer) 146
 Habermas and 27
 Minima Moralia 56
 repressive desublimination 16–22
 revisionist Freud 10, 12–15, 50
Althusser, Louis 183
 fear of non-existence 170
 ideological interpellation 58–62
 Reading Capital 170
Althusser, Louis
 'Lenin and Philosophy' 62
Altman, Robert
 Nashville 209
 Short Cuts 127, 209–10
Andersen, Hans Christian
 'The Emperor's New Clothes' 58
Aristotle 130
The Assault on Truth (Masson) 7
Austen, Jane 58
Austin, John L. 97

Bakhtin, M.M. 55
Balibar, Étienne 78
Bentham, Jeremy 73
Bradley, A.C. 176
Brecht, Bertolt 169
Buñuel, Luis 95–6
Butler, Judith 202–3
Byatt, A.S.
 Possession 191

Campion, Jane
 The Piano 192
Chion, Michel 118–19
Christianity
 Hegel on 38–42, 45–6
Chrysippos 123
The Company of Words (McCumber)
 47–9
Cronenberg, David
 M. Butterfly 105–8

Dahl, Roald 170
de Quincey, Thomas 74
Deleuze, Gilles 47, 91, 202, 212
 The Logic of Sense 122–3, 126–7, 128,
  130, 132, 153–4
Derrida, Jacques
 criticizes Lacan 193–6
 deconstruction 196–7
 returning to oneself 191
 Spectres de Marx 198
 violence 204
Dilthey, Wilhelm
 Habermas's argument 22, 24
Dostoevsky, Fyodor
 The Brothers Karamazov 80–81,
  176
Drury, M. 172
Ducrot, Oswald 97–8
Duras, Marguerite 153

Elster, Jon 65

Fichte, Johann Gottlieb 186, 188
Ford, John
    Searchers 215
Forman, Miloš 169
Foucault, Michel 198–9
Frankfurt School
    Freudo–Marxism 14
    Lacan and 50
    psychoanalytic process 22
    return to Freud 9–13, 18
    substance and subject 34
Freud, Sigmund
    cause 31
    contradiction and truth 13–15
    and Marxism 181–3
    naming 46
    repressive desublimation 16–22
    revisionism 9–13
    routine casting out 7–9
    Schreber 20
Fromm, Erich 10

Gadamer, Hans-Georg 129
Gilliam, Terry
    Brazil 63–4
Göring, Hermann 66
Gould, Stephen Jay 179

Habermas, Jürgen
    psychoanalytic process 22–7
    subjectivity 129
Hammett, Dashiel
    The Maltese Falcon 125
Havel, Václav
    'The Power of the Powerless' 63
Hawkes, Howard 75
Hegel, Georg W.F.
    cause and necessity 34–8
    Christianity 38–42
    Evil 212
    fighting evils 198
    identity 32, 97
    inversions of genus 158–9
    Jenaer Realphilosophie 46, 145
    Lessons on the History of Philosophy 156
    logic of the signifier 47–50

    mechanical memory 43–7
    the night of the world 122, 143
    Phenomenology 38, 147–8
    rails at Kant 187
    self-consciousness 188–9
    spirit 201
    teleology 189–90
    universality 146, 147–8, 156–7
Heidegger, Martin 98
    being-in-the-world 184–5, 200–01
    communication 129
    the gift 194, 195
    ontotheological metaphysics 157
Highsmith, Patricia
    'The Terrapin' 210–11
Himmler, Heinrich 66
Hitchcock, Alfred 58, 73, 176
    The Birds 180
    Murder 107
    Rear Window 208–9
    Rope 76
Hölderlin, Johann 201
Horkheimer, Max
    Dialectic of Enlightenment (with Adorno) 146
Hunt, William Holman 113–14
Husserl, Edmund 132
Huxley, Aldous
    The Grey Eminence 80–81
Hwang, David Henry 105

Ivory, James and Ishmail Merchant
    Remains of the Day 132

Jacoby, Russell 15
    Social Amnesia 9
James, P.D.
    A Taste for Death 93
Jameson, Fredric 194
Jordan, Neil
    The Crying Game 102–5, 109

Kafka, Franz 68
Kant, Immanuel 26, 146
    aesthetics 99
    antinomies 153–4, 159
    The Critique of Pure Reason 96

and cultural references 175–6
decentred subject 185–7
ethics 68, 69
experience of Sublime 74
identity 144
imperative 100
regulative Idea 197–8
Kieslowski, Krzysztof 170–71
Koresh, David 206
Ku Klux Klan 55, 81
Kundera, Milan 62–4, 212

Lacan, Jacques
big Other 42–3, 72, 77, 167,
178–80, 200, 207
cause 29–33
community of analysts 171–2
courtly love 89–95, 96–7, 99, 103
cynical enjoyment 57
Derrida criticizes 193–6
desexualization 154–5
and desire 216
discord of psychosis 19–20
Discours de Rome 29
enjoy-meant 156
ethics 68–70
existence 143–4
fantasy 78, 82, 131, 187, 214
Frankfurt School 50
identification 60–61, 62, 71
immixture of subjects 208
inconsistency of desire 150, 151–2
intersubjective communication 129
letter always arrives 60
naming 46
phallic signifier 201–3
popular culture 175–6
psychoanalysis 183–4
the Real 199–200
return to Freud 21
and the Sadeian fantasy 213
sexual differences 159
shifting ideas 173–5
signifier and signified 49, 131
subject 34, 185
superego 67–8
symbolic castration 127–8, 130, 153

topology 32
the unassimilable 70
unbearable surplus-enjoyment 75
and Weininger 142–3
women 105, 108–9
Laclau, Ernesto 147
de Laclos, Pierre Choderlos
Les liaisons dangereuses 68, 99–100
Laibach 71–2, 208
Lang, Fritz 75
Secret Beyond the Door 179–80
Lenin, V.I. 81
Longus
Daphnis and Chloe 155
Lukács, George 200
Lynch, David
Blue Velvet 114, 119–21
Chion's reading 118–19
Dune 116–17
The Elephant Man 115
pre-Raphaelitism 114–15
Twin Peaks 115
Wild at Heart 101, 119

Mad (magazine) 158
Malcolm X 147
Marcuse, Herbert
revisionist Freud 10–11
Marx, Karl
anatomy of man 84
Capital 49
class struggle 155–6
Derrida 197
labour and social life 157
Lafitte fantasy 194–5
Marxism and psychoanalysis
181–3
necessity 35–6
and political economy 216
psychoanalysis and 14
the Whole 97
Masson, Jeffrey
The Assault on Truth 7
McCumber, John
The Company of Words 47–9
Meinong, Alex 123–4
Miller, Jacques-Alain 8, 171, 172

Milner, Jean-Claude 58
Minnelli, Vincente
  Four Horsemen of the Apocalypse
  152–3
Morris, Jane 121–2
Morris, William 121–2
Mozart, Wolfgang A.
  Così fan tutte 42, 124–5, 132
Munch, Edvard 150

Noyce, Phillip
  Sliver 209

Orwell, George
  Nineteen Eighty-four 77, 168

Parmenides 184
Pascal, Blaise 59
  Pensées 132
Phenomenology (Hegel) 38
Plato 122–3, 184
Poe, Edgar Allan 98–9
  'The Purloined Letter' 74

Reiner, Rob
  A Few Good Men 54, 81
Rendell, Ruth
  King Solomon's Carpet 42–3
Rohmer, Eric
  Ma nuit chez Maud 101–2
Rorty, Richard 77, 214
Rosenberg, Alfred 146
Rossetti, Christina 90
Rossetti, Dante Gabriel 90, 121–2
Rostand, Edmond
  Cyrano de Bergerac 100–01
Russell, Bertrand 124

Sacher-Masoch, Leopold von 91–2
Schelling, Friedrich 129–30, 188
  Treaty on Freedom 201
Schnittke, Alfred
  Life with an Idiot 64

Scorsese, Martin
  Taxi Driver 215
Sellars, Peter 125
Shakespeare, William
  Coriolanus 78
  Hamlet 76
  Macbeth 176
  Richard II 118
Shelley, Mary
  Frankenstein 104
Siddal, Elizabeth 90
Social Amnesia (Jacoby) 9
Socrates 184
Spielberg, Steven 180–81
  Jurassic Park 180
Stalin, Joseph 57, 58, 81, 203–4
  Lacanian analysts 171–2
Stendhal
  Le Rouge et le Noir 200
Stoics 123, 132

Truffaut, François
  Day for Night 101

Wagner, Richard
  Parsifal 121–2, 150
Weininger, Otto 133, 160–61
  anti-Semitism 146
  and Lacan 142–3
  Sex and Character 121, 137
  striving for identity 144–6
  women dominated by sexuality
  137–43, 149–50
Welles, Orson 66
  Citizen Kane 175
Wharton, Edith
  The Age of Innocence 207–8
Wittgenstein, Ludwig 172
  Tractatus Logico-Philosophicus 124
Woolf, Virginia 58

Zupančič, Alenka 213